GLA

E.NA.03

The provincial Press and the community

Ian Jackson

The provincial Press and the community

Manchester University Press

Rowman & Littlefield, Totowa N.J.

© **1971 Ian Jackson**
Published by the University of Manchester at
The University Press
316–324 Oxford Road, Manchester M13 9NR
UK ISBN 0 7190 0460 8

USA
Rowman & Littlefield
81 Adams Drive
Totowa, N.J. 07512
US ISBN 0 87471 076 6

Printed in Great Britain by Butler & Tanner Ltd
Frome and London

Contents

Appendix

Illustrations

Preface

The idea for a specialised study of the evening and weekly regional Press first suggested itself in 1963, at a time when evening newspapers of Birmingham, Leeds, Leicester, Manchester and Nottingham were being closed down or merged in a general rationalisation of the few remaining competitive situations. It was then apparent that there was no available reference work that clarified the role of local newspapers in their communities—thereby showing what a community loses when its newspaper 'dies'. An opportunity to study the local Press occurred with the opening of the Centre for Contemporary Cultural Studies, University of Birmingham, where the years 1964–68 were spent gathering much of the material that has gone into this book.

The central aim is to analyse the functions that local newspapers fulfil, and to illustrate the main kinds of content that result. A further aim is to set the local Press in its historical and social context, and to examine the values and attitudes that inform it—special attention being paid to cultural and political attitudes. Of course, the emphases put and the selections made correspond to a personal response to this sector of the Press; it is for the reader to judge whether this response matches his or her own. No attempt is made to formulate a 'league table' based on comparisons of performance: local newspapers do not lend themselves to this sort of assessment.

It should be borne in mind that the analyses in chapters 5–12 refer to specific sampling periods within the years 1966–70; the description, and, at points, evaluation of practice should not be taken as having predictive validity. At least eight of the sixteen newspapers sampled in chapters 5 and 7 have seen a change of editor since 1966; this often results in fresh approaches and emphases which can take effect quite rapidly.

The study is limited to the evening and weekly Press, which have in common their appeal to all social classes; the majority of regional morning newspapers have a predominantly ABC1 readership—and well merit a separate, detailed account. In order to preserve a general

*

focus, no one newspaper's relationship to its community is studied in depth. There are, regrettably, very few books that explore this relationship; of these, Claud Morris's *I Bought a Newspaper* is one of the most stimulating.

But it is hoped that the succeeding chapters will assist in the mounting of further, detailed work on aspects of particular newspapers, and that they will contribute to the growing interest—in all spheres of education—in the nature and influence of the main communications media. For a fuller understanding of the strictly organisational and technical side of the provincial Press, the reader is referred to the late John F. Goulden's *Newspaper Management*; this contains chapters on management structures, paging and newsprint, relationships with trade unions and new printing techniques.

It remains to thank those in the respective spheres of the University and the local Press who unstintingly offered information, advice and helpful criticism. Their interest and encouragement proved invaluable, as did that of over one hundred local newspaper readers, in different parts of the country, who completed a comprehensive questionnaire.

Ian Jackson

University of Salford, 1971

To my mother and father

I Historical and social background

. . . the 'macro' analyst assumes that institutions, societies and cultures manifest laws and order beyond that apparent to large numbers of people at any one time, and that systems of artifacts express objective, even if subtle or implicit manifestations of this order. In his quest for the *system* behind the facts and forms of mass communication, the media analyst regards content as expressive of social relationship and institutional dynamics, and as formative of social patterns.

George Gerbner, in 'On content analysis and critical research in mass communications' (see L. A. Dexter and D. M. White's *People, Society and Mass Communications*)

The second kind* of modern newspaper in which there is a comparatively simple and visible social structure is the local paper: under some pressures, certainly, and with several contradictory features of chain ownership and monopoly; but still normally expressing a common experience which is there quite apart from the newspaper itself: of living in a particular place, sharing certain local needs and interests, facing certain local problems . . . The paper is to an important extent written *with* people if not *by* them; and in the sense that it is written *for* them this can be defined, quite reasonably, in terms of an interest larger than the paper itself: the interest of the local community.

Raymond Williams, in 'Radical and/or respectable' (see Richard Boston's *The Press we Deserve*)

* The first kind referred to is the quality national Press.

1 Historical background

Historical studies of the provincial Press from its origins in 1701 until the close of the Victorian period present it as an expanding institution that exercised growing social and—especially in the first half of the nineteenth century—political influence. It must suffice to cut into this history at two stages: the first halves of the eighteenth and nineteenth centuries. R. M. Wiles, in his study of the earliest provincial newspapers, sees their development in terms of a successful struggle against powerful odds: tiny profit margins, the stamp taxes, difficulties in distribution, metropolitan or regional competition and, in some cases, local vested interests. He speaks of them in a tone of admiring wonderment: 'a mighty struggle was in progress, the struggle of a force that burst its way into the open, thrusting aside all impediments, gaining momentum steadily, and bringing a new dimension into the life of England'.[1] Wiles considers the impact of the successive stamp taxes of 1712, 1725 and 1757, and concludes that these did not have more than a slight and temporary retarding effect: 'there were a few casualties among both city and country papers, but in the provinces momentum was quickly regained'.[2] As a result Dr Johnson could write in 1758 that 'now ... almost every large town has its weekly historian, who regularly circulates his periodical intelligence'.[3] In fact, in this year twenty-eight towns had at least one 'weekly historian'; five of them —Liverpool, Manchester, Nottingham, Coventry and Bath—had two, and Newcastle and Bristol had three. But the first two provincial papers, the *Bristol Post-Boy* and the *Norwich Post*, had faded from the scene before 1713.

The main news in these early weeklies was of international and national events. G. A. Cranfield has suggested that war reports constituted their main appeal: 'So long as a war was in progress, the newspapers were crammed with items about battles, sieges and grand strategy. Anything else was treated with scant respect, and domestic affairs in particular were almost completely ignored.'[4] Information about Parliamentary debates had great reader interest, the provincial

printers having to disguise their reports by removing direct reference
to persons—or run the risk of prosecution for violating the privilege
claimed by both Houses. News of murder and violence was also
popular; for instance, the famous trial of Miss Blandy in 1752—
she was accused of murdering her uncle—took up more space in the
thirty-three country newspapers then extant than any other news
story; for a month the *Cambridge Journal* devoted a whole page to it.

Local news, which in all its varied forms has become the staple
content of the provincial Press today, assumed an increasingly
prominent role in the period 1730–60; by 1750 many papers regularly included at least half a column of mixed local and regional
news, together with items culled from the London Press. By 1754
one finds the editor of the *Leeds Intelligencer* claiming that 'Accounts
of Occurrences, &c, in the Neighbourhood, whether serious or
jocose, of our rural Diversions, and the like would be more Entertaining to the Generality of Readers in the Country than any Thing
we have yet heard of the Routs, Riots, Drums and Hurricanes of
the Town'.[5] The growing provision of local news was obviously
one of the ways in which these early provincial newspapers became
organically connected with one particular community or region;
local advertising was another.

The pioneers of the provincial Press did not, for the most part,
take sides in local politics or offer much criticism of local institutions. One cause of this was the fear of prosecution by the authorities concerned; another was the understandable desire to alienate as
few potential customers as possible. One important exception was
Andrew Brice, editor of the Exeter-based *Brice's Weekly Journal*,
1725–32, who attempted to expose the keeper of a local gaol for
alleged cruelty and slovenliness. After a complaint from one prisoner who had been confined in 'the Dark house . . . double-gyved
with the largest Irons which could be got in Bridewell', Brice criticised George Glanvill (the keeper) in the issue of 27 October 1727.
R. M. Wiles notes that

Within a few days Glanvill had sued Brice for £500 damages. Brice
pleaded his cause in the columns of his own newspaper, later . . . complaining that the case had never come to fair hearing in court—'that is to
say, never a single Word of my Side was heard'. Yet penalties were
apparently imposed, and Brice had either to pay a fine of £103 or go to
jail. He absconded. During the many months he remained in hiding, Brice
suffered in many ways: his mother and his wife died, his business was left
to others to conduct, his health was impaired; but he deserves to be

remembered as a journalist who audaciously exposed a public scandal, insisting that a prisoner might as effectively be prevented from escaping by 'Stone Walls, and Pondorous Chains, and Iron Grates . . . above Ground, in comfortable Light and wholesome Air, as by his being buried alive, to rot, and perhaps engender a Pestilence, to the Destruction of the Nation'. This editor of an Exeter newspaper in 1727 showed admirable courage and alertness to appalling conditions which most of his fellow countrymen had long continued to ignore.[6]

Brice's heroic self-denial—and that of a few of his other contemporaries—served to pioneer that right to criticism now accepted as achieved. Thus Mackie & Co. Ltd, in written evidence to the 1947 Royal Commission, cited as amongst the rights of the Press 'the right to reveal and criticise decisions and acts which give advantage to the few to the prejudice of the community' and 'the right to argue in opinion columns the merits and de-merits of public decisions and acts'.[7] These rights came to be recognised in the course of the eighteenth century—thanks to the public-spiritedness of printers like Brice.

Nevertheless, the majority of provincial newspapers were anxious not to offend local institutions or influential individuals; this attitude affected correspondence as well as news columns. Thomas Cotton, printer of the *Kendal Weekly Courant*, wrote in the issue of 12 February 1732: 'I must entreat my Correspondents . . . to forbear sending me any private or public Scandal, or any Innuendo of either. . . . I will not suffer my Paper to be a Conduit to convey Envy, Detraction, Picque or Prejudice.'[8] This sort of guideline did not, however, apply to many letters of protest about Government legislation, social evils or unsatisfactory local conditions; then, as now, such topics as the need for road improvements, cruelty to animals and the incidence of profanity were included.

The early provincial Press also served as an indispensable means of promoting local cultural and social activity. This was done through advertising, whether of 'City-Musick' at the Norwich Assemblies in 1727—'particular care shall be taken to oblige the Gentlemen with a Glass of good Wine'[9]—or of horse races, cockfights or bull-baitings. Books, pamphlets, maps and prints (the 'number' books ranging from Milton's *Paradise Lost* to Dr Doddridge's *Family Expositor*) were also advertised and distributed by local printers; the following notice appeared in the *Portsmouth and Gosport Gazette* on 24 February 1752: 'Gentlemen and others living in the Country may be supplied by the Newsmen, with all

Sorts of New Books, Pamphlets, Maps and Prints, as cheap as in London, from the Printing Office and Bookseller's Shop on the New Canal in Sarum, where Books are bound either plain, or Gilt and Letter'd, at reasonable Rates.' Further, from about 1720 onwards many country newspapers contained essays, poems, serialised fiction, geography, history, criminal biography as part of feature content intended to divert or enlighten—or both. There was certainly a demand for what one reader in the *Gloucester Journal* termed 'some pleasant Amusements in Prose or Verse', which could be furnished by the 'many witty blades in Gloucestershire'.[10] But there were editors like Andrew Brice who took a strictly didactic view of their literary features; in the *Weekly Journal* of 14 October 1726, he wrote: '. . . it ought to be the aim of every (at least publick) Pen to instruct rather than divert, and inculcate the solid Rules of Piety and Good Manners, than titulate light and airy Fancies by ludicrous Vanities and sportive Trifles'. Other printers would aim at an individual 'mix' of both entertainment and instruction; they may not have set their sights quite so high as Joseph Addison in the *Spectator*, but the range of serious belles-lettres material was impressive— from translations of Propertius in the *Salisbury Journal* (March 1751) to Pope's *Messiah* in the *Worcester Journal*. Both newspapers also included lighter matter.

Thus by advertising local cultural activities, by publicising and distributing books, pamphlets and other printed matter, and by including miscellaneous literary features, the earliest local newspapers assisted in reducing the cultural imbalance as between the metropolis and the provinces. But neither in the news columns, the advertisements nor, in some cases, the feature content was a 'highbrow' concept of culture apparent; a wide range was made available, within which the reader could make his choices.

The attitudes of provincial newspapers towards national politics in the period 1701–60 warrant a brief comment before any consideration of the early nineteenth century Press can be effected. Their development was complex, and it must suffice to point to the main stages. From about 1726 onwards the local Press fell into two main groups *vis-à-vis* the Whig and Tory parties. Either they were wholeheartedly committed to one of the parties—Whig supporters being in the minority—or they tried to steer a middle course. The predominance of Tory support in the first group can be seen as linked to the fact that the majority of provincial readers were Tory, or at least, 'anti-Government', at this time. Whig support declined even further after the fall of Walpole in 1742, but when the 'Patriots' (the former Opposition) proved disillusioning in their turn, the provincial Press became generally sceptical about the competence of both parties; this disenchantment continued until the Earl of Chatham came to office. The Press then rejoiced in the new mood of national unity.

It is the role of the political advocate that is the most powerful determinant of our image of the nineteenth-century Press. If the primary appeal of the early eighteenth-century papers lay in their news columns, in the period 1790–1850 their attraction was largely associated with a commitment to a political programme. Competitive situations multiplied as a response to the need for local media of persuasion.

Donald Read's study of the middle-class reform newspapers of Manchester, Leeds and Sheffield[11] shows that these aimed to set out detailed programmes of solutions to the social problems of the new industrial society, editorial articles and reports of meetings constituting the principal means. The Northern manufacturers wanted a voice in Parliament to protect their interests; the corn law of 1815, heavy general taxation and imposts that affected their own trades had convinced them of their need for better representation. But whereas the middle classes were enthusiastic for the Reform Bill of 1832, the operatives tended to be opposed or indifferent—except in Sheffield, where there was a markedly higher degree of social and political unity, attributable to the status of the craftsmen in the steel industry. Elsewhere, the working classes concentrated upon the ten hours and the trade union movements—both strongly opposed by the manufacturers. After the Reform Act came the series of oppressive measures that led to the Chartist movement, whose origins Donald Read summarises as follows:

The Reform Act brought no relief from the burdens of the new society for the operatives. In 1833 the reformed parliament refused to pass a ten hours act; in 1834 it passed the stringent New Poor Law; in the same year the government upheld sentences of seven years' transportation passed upon six trade unionists of Tolpuddle in Dorset for administering illegal oaths. The new system seemed to the operatives only to have given government and employers greater power to oppress them. In a spirit of hatred of employers and government the ten hours and Anti-Poor Law movements were waged during the mid-'30s. In 1837 five years of intense trade depression began. The operatives now turned to political agitation.

In 1838 their discontent and class feeling expressed itself in the great Chartist movement.[12]

Of the biggest meeting in Lancashire—at Kersal Moor on 15 September 1838—the *Manchester and Salford Advertiser* wrote that its purpose was to effect 'those political changes which shall arrest their rapidly downward progress, and secure to them something like a reasonable proportion of the benefits which their own skill and industry so abundantly provide for others'.

Against this background provincial newspapers voiced their opinions—some speaking primarily to the middle classes, some to the working class, and yet others, with mixed success, to both. Donald Read singles out the *Manchester Guardian*, *Leeds Mercury* and *Sheffield Independent* as three middle-class reform newspapers that exercised considerable influence over their readerships:

The influence of the middle-class reform papers was confined to the middle-classes. Though they made many appeals to the operatives, they attracted few working-class readers. The *Manchester Guardian* and the *Leeds Mercury*, in particular, were identified by the operatives with the masters and the masters' political economy. An operative told the *Manchester and Salford Advertiser* that the workmen regarded the *Manchester Guardian* as 'the relentless enemy of their rights'. . . .
But among the middle-classes the influence of the *Manchester Guardian*, the *Leeds Mercury* and the *Sheffield Independent* was great. Samuel Smiles wrote in 1842 that the *Leeds Mercury* was 'looked upon by many as almost oracular . . . On almost all the great questions which have agitated the public mind during the last twenty years, the fiat of the *Leeds Mercury*, in the populous districts where it circulates, has generally been considered as satisfactory and decisive.'[13]

After making due allowance for the shortcomings of generalisation, one can still regard Samuel Smiles's comments as a yardstick for effecting comparisons with the provincial Press today. It is most unlikely that any workmen now regard the local newspaper as 'the enemy of their rights' or that the middle classes look upon it as 'almost oracular'. One reason for the change in attitudes is the current predominance of monopoly situations, whereby particular circulation areas have to be content with one newspaper unchallenged by rivals—a factor taken up again in the next chapter. Readers of all social classes and political persuasions now have to be courted, saturation coverage—and the inducement it affords to advertisers— acting as a powerful magnet. In general, the hortatory editorial postures common in the early nineteenth century have given way, with few exceptions, to more gently persuasive modes of argument—whether partisan or neutral. But in 1823 an editor could speak in terms and tones which would now seem only pompous and presumptuous; there is a hint of Dickens' Mr Pott ('The press is a mighty engine, sir') in the sonorous assumptions of Edward Baines, Jr., writing from the editorial chair of the *Leeds Mercury*:

> The press is alternately a cause and an effect of the growth of intelligence amongst the people. Its conductors are at once learners and teachers. They are themselves operated upon by the master-spirits of the age, who bring forth in their closets the moral and intellectual discoveries which have distinguished this period; and they, in their turn, after subjecting the new opinions to the ordeal of criticism, and establishing their correctness, diffuse them by the mighty agency of the periodical press.[14]

The *Leeds Mercury* may have been regarded as a 'mighty agency' by the middle classes, but the working-class section of the populace was far from convinced of the correctness of his opinions. Over the period 1830–31 Baines advocated an eleven-hour day for children under fourteen, as opposed to the ten hours sought by the operatives. The *Mercury* became so unpopular with them that, in Donald Read's words: 'On 28 April 1832 two hundred operatives marched through Leeds carrying a copy of the *Mercury* on a pole bound in crêpe. This was solemnly burned outside the *Mercury* office. In the evening an effigy of the elder Baines was likewise consigned to the flames "amidst the shouts and execrations of the assembled thousands".'[15] This episode shows clearly how a newspaper committed to a set of politico-economic principles could reinforce existing divisions within a local community and attract to itself a devoted middle-class readership on one side and the militant antagonism of the working man on the other.

In his account of the working-class radical Press of Leeds and Manchester, which included the *Leeds Patriot* (1824–33), the *Manchester Observer* (1818–22), the *Manchester and Salford Advertiser* (1829–48, when it was absorbed by the *Manchester Times*) and the great Chartist newspaper, the *Northern Star* (1837–52), Donald Read again sees the political content as the crucial sales factor and, referring particularly to the *Northern Star*, makes some significant observations about the extent of working-class literacy at this time:

> By February 1838 it was selling over 10,000 copies per week, more than the *Manchester Guardian* twice a week or the *Leeds Mercury* once a week. It had jumped spectacularly to the head of the provincial press. Its readers

were almost exclusively working-class, and the sudden success of the paper proved, as one editorial pointed out, 'that which was our first inducement to light up the *Northern Star* in the political hemisphere', that hitherto no single organ had satisfactorily voiced the grievances and aspirations of the new industrial working-classes.

. . . During the first half of 1839, while the National Petition was preparing and the National Convention sitting, the *Northern Star* sold unprecedented numbers for a provincial newspaper. Its maximum sale at this time was probably over 50,000 copies per week. This level was not maintained for long, but for several years the *Star* continued to be a markedly successful and profitable paper.

. . . As well as showing the extent of working-class political enthusiasm, these figures prove that illiteracy was not an obstacle to the success of a working-class newspaper, despite the low standard of educational provision for the poor at this time. It has recently been estimated that by the 1830s perhaps three-quarters of the operatives in the North could read.[16]

The sales figures of the *Northern Star*, particularly at the peak period of its success, should serve as a caution not to under-estimate the extent of literacy at this time. Some accounts of the growth of the national Press[17] do tend, in their explanations of the dramatic rise of the mass circulation dailies towards the close of the century, to give too much weight to the impact of the 1870 Education Act, which made school attendance compulsory. Changes in working conditions and in the nature of urban life were much more significant factors in this respect.

Thus far, the middle-class and working-class Press of three large Northern cities has been considered; the implication of two fictional allusions to the provincial Press is that the political role was also the predominant one in smaller towns and semi-rural areas. In both Dickens' Eatanswill and George Eliot's Middlemarch two competing newspapers supported opposing political platforms. Dickens implies through his satire that the two Eatanswill editors, Mr Pott and Mr Slurk, did not devote much of their time in 1827 to the intellectual discoveries of 'master-spirits'; they were too busy trading shrill invective and inflated declamation:

It appears, then, that the Eatanswill people, like the people of many other small towns, considered themselves of the utmost and mighty importance, and that every man in Eatanswill, conscious of the weight that attached to his example, felt himself bound to unite, heart and soul, with one of the two great parties that divided the town—the Blues and the Buffs.

. . . Of course, it was essentially and indispensably necessary that each of these powerful parties should have its organ and representative: and,

accordingly, there were two newspapers in the town—the Eatanswill
Gazette and the Eatanswill Independent; the former advocating Blue
principles, and the latter conducted on grounds decidedly Buff. Fine
newspapers they were. Such leading articles, and such spirited attacks!—
'Our worthless contemporary, the Gazette'—'That disgraceful and
dastardly journal, the Independent'—'That false and scurrilous print, the
Independent'—'That vile and slanderous calumniator, the Gazette'; these,
and other spirit-stirring denunciations, were strewn plentifully over the
columns of each, in every number, and excited feelings of the most intense
delight and indignation in the bosoms of the townspeople.[18]

One implication of this passage is that the competitive situation was
typical at the time; the inhabitants of Eatanswill were 'like the people
of many other small towns' and divided into two opposing political
camps—each of which had to have 'its organ and representative'.
This was also the case at Middlemarch, with its *Pioneer* and *Trumpet*;
in the course of the novel Mr Brooke purchased the *Pioneer* in order
to further his political aims. Sir James Chettam observed that Mr
Brooke's choice of editor, Will Ladislaw, soon became 'in everybody's
mouth'.[19]

   The provincial Press of the early nineteenth century, therefore,
was distinctive for its political partisanship and the supposed
magnitude of its influence. The editors of the larger urban newspapers
of the North saw themselves as intermediaries between political,
economic and social theorists and particular local readerships.
Those of smaller towns seem also to have been preoccupied with
political advocacy. Thus although international and metropolitan
events—and local news—continued to be reported, these and crime
and 'human interest' news are largely overlooked in the available
accounts of the newspapers of this period. The effect of competitive
situations was to divide communities into separate camps, and the
Press both stimulated and reflected the antagonism between the
two—as was the case with the *Leeds Mercury*.

   It might be thought that the provincial Press had reached the
peak of its possible influence in the 1820s; it was in 1823 that Edward
Baines Jr. referred to it as a 'mighty agency'. But James Grant, a
Press historian who published a three-volume study of the British
Press in 1871, felt that progress had been maintained and that even
greater power was accruing to the local newspaper; his primary
concern was with 'their influence . . . in relation to questions of
national interest and importance'; 'our existing provincial journals
exercise a mighty power over the public mind in the various localities

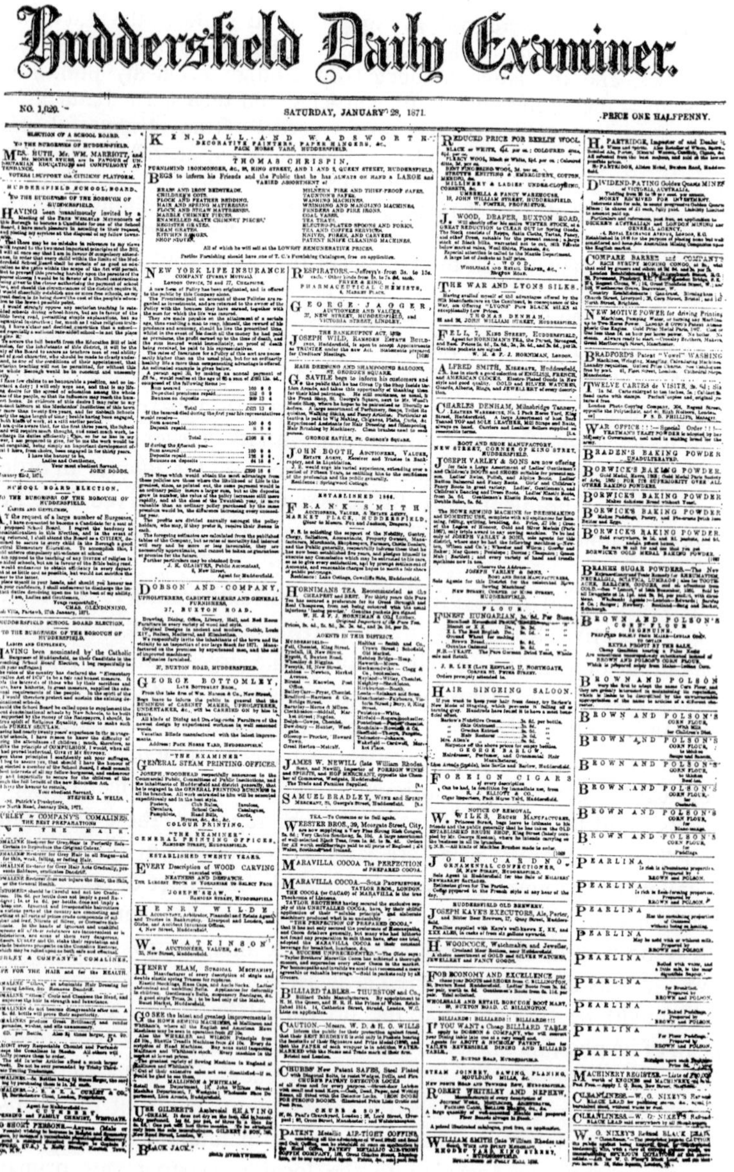
Huddersfield Daily Examiner.

NO. 1,020. SATURDAY, JANUARY 28, 1871. PRICE ONE HALFPENNY.

ELECTION OF A SCHOOL BOARD.

HUDDERSFIELD SCHOOL BOARD.

SCHOOL BOARD ELECTION.

KENDALL AND WADSWORTH

THOMAS CHRISPIN,

NEW YORK LIFE INSURANCE COMPANY

DOBSON AND COMPANY,

GEORGE BOTTOMLEY,

GENERAL STEAM PRINTING OFFICES.

HENRY WILDE

W. WATKINSON,

RESPIRATORS.

GEORGE JAGGER,

JOSEPH WILD,

JOHN BOOTH,

FRANK SMITH,

HORNIMANS TEA

JAMES W. NEWILL

SAMUEL BRADLEY,

MARAVILLA COCOA

BILLIARD TABLES

REDUCED PRICE FOR BERLIN WOOL.

J. WOOD, DRAPER, BUXTON ROAD,

THE WAR AND LYONS SILKS.

ALFRED SMITH,

CHARLES DENHAM,

JOSEPH VARLEY & SONS

FINEST HUNGARIAN,

HAIR SINGEING SALOON.

FOREIGN CIGARS

JOHN CARDNO,

H. WOODCOCK,

H. PARTRIDGE,

DIVIDEND-PAYING Golden Quartz MINES of VICTORIA, AUSTRALIA.

COMPARE BARNET and COMPANY'S

NEW MOTIVE POWER

BRADFORD'S Patent "Vowel" WASHING

TWELVE CARTES de VISITE,

WAR OFFICE!

BRADEN'S BAKING POWDER

BORWICK'S BAKING POWDER.

BROWN AND POLSON'S CORN FLOUR.

PEARLINA

MACHINERY REGISTER.

CLEANLINESS.—W. G. NIXEY'S

Fig. 1 A century of change: the front page of the *Huddersfield Daily Examiner*, 28 January 1871 and 21 July 1969. *By courtesy of the Huddersfield Daily Examiner.*

THIRD EDITION

BEAVERBROOKS
the jewellers

HUDDERSFIELD
DAILY EXAMINER

34,006 MONDAY, JULY 21, 1969 PRICE 5d.

"An honour and a privilege for us to be here"—Armstrong

MAN WALKS ON THE MOON

The Policy of Honesty—The Might of Right—The Expediency of Principle

Out of this world

SUPERLATIVES were, and are, superfluous. The deed speaks volumes for itself: man has landed and walked on the moon.

The words which were spoken were calmly simple: "Houston, Tranquillity Base here, Eagle has landed," followed a short time later by the comment from Neil Armstrong which, in a phrase, summarised the drama of man's first step on another planet and the whole Apollo programme — "One small step for man, one vast leap for mankind." Whatever happens now, and the sincere world hope must be that the mission will continue on its fine-far perfect way to the happiest of conclusions which one all three, Armstrong, Aldrin and Collins, safely back on earth, the awful fact remains; the old myth about "the man on the moon" has been made uniquely astonishing reality.

Astronauts unlock secrets of new world

HOUSTON.—Astronauts Neil Armstrong and Edwin Aldrin settled down to sleep in spaceship Eagle on Tranquillity Base today after their epic walk on the moon.

Meanwhile astronaut Michael Collins, who did not see the two-hour television spectacular of the first men on the moon, orbited in the mother ship Columbia.

Just before 7 o'clock tonight, after the flight plan switched to Armstrong and Aldrin will fire their ascent engine to lift off from the moon's surface and dock with Columbia.

Then at 5.57 a.m. tomorrow, safely aboard Columbia, they will fire the main engine to start their journey back to earth.

The lunar tasks

Earlier today, after Armstrong and Aldrin had re-entered Eagle, the television cameras kept faithfully transmitting pictures of the tragically moonscape and of a United States flag planted firmly in the lunar soil.

The two men performed all but one—and that minor—of the tasks assigned to them for their lunar walk—which included collecting soil and rock samples, planting a special laser-beam reflector, planting the flag and unveiling a plaque announcing that man came in peace to the moon in July, 1969.

The peace theme was stressed, too, in what US President Richard M. Nixon said was "certainly the most historic telephone call ever made."

He spoke to them from Washington, via the manned spacecraft centre at Houston, and the two astronauts replied while standing on the moon surface.

"As you talk to us from the Sea of Tranquillity, it inspires us to redouble our efforts to bring peace and tranquillity to earth," he added.

£62½m. a minute

Armstrong, who became the first man to step on the moon four minutes to beat the morning, spent almost two hours and forty minutes walking about, and was using his portable life-support system for two hours 47 minutes and 14 seconds.

His stay on the moon must have cost roughly 150m. dollars (about £62,500,000) a minute, averaging out the 24,000-mile journey.

And the two men certainly left their mark clearly—footprints about a half an inch to an inch deep in the slippery, powdery topsoil which they reported clung to their boots.

The tiny lightweight television transmitter beamed back pictures flawlessly and with extreme clarity for the whole duration of the almost unbelievable show from earth's airless satellite.

Before millions of people on earth watching Armstrong and Aldrin, leaping exuberantly across the dusty, rocky surface of the moon, underwent the ordeals of another world.

The two astronauts walked slowly and warily at first, aware that one false move could bring instant death to the airless, grey lunar desert.

Kangaroo hops

But as their confidence mounted, Armstrong and Aldrin—the only living souls in mankind's own true tradition—jumped, bounced and cavorted like a pair of their packing craft, taking advantage of reduced gravity.

With television's tested constantly on the astronauts the ordinary people of earth became almost matter-of-fact routine as Armstrong and Aldrin dug into the moon's surface, scooped up dust and rock samples, and erected their findings back on earth.

Ghostly figure

The astronauts spent the better part of two and a quarter hours bounding about on the moon's surface—each giving off a ghostly light.

With life support packs strapped to their backs, giving them about three hours of life on the moon, the astronauts carried out their duties, setting up a finality plan.

Their two astronauts returned constantly to a television camera positioned at the brink of the spacecraft's ladder recorded the scene as Armstrong's ghostly figure emerged from the moon craft and was guided down by his companion inside.

Armstrong's first words as he gingerly placed his foot across the moon's surface were, "That's one small step for man, but one giant leap for mankind."

Armstrong was placed on the moon's surface by Aldrin several minutes later.

NIXON'S HISTORIC CALL

WASHINGTON.—President Nixon told America's men on the moon in his telephone call: "For one priceless moment in the whole history of man all of the people on this earth are truly one."

The President spoke to astronauts Neil Armstrong and Edwin "Buzz" Aldrin from the White House.

Armstrong said, "It is a great honour and privilege for us to be here representing not only the United States but men of peaceable nations with an interest and curiosity and vision for the future."

Mr. Nixon told the astronauts, "This certainly has to be the most historic telephone call ever made from the White House."

"I just can't tell you how proud we all are of what you have done for every American. This has to be the proudest day of our lives.

"As you talk to us from the Sea of Tranquillity it inspires us to redouble our efforts to bring peace and tranquillity to earth."

Congratulations from the Queen

The Queen in a message of her warmest congratulations, also to the crew of Apollo 11, and to the American people. "I am filled with admiration for the fortitude of astronauts Armstrong, Aldrin and Collins whose exploits and a new dimension to man's knowledge of the universe," said her message.

The Queen, the Duke of Edinburgh and their children, watched the television programmes of the moon landing at Windsor Castle.

Blast-off from the moon on TV

The blast-off from the moon at 6.18 p.m. will be shown on both BBC and ITV television. The BBC programme will begin at 4.30 and once on the outward journey from earth.

On BBC1 at 6.5 Panorama will review the implications of the flight and in future years will deal with the manned landing, showing the ten-craft being recalled.

Second industrial revolution?

The British Interplanetary Society stated that the moon landing presaged a new age heralding the second industrial revolution and making manned spaceflight a great commercial proposition, date promoting machine-made, industrial commercialisation process source and much more.

Vice-President Mr Kenneth Gatland said, "We are particularly interested in using satellites as communication links and the whole communication in space as becoming more rapidly into the twentieth century."

The voices from another world

PARTICULARLY fascinating to TV viewers were the conversations between the two astronauts and their link-up with Capcom (ground capsule communicator) and Pan Space Agency public affairs officers. Here are some very brief extracts:

Armstrong: The hatch is coming open...
Aldrin: O.K. stand by...
Armstrong: I know how it's coming now...
Aldrin: I'm a little tired...
Armstrong: O.K. Houston, I'm on the porch...
Aldrin: O.K. That's good...
Armstrong: It's quite dark here in the shade...
Aldrin: Roger...
Armstrong: I'm at the foot of the ladder...

LIKE POWDER

Armstrong: I'm at the foot of the ladder. The legs foot pads are only depressed on the surface about one or two inches, although the surface appears to be very, very fine grained as you get close to it. It's almost like a powder...

Capcom: Roger, Neil.

Aldrin: I'm going to step off the LM now.

Armstrong: That's one small step for man, one giant leap for mankind...

LIGHT-FOOTED

Aldrin: I'm moving off and hanging around the surface and I'm quite lighthearted...

Armstrong: You've found a purple rock?

How the news was given in Russia

MOSCOW RADIO today broadcast a report of Apollo II's landing on the moon. It gave terse details of the activities of the astronauts.

The report said: "We have just received a report that the lunar module of the Apollo II spaceship landed on the moon in the Sea of Tranquillity."

"After landing on the moon an American astronaut, Neil Aldrin, prepared all stations and carried out the necessary technical work.

"Then, for about an hour, the two men carried out the visual observation of the lunar surface from the landing point, they took samples of lunar rocks, and, for particular investigation, the first soil samples.

"Pravda," the Communist Party newspaper, also carried a report of the moon landing.

Luna 15 still a mystery

THERE was mystery early today over the Russian Luna 15 spacecraft, which was put into an orbit around the moon twenty hours before the US astronauts, and no signs that it was about to land.

Sir Bernard Lovell, director of Jodrell Bank, said last night that Luna 15 could not be left in its present orbit for many days.

It could, as far as he knew, land or return to earth, but nothing was certain.

NEIL ARMSTRONG

EDWIN E. ALDRIN

MICHAEL COLLINS

Britain's "heartfelt relief"

—PREMIER

THE PREMIER, who watched the moon landing on television at 10, Downing Street, shortly afterwards said in a television broadcast to America that Britain's feeling was one of "heartfelt relief" that the landing had been safely accomplished.

Mr. Wilson later told ITV Viewers at a breakfast, "All of us were anxious over the dangerous parts of the other dangerous parts of the mission will have to stand before, it not too great."

"It is right to say that our other great feeling is one of great admiration for the way in which this was been planned and worked out..."

Sir Bernard Lovell, director of Jodrell Bank, said after he watched the breakdown of Eagle in the Sea of Tranquillity: "The moment of touchdown was one of the moments of greatest drama in the history of man.

"The moment is this part of the enterprise opens the most spectacular experiences for the future explorations of the universe..."

Timetable of events

Here is a timetable of outstanding events after the two dots men in history landed on the moon.

2.36: Armstrong descends.

3.56: Aldrin descends.

3.39: TV picture of figure on moon.

4.15: Aldrin down-walks ladder.

4.15: Aldrin deserves landing.

4.15: Aldrin steps on moon.

4.51: Sets up flag.

4.51: Stars and Stripes placed.

5.35: President Nixon speaks to moon.

5.51: Scoopfuls of lunar soil picked up.

6.11: Armstrong and Aldrin back in Eagle and hatch closed.

POWER SURGE

CRIMES dropped to less than one-third of the normal level in Milan during the night, industrialists disappeared and offered to pay higher wages.

CHAMPAGNE BREAKFAST:

Interplanetary Television took production teams who worked on the all-night programmes, celebrated with champagne delivered by house and eggs.

in which they are published. . . . I look forward to the publication . . . of daily papers in every town containing a population of
20,000.'[20] This comment confirms yet again that the characteristic
way of looking at the nineteenth-century Press was to see it in terms
of its influence on social and political attitudes; the newspaper could
be a 'mighty agency' or 'mighty power' in relation to 'the people' and
'the public mind'. This capacity to influence, as opposed merely to
inform, was perceived as the key function and acts as the shaper of
the image that the modern reader has of the nineteenth-century
Press. It was a function that corresponded to the view that the Press's
mission was 'to Enlighten, to Civilize, and to Morally Transform the
World'.[21] Since 1871—when this view was propounded—there has
been a gradual shift of emphasis from comment to information, so
that now the primary task, or mission, of the local Press is to present
the facts and, while not entirely abandoning the attempt to mould
political opinion,[22] to leave the reader much more to draw his own
conclusions. In effect, this represents a return to the role of the
eighteenth-century newspapers, although the ratio of local to
national and international news is, in the evening Press, almost the
inverse of that two hundred years ago, and the relationship of
the local Press to the institutions has undergone considerable,
emancipating, change.

Grant's optimism about an ever-growing number of daily local
newspapers, and about the missionary power of the provincial
Press, proved unfounded; the major developments were to take
place in Fleet Street. *Lloyd's Sunday News*, which had been selling
100,000 copies a week in mid-century, became the first newspaper
to sell a million copies in 1896. It seems that once the goals of male
franchise and the amelioration of the harshest aspects of working-
class life had been met—through the Reform Act (1832), Ashley's
Factory Act (1844), Ashley's Act for a ten-hour day (1847), the
second and third Reform Acts (1867, 1884)—the great days of the
provincial Press as an articulator of keenly felt social and political
attitudes, and shaper of these attitudes, were on the wane. Its most
telling sales factor was to be the provision of information about the
local scene—its institutions, its culture, its commerce and its currently
newsworthy citizens.

Nevertheless, for at least two more decades the numbers of provincial newspapers continued to grow, as the list of establishment
dates for the evening Press (see Fig. 2) indicates. The city papers

especially reflected the rising interest in sport, and some placed increased stress on crime and 'human interest' stories—in these latter cases reverting to the news values of the early eighteenth-century printers. In most provincial towns and cities the process of change was by no means abrupt or dramatic; local newspapers tend to be conservative communications media and the influence of community leaders would act as a decisive check on any concept of wholesale popularisation.

This brief outline of the history of the provincial Press enables the following points to be made. First, there has been a marked shift from non-local to local content. No local newspaper reader would now assume that the heading 'Town talk' referred to items from London. Second, the period of its greatest growth and claimed influence was characterised by competitive situations and the vigorous propagation of political opinion. Third, amongst its pioneers were printers of the calibre of Andrew Brice, prepared to face the deterring consequences of exposing the shortcomings of particular local institutions.

The next chapter discusses the decline, during the past fifty years, in the number of competitive situations, and the rise of new forms of ownership.

Notes

1 R. M. Wiles, *Freshest Advices: Early Provincial Newspapers in England* (Columbus, Ohio: Ohio State University Press, 1965), p. 25.
2 *Ibid.*, p. 22.
3 Dr Johnson, *The Idler*, No. 31.
4 G. A. Cranfield, *The Development of the Provincial Newspaper, 1700–60* (Oxford: Clarendon Press, 1962), p. 65.
5 *Leeds Intelligencer*, 12 July 1754.
6 Wiles, *op. cit.*, pp. 291–2.
7 *Memoranda of Evidence submitted to the Royal Commission on the Press* (London: HMSO, 1947), p. 82.
8 See Wiles, *op. cit.*, pp. 275–6.
9 See Cranfield, *op. cit.*, p. 217.
10 See Wiles, *op. cit.*, p. 308.
11 Donald Read, *Press and People* (London: Edward Arnold, 1961). For a useful general survey of available sources of information about the Victorian provincial Press, the reader is referred to chapter 3 of Lionel

Madden's *How to find out about the Victorian period* (Oxford: Pergamon Press, 1970), pp. 22–38.

12 Read, *op. cit.*, p. 49.

13 *Ibid.*, p. 205.

14 *Ibid.*, p. 116.

15 *Ibid.*, p. 124.

16 *Ibid.*, pp. 99–101.

17 See, for example, Cecil King, *The Future of the Press* (London: MacGibbon & Kee, 1967), p. 14. A much more convincing account is offered by Raymond Williams in *The Long Revolution* (London: Chatto & Windus, 1961), pp. 166–7, 173 ff.

18 Charles Dickens, *The Posthumous Papers of the Pickwick Club* (London: J. M. Dent & Sons, Everyman edition, 1913), pp. 159–60.

19 George Eliot, *Middlemarch* (Harmondsworth: Penguin Books, 1965), pp. 392–3.

20 James Grant, *The Newspaper Press: its Origin, Progress, and Present Position*, I (London: 1871), p. 158.

21 *Ibid.*, p. vi.

22 See chapter 12.

2 The monopoly situation; the growth of chain control

The monopoly situation

Since the end of the first world war there has been a decline in the overall numbers of provincial newspapers. The figures for 1921, 1937, 1947,[1] 1967 and 1969 follow:

	1921	1937	1947	1967	1969
Provincial morning	41	28	25	22	22
Provincial evening	89	79	75	77*	79*
Weekly	1,485	1,303	1,162	1,173†	1,163†

* The two London evening newspapers not included.
† Includes the metropolitan weeklies.

Over the forty-eight year period, it is apparent that the provincial morning Press has suffered the most serious decline, down 46 per cent; the evening Press has diminished by 11 per cent and the weeklies by 21 per cent. There has, however, been a slight increase over the past twenty years in the number of evening newspapers (+4).

During the years 1963–64 a spate of evening newspaper closures and mergers was commanding the attention of Press commentators; one of them—a *Financial Times* correspondent—referred to this as 'basically a tidying-up operation'.[2] The process had simply been one of 'rationalisation'; in his conclusion he suggested that since monopoly situations now existed everywhere except Glasgow, there was 'very little point in more rationalisation, just yet'. The term 'rationalisation' implies that an eventual gain will justify any immediate loss, but gain here seems to be gauged in terms of profitability alone. The demise of six city evening newspapers in 1962–64 (at Birmingham, Edinburgh, Leeds, Leicester, Manchester and Nottingham) was therefore presented as a matter for approval: '. . . it has been apparent for some time that where two papers are in competition in an area, one eventually gains the upper hand. From that point, as Mr Roy Thomson put it, "the strong get stronger and the weak get weaker", and advertisers are naturally attracted to the paper which gives them the bigger coverage. The only course is to close down the loser—and a lot of owners have done the inevitable this year.'[2] Lord Thomson's formulation of newspaper 'strength' (i.e. its advertising pulling power) affords the logic here; strength is clearly not primarily perceived as a matter of *quality* when rationalisation is afoot. The 'loser' is the paper that has a declining readership; whether it might be worth trying to preserve for its editorial content or not, it must—unless it has the status of *The Times*—bow to the 'inevitable'.

Every effort, certainly, was made to save the *Manchester Evening Chronicle*, and a brief consideration of the background to its closure will serve to illustrate the process of rationalisation. Between July and November 1960, negotiations were proceeding between the Manchester Guardian and Evening News Ltd and Thomson Newspapers Ltd (the then owners of the *Chronicle*) with a view to collaborating in 'the joint operation of the two Manchester evening papers'.[3] The intention was to improve the financial position of both the *News* and the *Chronicle* by integrating financial and operational control within a new company—North News Ltd—in which the Manchester Guardian and Evening News Ltd would have a controlling interest. Arrangements between the two companies were completed in November 1960. But by June 1962 Mr L. Scott (the chairman) was appealing to the general secretaries of trade unions affiliated to the Printing and Kindred Trades Federation to join in an attempt to save the *Chronicle*; 'the gap between costs and revenue had to be substantially closed during the next few months'. There was at present 'no intention of merging the two papers, much less of closing the "Evening Chronicle" '.[4]

Nevertheless, the last issue of the *Chronicle* appeared just over a year later, on 26 June 1963; its ironic main headline (referring to a Yugoslavian earthquake) ran 'Wiped out'. The *Chronicle*, explained Mr Scott, had been costing some £300,000 a year to keep alive— 'a sum that is far greater than we can afford'.[5] The key to the situation was declining advertising revenue, as Mr Scott pointed out:

'Local advertisers get better results from one paper and make more use of it; that newspaper becomes fatter and full of advertisements; those readers who are interested in advertising prefer it to the other paper, and so more advertisers get even better results from using it. This is a vicious circle that a second newspaper finds hard to break.

The problem of the *Evening Chronicle* in Manchester has not been a failure to hold a substantial readership, but a failure through that readership to give advertisers a worthwhile return.'

They had tried to break down advertisers' resistance and to provide financial inducements for them to use the *Evening Chronicle*, but with depressingly little effect. The following figures showed what had happened to the advertising in the *Chronicle* for a typical period (Saturday excluded):

> Jan. to Mar. 1961, 5,475 col.
>   ,,   1962, 4,693 col.
>   ,,   1963, 4,029 col.[5]

Thus the volume of advertising declined by approximately 26 per cent over a two-year period. The readership fell by about 11 per cent (24,000) during this time, but was still over 258,000 as against the *News*'s 323,000. The then mayor of Manchester referred to the closure as a 'tragedy'; the *Chronicle* and the *News*, he said, 'represented two completely separate approaches to journalism and now there will no longer be a choice'.[6] But the advertiser pays the piper more than the reader, and therefore calls the tune.

The pattern of closure and the diminishing number of competitive situations in the provincial Press were assessed as an unhealthy trend by Francis Williams in his book *Dangerous Estate*. Of the period 1918–57 he wrote:

> Great provincial journals of opinion have suffered in even greater number. In scores of towns and cities where once the battle for freedom of news and opinion found its daily reflection in the challenge and counter-challenge of competing morning and evening newspapers with deep roots in local interests and loyalties, the position has so altered that in fifty-six of the sixty-six cities which are still capable of sustaining any sort of daily newspaper press those who wish to read a paper must content themselves with what is offered to them by one evening paper only. Nor in this time of vastly increasing newspaper readership, and of town and country planning with its stimulation to civic consciousness, have even the provincial weekly newspapers, for so long the traditional voices of their communities on matters of local concern, fared any better. At least 225 such papers have been forced to cease publication during these thirty-eight years.[7]

It has already been noted that further closures since 1957 have resulted in the elimination of evening newspaper competition in England and Wales; the era of 'challenge and counter-challenge'—Baines versus O'Connor—has passed for this sector of the provincial

Press. Williams' point is that the pattern of change has produced a situation unsuited to contemporary community needs; it appears that he has local politics particularly in mind, and feels that competing newspapers could do much to promote greater interest in them. He seeks vigorous debate, and sees this as essential for the healthy functioning of democracy: 'democracy operates best where the strong clash of divergent opinions compels the lively examination of great issues. It was through the stimulation of debate that the provincial press best served the nation in the great flowering of journalism that followed the abolition of the taxes on knowledge.'[8]

In chapter 12 it is shown that approximately 40 per cent of the evening newspapers sampled, and 90 per cent of the weeklies, are politically neutral; a further 40 per cent of the former are Conservative-leaning, and up to 10 per cent of the latter. Thus the majority (at least 80 per cent) of the evening Press is either neutral or variously Conservative, as is almost the entire weekly Press. Only in a minority of Conservative-supporting newspapers is the advocacy at all vigorous, so that Williams' charge that the provincial Press opts for a 'circumspect neutrality in many matters where the clash of opinion is desirable'[8] is a largely valid generalisation.

The ideal that Williams has in mind is the typical competitive situation of the first half of the nineteenth century. He sees the monopoly newspaper as incomplete—an army without an opposing force. He wants 'clashes'—the 'strong clash' of conflicting opinions. In effect, he wants a rebirth of the radical provincial Press which largely breathed its last breath in the inter-war period. At present, the monopoly newspaper (i.e. all regional evening newspapers in England and Wales, and most weeklies)—whether partisan or neutral—does not have to face the counter-challenge of a competitor. Contradiction of its opinions is confined to those news reports that contain opposing views and to the correspondence column, except at election time, when all parties may be given feature space. One effect of the drastic reduction in competitive situations, therefore, is a significant impairment of one newspaper function cogently advocated by Kemsley Newspapers Ltd in their evidence to the 1947 Commission: 'Just as Parliament is made alive by the cut and thrust of debate, so in the country at large, the Press provides a great forum of opinion out of which, if expression be free, truth will emerge.'[9] The public's right to dissent may still be free, but the trend towards 'circumspect neutrality' and the gradual loss of rival voices mean that the old cut and thrust of debate has virtually departed.

It is probable that the principal motive behind the adoption of a neutral or anaemically partisan position, as opposed to full-blooded partisan commitment, is that of securing maximum sales; there is then no risk of alienating readers who strongly support one of the main political parties. Spokesmen for such positions claim that they are more likely to present political news 'straight', and offer opinions arrived at after objective evaluation, than the newspaper tied to one party. As the Bristol Evening Post Ltd put it in their evidence to the 1947 Royal Commission, 'a non-party newspaper is in a happier position, because it draws its readers from supporters of all political parties, and it is not to its advantage to temper its selection of news to the prejudices of any section of its public'.[10] There are also a number of secondary reasons for the widespread withdrawal from partisanship. First, the majority of readers will be exposed to the political persuasions of the *Express*, the *Mirror* or the *Mail*; they may welcome the absence of such persuasion in the local Press. As Mr W. A. McWhirter, the then managing director of Northcliffe Newspapers Group Ltd, suggested to the 1947 Commission, 'people do not want politics shoved down their throats day after day'.[11] Second, evening newspapers are now printed earlier than formerly so that the effect of rush-hour traffic can be minimised; as a result, the main Parliamentary debates of the day must at best be briefly reported in the 'stop press' column. Thus the actual volume of political reporting has undergone a reduction, and the formerly close association between the evening Press and Parliamentary controversy, as a sales factor, has been almost lost.

There is not, in fact, any evidence to support the theory that vigorous partisanship on the part of a provincial newspaper impairs its sales figures. In 1964 the percentage of local households covered by the strongly Conservative *Yorkshire Evening Post* was 90·08 per cent; this figure was in fact slightly higher than the average for the ten biggest members of the Evening Newspaper Advertising Bureau —88·7 per cent. Even so, neutrality burgeons. Interestingly, those newspaper companies that adopt the 'non-party' posture (to which might be added those with a virtually nominal partisan commitment) have reverted to that preferred by the earliest eighteenth-century printers. For instance, on 21 February 1734, the printer of the *Derby Mercury* announced that 'as it is undoubtedly my

Interest to be equally willing and faithful in serving all Parties, so I hope all who read my News Paper may be convinced that I am so far from being such a Bigot as to act contrary to that Interest'. Non-party newspapers today would no doubt echo these sentiments in spite of the point made about the *Yorkshire Evening Post*.

Much as one may regret the passing of the old kind of 'challenge and counter-challenge', there is no prospect of any return in the foreseeable future to the old pattern of keen local rivalry. Even if there were, the continuing and dominant impact of the national media must surely mean that the early nineteenth-century level of interest and involvement on the local Press's part can never return in relation to Parliamentary politics. Yet a resurgence of competitive situations might well spark off a much livelier interest in town hall affairs; public involvement could hardly fail to be stimulated if newspapers of the Left were to be established in cities like Birmingham or Leeds.

However, the monopoly newspaper of today enjoys at least one important advantage over its Victorian predecessors. For competing newspapers now would, in most cases, aim their content at part, and not the whole of the available readership; one, perhaps, at the 'intelligent layman', and the other at the 'man in the street'—to use two rather crude and partially overlapping descriptions. The former might resemble a localised *Daily Telegraph*; the latter might correspond more nearly to the *Daily Mirror* in its pattern of content selection and presentational techniques. 'Challenge and counter-challenge' could merely take the form of an insipid Conservatism confronting a flimsy radical platform. If competition were to take this form, neither paper would speak to and for the community as a whole in the way that, say, the weekly *Buxton Advertiser and Herald and High Peak News* does in its circulation area. In such a town the local newspaper is very much 'our paper'; as Westminster Press Provincial Newspapers Ltd pointed out in evidence to the 1947 Commission, this type of paper is 'often regarded by the public . . . as "their paper" in a much more personal sense than is a national paper'.[12] Obviously this comment would apply to one of two competing local newspapers, but here 'our paper' might signify 'the paper that serves the interests of our socio-cultural sector'. It would have been in this way that the middle classes of Leeds might have referred to the *Leeds Mercury* in its hey-day as 'our paper'. So a provincial newspaper's monopoly situation does put it in the position of being able to speak for and to a whole community of readers; this represents a possible gain to offset the loss of 'challenge and counter-challenge'. Even so, competition between two vigorously conducted and journalistically responsible local papers would seem to be the state of affairs most likely to promote a community's best interest.

Chain control

Before discussing the growing hold of the major London-based chain groups on the provincial Press, it is important to stress that about 45 per cent of evening newspapers, and at least 75 per cent of weeklies, are still owned by regional groups or individual pro-prietors. Evening newspapers like the *Huddersfield Daily Examiner*, Bolton *Evening News*, *Manchester Evening News*, *Liverpool Echo*, *Birmingham Evening Mail*, Wolverhampton *Express and Star*, *Nottingham Evening Post*, Portsmouth *Evening News* and *Cambridge Evening News* are amongst those that remain independent. The range of newspapers in the independent sector can be indicated by some comparisons between the small circulation weekly *The Epworth Bells* and a regional evening newspaper like the *Birmingham Evening Mail*. *The Epworth Bells* still gives its front page over to local advertising and has a circulation of 7,000—largely in the fifty square mile area of the Isle of Axholme, east of Doncaster. It is estimated that 99 per cent of homes in the Isle take the *Bells*. The editor is the only full-time member of the editorial staff; he is supported, of course, by district correspondents. The *Bells* celebrates its centenary in 1972; the editor writes that 'it is profitably successful and has a high reputation among the local population'. In contrast, the *Birmingham Evening Mail*—centenary year, 1970—is housed in a £7½ million building in the city centre; with its sister paper, the morning *Post*, it occupies a total floor space of ten and a half acres. Its editorial staff in September 1970 numbered 113 (excluding clerical staff and artists): thirty head office reporters and news desk staff, twenty-three news sub-editors, twenty-five district staff reporters, fifteen executive and features staff, twenty sports staff and nine photographers. It sells up to 400,000 copies daily and covers 80 per cent of households in the main city areas. The group's 1970 statement showed pre-tax profits of £1,328,000 for the year ending 30 June 1970.

There is a similar, but not quite so extreme, range of newspapers within four of the five major chains, whose potential influence on editorial opinion and content has intermittently prompted expressions of anxiety and concern. Anxiety about the powers of the proprietor in control of a large group of newspapers largely inspired the demand for the 1947 Royal Commission on the Press; the Commission's terms of reference therefore laid special stress on the forms of newspaper ownership, and it sought particularly to examine monopolistic tendencies in control. The 'chains' (a 'chain' being defined as an 'organisation having single or multiple units in several widely separated places') therefore came in for close scrutiny. The Commission concluded that the current level of chain ownership did not call for any remedial action, but added that further concentration of ownership would be undesirable.

Nevertheless, the groups have been slowly adding to their numbers and the pace of expansion has, in the case of the Thomson and United Newspapers groups, accelerated during the 1960s. Another national group, the International Publishing Corporation Ltd (owners of the *Daily Mirror*) has also entered the provincial field. Before considering the implications of this expansion, a brief analysis of the extent of chain ownership as it stood in 1969 is necessary. At the end of this year about 55 per cent of English and Welsh provincial evening newspapers were owned by five London-based groups:

1. News of the World Organisation Ltd

    Hereford Evening News, Worcester Evening News. Twenty-three weeklies.

2. Associated Newspapers (Northcliffe Group)

    Daily Mail (Hull), *Grimsby/Scunthorpe Evening Telegraph Lincolnshire Echo, Evening Sentinel* (Stoke on Trent), *Derby Evening Telegraph, Leicester Mercury, South Wales Evening Post* (Swansea), *Citizen* (Gloucester), *Gloucestershire Echo* (Cheltenham), *Western Evening Herald* (Plymouth), *Express and Echo* (Exeter), *Herald Express* (Torquay). Also twenty-nine weeklies.

3. United Newspapers

    The Star (Sheffield), *Yorkshire Evening Post* (Leeds), *Doncaster Evening Post, Lancashire Evening Post* (Preston), *West Lanca-*

shire Evening Gazette (Blackpool), *Chronicle and Echo* (Northampton). Also thirty-five weeklies.

4. The Thomson Organisation

Lancashire Evening Telegraph (Blackburn), *Evening Star* (Burnley), *Evening Chronicle* (Newcastle), *Evening Gazette* (Middlesbrough), *South Wales Echo* (Cardiff), *Evening Echo* (Watford), *Evening Post* (Luton), *Evening Post* (Reading), and—jointly with the Westminster Press Group—*Evening Mail* (Slough). Also twenty-two weeklies.

5. Westminster Press Group

North Western Evening Mail (Barrow), *Telegraph and Argus* (Bradford), *Evening Despatch* (Darlington), *Yorkshire Evening Press* (York), *Shields Gazette* (South Shields), *Oxford Mail*, *Bath and Wilts Evening Chronicle*, *Evening Advertiser* (Swindon), *Evening Argus* (Brighton), *Evening Echo* (Southend on Sea). Also eighty-three weeklies.

In 1964 the weekly Press was at the most 18 per cent owned by the major groups, as the following extract from a *Financial Times* article indicates:

... the vast majority of weekly newspapers are still published by family firms. They have—so far—effectively resisted the offensive by the big groups. . . . In 1948 five groups, controlling 19 or more weeklies each, owned 6·7% of the total. By 1961 this percentage had increased, but was still no higher than 11·2%. It is very doubtful whether the 18% mark has yet been reached.
Some of the family firms are, of course, groups in themselves, owning more than one local paper. Nevertheless, there is still a strong core of one-man proprietors. [But] Lord Thomson would like to have many more—'put in better management, make them better papers, and they will be more profitable still' was his comment.[13]

By the end of 1969 at least 200 weeklies were owned by the major groups, then well on the way to controlling 25 per cent of the weekly total.

It is important to consider the implications of this pattern of change. In recent years the main anxiety of those who oppose the further extension of chain ownership has arisen very much from the way that a proprietor like Lord Thomson talks about his newspapers: 'put in better management, make them better papers, and

they will be more profitable still'. There is a confident assumption
here that Thomson House has all the answers; it seems to be held
as axiomatic that a local newspaper can be made better through
membership of a large London-based organisation. In this respect,
the tone is condescending; the relationship implied is that of the pike
to the minnow. The order of priorities in 'better . . . more profitable
still' is ominous; the effect is to make the higher degree of profitability the ultimate end in view. Such an end denotes a commercial
orientation that contrasts with the position recommended by the
Manchester Guardian and Evening News Ltd in their evidence to
the 1947 Commission: 'newspaper ownership should be conceived
of rather as a public trust than as an instrument for making the
maximum private profit'.[14]

Contemporary critics of the chains, then, fear an excessive
emphasis on profitability; twenty years ago the case against them
was lodged mainly in terms of the potential political influence that
they afforded their respective proprietors. It was feared that the
latter were in a position to impair the objectivity that should characterise news reporting, and to intrude their own political attitudes into
the columns reserved for comment. Accordingly, the Royal Commission of 1947 included the following question in its questionnaire
to ninety-five newspaper companies: 'Do you consider that the
concentration of control of organs of the Press works for or against
the accurate presentation of news and the adequate expression of
opinion?' In their replies, about 40 per cent of the fifty-nine English
provincial newspaper companies addressed evinced some degree of
concern at group control; 38 per cent felt that any assessment must
depend on the motives or performance of particular chains, or were
non-committal; 22 per cent (including the major chains themselves)
were on the whole favourably disposed towards this form of management. Most of the adversely critical comments were on the lines
of the following extract from the reply submitted by the Norfolk
News Co. Ltd: 'the chief objection in our view is that unless central
control is exercised very lightly and with much public spirit there is
bound to be a sterile uniformity in editorial outlook, leaving the
impression on the public that all the strings are pulled by a Press
magnate remote from and impervious to local opinion'.[15]

Turning again to the provincial Press of today, it is important
first to enlarge on one's view that critics now are predominantly
concerned at the evidence of an accentuation of commercialism.

non-'trivialisation' of Regs. v. Sun!

Raymond Williams, for instance, fears that 'all the basic purposes of communication—the sharing of human experience' may become subordinated to the drive towards the saturation coverage that will command the attention of advertisers. 'The pressure here is actually increasing. The old kind of newspaper proprietor, who wanted control so that he could propagate his opinions, is being replaced by a kind of proprietor who says he is not interested in opinions but simply in selling as many papers as he can. What was once a means to some larger policy has become in many cases the policy itself.'[16]

In terms of newspaper content, the danger is that a proprietorial demand for increased sales may induce an editor whose journalistic standards are high to compromise them. 'Hard' news reporting about politics, local government and so on may be reduced, and more emphasis put on crime, violence and lightweight 'human interest' stories. Similarly, responsible feature material aimed at the intelligent layman may slowly give ground to supposed circulation boosters, such as syndicated features about non-local celebrities— 'pop' stars and 'sex symbols'. Effort and imagination that should be focusing on new and relevant ways of exploring and evaluating local community life will tend to be diverted to the devising of undemanding circulation-raisers.

The editor who is 'pressured' along these lines may have to face some local cynicism about the resulting changes, but the proprietor is virtually immune in his capacity as 'a Press magnate remote from and impervious to local opinion'. It is for this reason that a number of provincial companies, in their evidence to the 1947 Commission, sketched out the sort of ideal organisational structure proposed by the Holmesdale Press Ltd: 'I believe in local newspapers being in the hands of local people who have at heart the welfare of the district in which they work, and have their recreation and interests in the district in which they spend their lives.'[17] The proprietor who is in regular contact with the community leaders in his circulation area may well be much more wary of the effect of any trivialisation than the London-based chain owner.

The argument thus far has stressed the potential dangers in chain control; it would be unfair to the groups concerned not to stress equally that these dangers need only be latent. Furthermore, a number of advantages are attendant upon group membership. The chain newspaper stands to enjoy a much more comprehensive news service—a point put to the 1947 Commission by Mr F. M. Inwood,

then the London editor of Westminster Press Provincial Newspapers Ltd:

A paper in a group has a very much better service than individual
papers. For example, something happened a few weeks ago at Bradford.
We were able to put three men on it, for one small Bradford item. Where-
ever you can now you send out a couple of men to a job, to a conference,
for instance, to look out for local points, whereas when the papers were
on their own they were able to send only one. You get a much wider special
coverage.[18]

Mr Inwood also showed how an official White Paper could be
assessed in a way that would be beyond the compass of most independent newspapers: 'We should have a man in London examining the
White Paper from the political standpoint, another from the industrial standpoint, and so on; and if there is an ordinary news angle,
that will be there too.'[18] If this editor's analysis of his group's
practice is, as seems likely, valid for other chain organisations, then
the chain can offer more coverage in depth of some types of news
story and a more comprehensive evaluation of national plans,
policies or events than all but the largest of the independents.

Again, although the concept of rationalisation ('close down or
merge a "loser" ') seems to be fashionable at the present time, it is
still open to a chain proprietor to nurture a failing newspaper in the
hope that it will revive—and without necessarily demanding changes
of a kind that might be seen as qualitative impairments. The Westminster Press group, for instance, did its utmost to restore the
fortunes of several ailing Liberal newspapers in the period that followed the first world war; between 1921 and 1934 the group paid no
dividend to its shareholders, and showed a profit only in 1930 and
1933. In 1923 the total loss was £337,403.[19] The majority of these
radical newspapers have since been merged with competitors or
closed down, but their lives were certainly prolonged.

Finally, the principal chains are, if their profits are healthy, in an
advantageous position to develop new papers as and when oppor-
tunities present themselves; during the period 1964–69, for instance,
the Thomson Organisation launched new evening newspapers at
Burnley, Reading, Watford, Luton and Slough. These have helped
to arrest the trend of numerical decline that has characterised the
recent history of the provincial Press.

These, then, are amongst the possible positive contributions that
the chains can make to the well-being of the provincial newspaper

industry—itself a descriptive term to which Scarborough and District Newspapers Ltd took exception in comments to the 1947 Commission: 'there are some of us engaged in journalism who are old-fashioned enough to regard it not as an industry, but as a profession'.[20] The principal theoretical dangers that lie in chain control stem from the power that is conferred upon the owners; power to try to shape public opinions and attitudes from the centre, and to elevate the profit motive above all others. In the final analysis the quality of the chain newspaper must reflect the journalistic criteria of its proprietor(s), whose duty ought to be to 'conform to the proper standards of newspaper integrity'.[21] It is up to him to heed C. P. Scott's assessment of the 'business' of the Press:

> . . . a newspaper has two sides to it. It is a business like any other, and has to pay in the material sense in order to live. But it is much more than a business; it is an institution; it reflects and it influences the life of a whole community; it may even affect wider destinies.
> . . . It may educate, stimulate, assist, or it may do the opposite. It has, therefore, a moral as well as a material existence, and its character and influence are in the main determined by the balance of these two forces. It may make profit or power its first object, or it may conceive itself as fulfilling a higher and more exacting function.[22]

In spite of the contemporary predominance of the monopoly situation and the steady growth of the chain organisations, it is still the case that a community's best interests would be served by two locally owned competing newspapers—with the proviso, of course, that these cultivate the moral as well as the material dimension. Such competition should serve to foster public interest in local institutions, and to make the achievement of local consensus a less compelling goal. Although a 1970 survey showed that there were as many as twenty radical community journals, such as *The Mole* (Brighton) and *Crab* (*Chelmsford Radical Bulletin*)—papers that are 'spurred on by community action, and themselves stimulate it further'[23]—the established monopolies are hardly likely to see any significant challenge in these at present. But they may well gather momentum, and attract increasing attention, during the 1970s.

Fig. 2 The centres of evening newspaper publication in England and Wales, 1969. *By courtesy of the Evening Newspaper Advertising Bureau and Map Productions Ltd; map Crown copyright.*

Publication centre	Newspaper	1969 circulation	Year of establishment
Barrow	*North Western Evening Mail*	28,935	1898
Bath	*Bath and Wilts. Evening Chronicle*	32,879	1760
Birmingham	*Birmingham Evening Mail*	396,743	1870
Blackburn	*Lancashire Evening Telegraph*	68,974	1886
Blackpool	*West Lancashire Evening Gazette*	72,369	1929
Bolton	*Evening News*	85,796	1867
Bournemouth	*Evening Echo*	63,756	1900
Bradford	*Telegraph and Argus*	124,761	1868
Brighton	*Evening Argus*	100,135	1880
Bristol	*Evening Post*	183,371	1932

Burnley	Evening Star	26,275	1965
Burton on Trent	Burton Daily Mail	25,125	1898
Cambridge	Cambridge Evening News	47,615	1888
Carlisle	Cumberland Evening News and Star	29,573	1914
Chatham	Chatham/Rochester/Gillingham		
	Evening Post	19,343	1968
Cheltenham	Gloucestershire Echo	35,000+	1873
Coventry	Coventry Evening Telegraph	122,665	1891
Darlington	Evening Despatch	22,696	1914
Derby	Derby Evening Telegraph	98,000+	1879
Doncaster	Doncaster Evening Post	35,161	1966
Exeter	Express and Echo	38,969	1864
Gloucester	Citizen	40,000+	1876
Grimsby	Grimsby Evening Telegraph	73,000+	1897
Halifax	Halifax Evening Courier and		
	Guardian	43,217	1892
Hartlepool	Northern Daily Mail	33,839	1877
Hereford	Hereford Evening News	8,785	1959
Huddersfield	Huddersfield Daily Examiner	51,660	1871
Hull	Daily Mail	133,000+	1885
Ipswich	Evening Star	48,443	1885
Ketley	Shropshire Star	46,970	1964
Kettering	Northamptonshire Evening Telegraph	49,550	1897
Leeds	Yorkshire Evening Post	253,330	1890
Leicester	Leicester Mercury	180,000+	1874
Lincoln	Lincolnshire Echo	37,000+	1893
Liverpool	Liverpool Echo	389,367	1879
Luton	Evening Post	53,766	1967
Manchester	Manchester Evening News and		
	Chronicle	450,204	1868
Middlesbrough	Evening Gazette	119,465	1869
Newcastle on Tyne	Evening Chronicle	236,511	1885
Northampton	Chronicle and Echo	56,021	1880
Norwich	Eastern Evening News	74,149	1882
Nottingham	Evening Post and News	n.a.	1878
Nuneaton	Nuneaton Evening Tribune	17,637	1914
Oldham	Oldham Evening Chronicle	46,650	1880
Oxford	Oxford Mail	44,091	1928
Peterborough	Peterborough Evening Telegraph	22,351	1960
Plymouth	Western Evening Herald and		
	Western Evening News	67,213	1895
Portsmouth	The News	103,373	1877
Preston	Lancashire Evening Post	138,910	1886
Reading	Evening Post	50,876	1965
Scarborough	Scarborough Evening News	15,678	1876
Sheffield	The Star	202,206	1887
South Shields	Shields Gazette	36,900	1849
Slough	Evening Mail	23,409	1969
Southampton	Southern Evening Echo	99,683	1888
Southend	Evening Echo	50,000	1969
Stoke on Trent	Evening Sentinel	125,000+	1873
Sunderland	Sunderland Echo	84,668	1873
Swindon	Evening Advertiser	35,366	1898

Torquay	*Herald–Express*	25,579	1921
Watford	*Evening Echo*	53,623	1967
Weymouth	*Dorset Evening Echo*	22,495	1921
Wolverhampton	*Express and Star*	233,278	1874
Worcester	*Worcester Evening News*	31,752	1880
York	*Yorkshire Evening Press*	60,812	1882
Cardiff	*South Wales Echo*	148,031	1884
Newport	*South Wales Argus*	57,396	1892
Swansea	*South Wales Evening Post*	71,000+	1861

The data are drawn from Benn's *Newspaper Press Directory*, 1970, *Willing's Press Guide*, 1970, and the ENAB publication *Where?* for 1970.

Notes

1 The figures for 1921, 1937 and 1947 are taken from Raymond Williams, *The Long Revolution* (London: Chatto & Windus, 1961), p. 210; those for 1967 and 1969 from Benn's *Newspaper Press Directory*.
2 *Financial Times* correspondent, 'Provincial newspapers after the pruning season', *Financial Times*, 28 November 1963.
3 *Manchester Guardian*, 23 September 1960.
4 *Ibid.*, 8 June, 1962.
5 *Manchester Evening News*, 27 July 1963.
6 *The Guardian*, 27 July 1963.
7 Francis Williams, *Dangerous Estate* (London: Arrow Books, 1959), pp. 11–12.
8 *Ibid.*, p. 152.
9 *Memoranda of Evidence* (1947 Royal Commission), p. 103. There are still a few competitive situations in the weekly sector, e.g. at Chester, Stockport and Brighton.
10 *Ibid.*, p. 56.
11 *Minutes of Evidence taken before the Royal Commission* on the Press, 21 January 1948 (London: HMSO, 1948), Minute 5395, p. 18.
12 *Memoranda of Evidence*, p. 200.
13 *Financial Times* correspondent, 'Plenty of life in local weeklies', *Financial Times*, 4 May 1964.
14 *Memoranda of Evidence*, p. 130.
15 *Ibid.*, p. 137.
16 Raymond Williams, *Britain in the Sixties: Communications* (Harmondsworth: Penguin Books, 1962), p. 24.
17 *Memoranda of Evidence*, p. 93.
18 *Minutes of Evidence*, 4 February 1948, pp. 20–1.
19 *Memoranda of Evidence*, pp. 197–8.
20 *Ibid.*, p. 168.
21 *Ibid.*, p. 78.
22 *Ibid.*, p. 131.
23 See K. Worpole and R. Hudson, 'Community Press', *New Society*, 24 September, 1970.

3 The nature and influence of the provincial newspaper readership

The popular national dailies are so often described as amongst the 'mass media' (media, presumably, of appeal to 'the mass') that it is easy to overlook the fact that, within their main circulation areas, some provincial newspapers are bought by a higher percentage of readers than the combined percentage readership of the *Daily Mirror*, the *Daily Express* and the *Daily Mail*. (Between July 1963 and July 1964 88 per cent of all adults read at least one of these three papers.) They are therefore 'mass media' within the confines of particular localities or regions—if 'mass' is freed from any acquired overtones tending to make it synonymous with 'the herd'. Their appeal, in many instances, is to a large majority of local people; the provincial newspaper operates on this assumption, as Hirst Kidd & Rennie Ltd pointed out to the 1947 Commission: 'We are a local paper, and our circulation is therefore not confined to any one section of the community, either politically or economically.'[1]

This claim can be rooted in hard fact. A necessary preliminary is to survey the circulation sizes of the sixty-five English provincial evening newspapers, as these stood at the end of 1969. The following figures result after their distribution into five categories:

(*a*)	Below 25,000	8
(*b*)	25,000–50,000	22
(*c*)	50,000–100,000	17
(*d*)	100,000–250,000	13
(*e*)	250,000–500,000	5

The fact that almost half the newspapers in question have circulations under 50,000—categories (*a*) and (*b*)—serves as a caution not to think of the evening Press solely in terms of the 'big city' newspapers. Three main groupings can be made: (1) the small towns, with circulations from 8,500 to 25,000, (2) the medium-sized town, with circulations from 25,000 to 100,000 and (3) the large town or

city with circulations over 100,000. The totals of evening newspapers
in each category are eight, thirty-nine and eighteen respectively.
Numerically, the newspapers of medium-sized towns (e.g. Blackpool,
Huddersfield, Norwich and Oxford) constitute the single largest
category—60 per cent of all.

The 'big city' evening newspapers are characterised by a very high
percentage household coverage in the central urban areas; taking the
ten largest of the forty-eight members of the Evening Newspaper
Advertising Bureau in 1969, the range was from 78·84 per cent
(*Yorkshire Evening Post*) to 93·28 per cent (*Lancashire Evening Post*).
The average percentage for the ten newspapers of Manchester,
Birmingham, Leeds, Newcastle upon Tyne, Wolverhampton,
Sheffield, Preston, Bristol, Bradford and Coventry was 82·8. The
total number of copies sold daily in the entire circulation areas of the
ten was 2,341,979—or almost half the national daily sales of the
Daily Mirror (4,924,157) during the same period. Considering all
forty-eight members of E N A B, thirty-seven were taken by not less
than two-thirds of all households (i.e. in the main distribution areas),
and thirty-two by 75 per cent or more of all households. This last
figure, together with that for the ten largest members (82·8 per cent),
suggests that the evening newspaper can properly be regarded as one
that is taken by all sections of the community.[2] Further proof of this
is afforded by the data of the Newspaper Society's regional readership and markets survey of 1961, which shows that there is a fairly
close correspondence between the sizes of social groups within the
country as a whole and the sizes of these groups in terms of evening
newspaper readers. In 1965, the ratio of ABC1 (i.e. upper middle,
middle and lower middle) population numbers to C2DE (i.e. skilled
working class, working class and those at the lowest levels of sub-
sistence) was approximately 1 : 2·3; the ratio of ABC1 to C2DE
readers of evening newspapers was 1 : 2·6—a weighting slightly in
favour of the working-class groups. Slight variations occur from
region to region; for example, 1 : 2·7 in Yorkshire, 1 : 2·6 in the
Midlands and 1 : 2·5 in the South. Thus the evening newspaper is
marginally more popular with the working classes in the North than
in the South.

It is important to relate the ratios elicited rather more closely to
the educational background and the national newspaper reading
preferences of the various social groups. Focusing on the evening
newspaper readers of the Midlands region, table 1 shows how many

readers in each social grade had a terminal education age of fifteen or less.

Table 1

Social class	Total numbers of readers	Number whose education ended at 15 or less
A (approx.)	18,525	2,779
B (approx.)	55,575	17,228
C1	177,000	100,890
C2	350,400	304,848
DE	269,770	248,188
	871,270	673,933

Expressed as a percentage, 77 per cent of Midlands evening newspaper readers completed their formal education at fifteen or earlier. A percentage as high as this can therefore be assessed as a majority; the remaining 23 per cent are the minority who do not leave school or complete their education until sixteen or later. Thus, when provincial newspaper editors refer to majorities and minorities of readers in a way which points to their assumed level of education, these are the proportions they will broadly have in mind (the figures refer, of course, to the early 1960s).

The national newspaper reading habits of the majority and minority groups outlined show marked differences as well as some overlaps. In *Education, Social Class and the Reading of Newspapers and Magazines*[3] Mark Abrams shows that the most popular national daily with readers having a TEA (terminal education age) of nineteen or more is the *Daily Telegraph*, readers having a TEA of sixteen–eighteen the *Daily Express*, and readers of TEA fifteen or less the *Daily Mirror*. In all three sections the *Daily Express* is read by at least one-quarter of the total and the *Daily Mail* by approximately one-sixth. The paper most likely to be read by the 15·5 per cent of all adults with a TEA of sixteen–eighteen is the *Daily Express* (38 per cent), followed by the *Daily Telegraph* (27 per cent), the *Daily Mail* (24 per cent) and *Daily Mirror* (23 per cent). The paper most likely to be read by the 81 per cent of all adults with a TEA of fifteen or less is the *Daily Mirror* (42 per cent), followed by the *Daily Express* (32 per cent).

Accordingly, the Midlands evening newspaper editor is confronted by a readership which consists of a majority (77 per cent) and a minority (23 per cent)—the division being determined by the TEA of each. Of the majority roughly 42 per cent take the *Mirror*; of the minority, again approximately, 40 per cent take either the *Telegraph* (27 per cent), the *Times* (7 per cent) or the *Guardian* (6 per cent). This leaves out of the account the *Birmingham Post*, a 'quality' regional daily with a 1964 circulation of 73,544. The paper that most links the 'majority' and 'minority' is the *Daily Express*, taken by 38 per cent of the former and 32 per cent of the latter. This national daily, on the face of things, would seem to afford a viable 'model' for the provincial editor to consider. But in practice the factors discussed later in this chapter that make the typical local newspaper distinguishable—quite apart from the local emphasis of the content—from the popular national dailies result in its being closer to the *Daily Telegraph* in the tone and style of its reporting, although the parallel cannot be pressed further. The detailed coverage of political and cultural matters in the *Telegraph*, for instance, is less in evidence.

Turning briefly to the weekly newspaper, Newspaper Society statistics show that this is particularly favoured by middle-class readers, and by the inhabitants of towns with a population under 100,000 and rural areas; further, there is a general trend (to which there are some exceptions) of a higher percentage of households taking a weekly as one moves from North to South. These generalisations emerge from the figures in table 2.

Table 2

Region	Percentage of particular social grades taking a weekly newspaper
Yorkshire:	ABC1, 51 per cent; C2, 47 per cent; DE, 38 per cent.
Midlands:	AB, 64 per cent; C1, 50 per cent; C2, 41 per cent; DE, 46 per cent.
South:	ABC1, 70 per cent; C2, 59 per cent; DE, 56 per cent.

The proportion of ABC1 to C2DE readers of weekly newspapers in Yorkshire is the same as the proportion of ABC1 to C2DE social

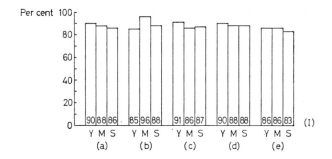

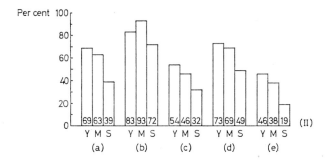

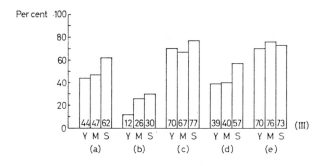

Fig. 3 Community coverage of the evening and weekly Press in Yorkshire, the west Midlands and the South, 1961: proportion of housewives reading (I) any local paper, (II) any evening newspaper, (III) any weekly newspaper. **Key** (*a*) All housewives, (*b*) towns over 100,000, (*c*) towns under 100,000, (*d*) all urban areas, (*e*) all rural areas. *Y* Yorkshire, *M* Midlands (Herefordshire, Shropshire, Staffordshire, Warwickshire, Worcestershire), *S* South (Berkshire, Buckinghamshire, Dorset, Hampshire, Oxfordshire). Note: these statistics pre-date the establishment of the *Doncaster Evening Post* (Yorkshire), the *Shropshire Star* (west Midlands) and the Reading *Evening Post* (South). *By courtesy of the Newspaper Society*

groups in the population as a whole—1 : 2·3. Lower proportions of C2DE readers obtain in the Midlands (1 : 1·9) and the South (1 : 1·6).

The relative popularity of the evening newspaper in the urban North, and of the weekly in the comparatively rural South, is easily demonstrated. The lowest percentage, of any social grade, taking an evening newspaper in Yorkshire was 68 (C2 group); in the South only 48 per cent of the C2 group took one. The lowest readership for the weekly in the South was 56 per cent (DE groups); in the North only 38 per cent of the DE groups took one.

One further point about the overall coverage of the evening and weekly Press is worth making, namely, that taking into account three community classifications—towns over 100,000, towns under 100,000 and all rural areas—wherever the evening newspaper coverage is less than 68 per cent of households, the weekly coverage will usually be not less than 57 per cent. Thus in the majority of communities *either* the evening newspaper *or* the weekly is taken by 57 per cent or more of local people. This figure represents the minimum extent to which the provincial newspaper can be regarded as a mass medium; it will be recalled that, of the forty-eight communities served by English members of ENAB, household coverage in the main distribution areas was over 75 per cent in thirty-two cases. As a generalisation, one may say that in any given type of community it is probable that either the evening or the weekly newspaper will be at least as 'mass circulating' as the *Daily Mirror* and *Daily Mail* circulations combined, i.e. 55 per cent of all adults. In the light of these figures it is appropriate to move on to a consideration of the ways in which provincial newspaper readerships—including majorities and minorities variously defined—influence the choice of content and the working principles of editors.

The influence of provincial newspaper readers

All provincial newspaper readers may be said to share the areas of interest denoted by main headlines. Referring particularly to evening newspapers, the editor of the *Oxford Mail* has said: 'The variations in street sales show that absolutely major national and international events, accidents and crime provide a basic impulse to buy a newspaper.'[4] The analyses of main headlines (see chapter 5) show more fully what kinds of news provide this basic impulse: news of wars, riots, accidents and disasters; deaths of public figures; Government policies, plans and decisions—especially where these affect the reader as consumer; murders, prison escapes and so on. Main news stories are selected for their capacity to involve the reader—either by directly affecting his own life or by stimulating his imagination. Some of the types of news that command involvement have not changed significantly over the 266 years of provincial newspaper history; the editor of the *Bristol Evening Post*, in his evidence to the 1947 Commission, might—apart from his inclusion of sport—have been writing of the eighteenth-century reading public: '. . . it would be absurd to deny that there is a vast public interest in sport, in the absorbing trial or gripping crime or human interest story and the like . . .'[5]

Having pointed to some of the continuing areas of news appeal, one must add that in every age the nature of social and technological change may result in a particular emphasis on one or more kinds of news within or outside the traditional news staple. In order to discuss the contemporary situation more effectively, it is necessary to sketch out two broad categories of main headline news. The first may be styled 'institutional informative'; it includes, for example, news of national government policies and decisions and of local government. The second category contains some element of drama— news of conflict, disaster, accidents, crime and some sports news and human interest stories belong in this general area.

As a means of assessing the nature of any changes in reader interests in the post-war years, nine evening newspaper editors were asked whether public enthusiasm for the two categories specified had increased, remained constant or diminished during the past two decades.[6] The majority (two-thirds) felt that there had been a marked growth of interest in 'institutional informative' news stories; the remainder discerned a slight shift in the same direction. The relatively greater affluence of contemporary society was regarded as the principal cause; readerships, having more money, were more eager to assimilate information of the kind that had bearing on their choices as citizens and consumers. One editor suggested that 'interests have widened to social questions affecting family life and health, holidays, children, schools, home budgets—these are questions that are of immediate and absorbing interest today'. The

extension of educational provision and the 'window opening' effect
of television were seen as factors tending to strengthen the growing
appetite for informational material. A further feature of change was a
slight decline of interest in crime, the lives of the rich and some of the
professional sports.

Several editors expressed the opinion that women were now much
more interested in provincial newspaper content than they had been
in 1947, as a result of the social changes referred to above; this
interest has been encouraged by an expansion of feature content
aimed at women readers of the evening Press. The so-called 'teenage
revolution' had also made its impact on news and feature content; it
was necessary to heed their interest in 'pop' stars, fashions and
current crazes. This apart, the dominant editorial assumption is that
readerships are now moving—albeit very slowly—in the direction of
greater seriousness of outlook; editors claim that they do more than
merely keep pace with this movement. They endeavour to accelerate
it by 'taking the lead in levelling up rather than down'.[7] An assessment of the genuineness of such sentiments is offered in the concluding chapter.

Quite apart from their influence on the nature and level of news
and feature content, readerships are perceived as the ultimate
determinants of the overall network of values and of the ideals to
which provincial newspapers subscribe. They also constitute a
permanent 'pressure group' demanding reliability and accuracy.
Considering values first, it is apparent that the local Press, in endorsing the values of the institutions (an aspect discussed below),
believes it is also upholding the family values of its readers. The
operative assumption is that the family, as a social group, actively
or passively accepts institutional values—including, for example,
community progress and service, law and order, and morality. The
institutions and the family readership are therefore seen as a joint
influence on what (in many respects) editors include or omit, em-
phasize or play down.

Provincial newspapers are aimed at all members of families:
teenagers and adults, men and women. The editor of one of the
largest Northern evening newspapers stated that the concept of 'the
family newspaper' meant, in effect, that 'it must be acceptable in as
many households as possible and also to as many members of the
household as are interested in reading a newspaper. These objectives
form a basis for value judgments on news, pictures and features and

offer a guideline on matters of taste.' Thus a number of provincial companies, in written evidence to the 1947 Commission, observed that the family readership served as a pressure against the reporting of some kinds of sex crime, scandal and gruesome violence; Black-pool Gazette and Herald Ltd made this point as follows:

> There is, of course, always a market for sex and sensation, but contrary to the view widely held, sex and sensation are *not* in the best interest of a reputable paper which values its family reader interest. Our papers have never suffered from the absolute instruction that they must be kept clean.[8]

Kentish District Times Co. Ltd noted that 'there is a rule of the house . . . that certain cases in magistrates' and higher courts are not to be reported extensively (e.g. affiliation, incest, indecent exposure, etc.). This is to maintain the high standard we set ourselves as a "family newspaper".'[9]

There is no evidence of any major change of attitudes in this respect since 1947. Provincial newspaper editors clearly feel that local newspaper readers hold quite different expectations of local as compared with some popular national media. Even if they welcome the inclusion of 'sex and sensation' content in the national newspapers they take, they nevertheless prefer the local Press to have a separate, 'family value' oriented identity. This point was made by the editor of the Wolverhampton *Express and Star*, who added that in any case local newspapers could hardly compete effectively with the nationals in the provision of 'sex and sensation': 'the people who want it seem to prefer to obtain it in concentrated form from those national and Sunday newspapers that can deal with it with a greater degree of expertise that can a regional newspaper. We do not consider ourselves the right medium for this sort of thing.'[10].

The family readership, then, is seen as working against the inclusion of detailed reports that might be construed as salacious or distasteful; as a result, the image that a community is given of itself is enhanced. In the long term, particular readerships may conclude that their communities, at least, are 'respectable'—even if the rest of the country seems to be degenerating.

Collectively, readers also serve to define the provincial newspaper's relationship to local institutions; they have traditionally looked to the local Press to articulate any grievance or gratitude they may feel in respect of institutional policies and actions. They are seen as a pressure towards the ends of community progress and value for money. The Holmesdale Press Ltd in evidence to the 1947 Commission, observed that rate-payers look to their newspaper to 'draw attention to matters which they think want putting right'.[11] F. J. Parsons Ltd suggested that their responsibility to readers lay in their being 'accurate, honest and fair'.[12] Criteria of honesty and fairness may necessitate criticism—whether explicit or implicit—of local institutions, whether voiced in a leading column or through a news report or feature article. The openness of the correspondence column is essential as a symbol of a newspaper's criteria of accuracy, honesty and fairness, for it is here that its discoveries and assessments (or, indeed, omissions) are susceptible to comment.

Provincial readerships are further seen as a rigorous check on the accuracy of news reports and features where these concern the local scene. For collectively readers have a detailed knowledge of all the local material. They act as a check not only on factual accuracy but also on any distortion or exaggeration that may result from the mode of selection or the manner of presentation. In its evidence to the 1947 Commission the Burton Daily Mail Ltd claimed that accuracy was essential if its two newspapers were to remain in business:

> The newspaper which wilfully distorted its news would soon go out of business. This particularly would apply to provincial newspapers, which have more intimate relations with their readers than the national Press. Provincial readers are more critical and discriminating and have more knowledge of events in their immediate vicinity and are thus good judges of the standard of accuracy of their local newspapers.[13]

In their evidence, Mackie & Co. Ltd noted that in the provinces 'few inaccuracies escape notice and complaint by readers'. This company added that if inaccuracies were frequent, 'local staffs in small towns would be deprived of access to essential news channels . . .'[14] The effect of inaccuracy, therefore, is not confined to diminished prestige; it may result in the withholding of information and, in consequence, the impairment of content.

The influence of readerships as a whole can be summed up as follows. First, it is claimed by newspaper spokesmen that the local Press adjusts its content, in terms of subject matter and depth of presentation, in accordance with a continuing assessment of its readers; a further claim is that the Press endeavours to level up, and to accentuate any discernible trend towards greater maturity in taste. Second, readerships are perceived as collocations of family units, the majority of whom prefer reticence rather than boldness in the handling of 'sex and sensation' material and expect institutional and family values to be endorsed. Third, readers' expectations place an obligation on the Press to adopt a critical posture towards local institutions—especially those which concern the reader as rate-payer. Finally, the readership acts as a permanent check on the standards of accuracy of local newspapers; mistakes are soon followed by demands for rectification or, in the case of minor errors, by straightforward notice.

The influence of local institutions and community leaders

Thus far the influence of readers that devolves from their common interests, their educational background, their family membership and their local habitation and knowledge has been considered. It is now necessary to discuss the impact of particular groups within every community: the local institutions, and minority organisations.

Institutional leaders, amongst whom are the elected councillors, local government officials, the clergy, headmasters, magistrates, police officers, leading businessmen, officers of the main social and cultural organisations, trades union officials, etc., exercise a decisive influence on local newspaper content and its presentation. In the course of their evidence to the 1947 Commission many provincial companies revealed that they recognised the power and influence of the principal community leaders. Sometimes these were referred to directly as the 'leaders of thought'; sometimes the allusion was to the institutions within which they exercised authority. Two instances of the recognition of their influence must suffice.

Home Counties Newspapers Ltd:

It appears to us that the influence of a newspaper on public opinion does not necessarily increase with increasing circulation. What matters is the assessment by leaders of thought of the value of the newspaper's opinions. It is the notice taken by these leaders of thought and the extent to which they transmit them to the public that is the indication of a newspaper's influence.[15]

Express and Independent Newspapers Ltd:

So far as local newspapers are concerned, local knowledge and experience and a sense of responsibility to local institutions and local 'feeling' are essential to successful management, editorial and otherwise.[16]

The assessment of local 'leaders of thought', then, is regarded as the assessment that matters. Three main reasons for this attitude are apparent.

First, if the general opinion of community leaders is favourable, it can be deduced by the local Press that it is perceived as a communications medium upholding the dominant values of the institutions taken as a whole: law and order, morality, social welfare, community progress and pride, etc. Second, the institutions are key sources of news, and especially of the background information that gives a journalist, and thence, if he passes it on, his readers, the feeling of being 'in the know'. It has already been seen that one provincial company feared a curtailment of its news supply if its newspapers contained frequent inaccuracies, and that this might ultimately result in its closure. The community leaders' hold on much vital local news and background accounts very largely for Morris Janowitz's comment on the local weeklies of Chicago: 'the integration of the local paper with the political party, business interests and the dominant churches spells success or failure for the paper, and the community editors speak for and to the leaders of these groups'.[17] Institutional leaders are in a position to promote the flow of news or to obstruct it; they may also influence the attitudes of others in their respective networks. Thus a third reason why the good opinion of these leaders is valued is that it acts as an important determinant of a local newspaper's prestige—and hence that of the proprietor and editor, who will seek an affectionate, and not contemptuous, usage of the phrase 'the local rag'.

The 'sense of responsibility to local institutions' does, it has been suggested, assist in defining the local newspaper's value system; it reflects institutional values in many types of news report and, by and large, will be disposed to endorse them in its expression of opinion. In theory, the necessary condition for such an endorsement will be that the institutions are acting in the best interests of the community as a whole, and are not in conflict with 'family values'. Complications arise when two or more institutions are in a state of conflict, but here again (theoretically) the welfare of the community at large should afford the yardstick for assessment. Thus in the course of their evidence to the 1947 Commission, Home Counties Newspapers Ltd saw their 'paramount concern' as 'the good of the community';[18] the Kentish District Times Co. Ltd stated that editorial comment in their newspapers was offered from 'the point of view of the general weal, and not from any party-political or sectarian viewpoint'.[19]

It is claimed, then, that the interests of the circulation area as a whole carry more weight than any merely sectional interest; this is the ideal ordering of priorities. At least three possible reasons why this ideal may not always be fully attained suggest themselves. First, an editor or proprietor may to some degree be vulnerable to the influence of particular social or professional contacts. Second, a newspaper's acknowledged or unacknowledged political affiliation may make a fully objective appraisal of local government policies and decisions more difficult to effect—even where objectivity is the criterion. And third, editors may feel disposed to avoid too close a scrutiny of local commercial practice, since commercial concerns afford an indispensable, major source of revenue. The first two hypotheses are not tested in this study; adequate discussion of them could take place only in the context of long-term surveys, and intimate knowledge, of particular newspapers serving communities fully familiar to the researcher. However, the third hypothesis is considered in chapter 10.

Provincial newspapers and minority groups

Readers as member of minority groups also make their impact on provincial newspaper content. There are, of course, various kinds of minority group within any one circulation area; quite apart from the so-called 'intelligent minority', there will be political, religious, cultural, social and vocational minority groups—and minorities interested in particular sports and hobbies. The majority (explicitly, 71 per cent) of the fifty-nine provincial companies that submitted evidence to the 1947 Commission claimed to include news and views of minority groups; their reason was the desire to present a complete and balanced picture of local life. The Birmingham Post and Mail Ltd offered a typical comment: 'A well-balanced paper is bound to publish much that is of interest and importance to only certain sections, not always large sections, of its readers. This is done on the grounds that a good newspaper must present a proper picture of thought and opinion in general.'[20]

News and features of interest to minority groups, therefore, are regarded as essential balancing elements if a 'proper picture' of local life is to be presented. The provision of a platform for the expression of minority opinion (e.g. political, religious, social) is widely accepted as obligatory; this platform consists of both the news and correspondence columns. Thus Berrow's Newspapers Ltd suggested to the 1947 Commission that 'a newspaper would fail in its duty if it suppressed other points of view and the usual channel for such opposing views is the "Letters to the Editors" or reports of speeches published by our newspapers as a matter of course'.[21] At the same time, the values and interests of the majority of readers may be invoked as a basis for making decisions about minority opinion that might be construed as offensive, cranky or tedious. Too much concession to the writers or speakers classed by Scarborough and District Newspapers Ltd as 'cranks and propagandists' would, it is felt, serve to diminish the newspaper's prestige *vis-à-vis* the readership as a whole. The same company was of the opinion that the degree of concession was not, and could not be, uniform throughout the provincial Press; it was 'a question that each paper alone can decide . . . having regard to its own particular circumstances'.[22]

Obviously, the factor of prejudice may, in respect of minority interests and opinions, act as a conscious or unconscious influence on what to include and what to omit, or on the degree of prominence judged to be appropriate. A political, religious or socio-cultural opinion with which one does not agree is easily dismissed as bigotry or crankiness if personal convictions are permitted to usurp the criterion of impartiality; but there are three important external checks on any tendency to discriminate in a prejudicial way. First, the members of minority groups are likely to be local newspaper readers, and might take offence at any sign of seemingly unwarranted bias against them; their resulting attitude to the local Press may, in some cases, influence the attitudes of others either within or outside the minority group concerned. Second, certain kinds of minority activity and opinion do have appeal to a wider range of readers, and may stimulate a lively interchange in the correspondence column. Finally, the reader who feels that his, or his group's, activities and opinions have been unfairly suppressed can now lodge an appeal with the Press Council.

Prejudice apart, there are of course a number of possible editorial interpretations of what the proper balance—as between items of majority and minority interest—should be. In communities served by both weekly and evening newspapers, editors may evolve a division of labour which enables them to avoid duplicating some kinds of news of minority appeal. For instance, the *Cambridge Evening News* leaves much routine, secondary local news (anniversaries, presentations, etc.) to its weekly sister paper, the *Cambridge Independent Press and Chronicle*. Such a division of labour undoubtedly assists the sales of the weekly newspaper; in towns where the weekly is largely a re-working of the previous week's local news as reported in the evening Press, sales are often unimpressive.

Of course, provincial newspaper coverage of minority activities and opinions need not be thought of as merely disinterested altruism on the Press's part. The members of minority groups are likely to be among the most faithful purchasers of local newspapers, ever keen to read about events that closely concern them; furthermore, these groups may collectively constitute a majority of the total readership in all but the most moribund of circulation areas.

In this chapter several of the ways in which readerships influence the content of the local Press have been suggested. Corroborating evidence has been confined very largely to the views of newspaper spokesmen, and it remains to measure practice against precept in succeeding chapters. But if it is the case that community leaders and minority groups are as influential as provincial newspaper companies claim, then they must act as crucially important contributors to the overall ethos of the local Press. How editors define and, indeed, can help to consolidate this ethos is the subject of the next chapter.

Notes

1 *Memoranda of Evidence* (1947 Royal Commission), p. 91.
2. Evening Newspaper Advertising Bureau, *Where: an Analysis of Regional Evening Newspaper Sales* (London, 1970).
3 Dr Mark Abrams, *Education, social class and reading of newspapers and magazines* (IPA booklet No. 5, January 1966).
4 Comment submitted to the writer by M. Barrington-Ward, editor of the *Oxford Mail* (January 1966).
5 *Memoranda of Evidence*, p. 57.
6 The editorial comments referred to were submitted in January 1966 by the then editors of the Darlington *Evening Dispatch*, *Oxford Mail*, Wolverhampton *Express and Star*, Bristol *Evening Post*, *Yorkshire*

Evening Post, Leicester Mercury, Cambridge Evening News, Nottingham Evening Post and *Bolton Evening News.*

7 W. D. Barnetson, 'The Press, the public and the future', *West Lancashire Evening Gazette*, 28 October 1968.

8 *Memoranda of Evidence*, p. 54.

9 *Ibid.*, p. 116.

10 Comment submitted by J. Clement Jones, editor of the Wolverhampton *Express and Star* (January 1966).

11 *Memoranda of Evidence*, p. 94.

12 *Ibid.*, p. 151.

13 *Ibid.*, p. 58.

14 *Ibid.*, p. 127.

15 *Ibid.*, p. 96.

16 *Ibid.*, p. 82.

17 Morris Janowitz, *The Community Press in an Urban Setting* (Glencoe, Ill.: Free Press, 1952), p. 85.

18 *Memoranda of Evidence*, p. 95.

19 *Ibid.*, p. 115.

20 *Ibid.*, p. 52.

21 *Ibid.*, p. 44.

22 *Ibid.*, p. 167.

4 Editorial assumptions and approaches

In the previous chapter it was suggested that provincial editors assess 'sex and sensation' material in the light of family and institutional values, and feel that accuracy and reliability are indispensable to their commercial success as well as to the sort of reputation they seek. These attitudes can be seen as pointers to the overall view of the provincial Press that its chief spokesmen hold. They see it as, by and large, a particularly trustworthy and 'respectable' sector of the Press. Accordingly, they resent being lumped together with the popular nationals in generalising surveys of the newspaper industry as a whole. In their evidence to the 1947 Commission, Scarborough and District Newspapers Ltd rightly pointed out that such surveys ignored 'some very wide and important differences' as between differing types of newspaper; as a result, mud thrown at a small number of sensation-peddling popular nationals did not fail to 'stick to the relatively large number of small newspapers'.[1] In 1967 Mr W. G. Ridd (then Director of the Newspaper Society), commenting on the reception of *The Economist* Intelligence Unit's report on national newspaper production drew attention to 'the unfortunate fact that those who are currently taking part in the public discussion concerning the state of the British Press make no distinction between the national newspapers and the regional Press'. There might be inefficiencies in the production methods of the nationals, but in the provinces there had been 'considerable technical progress in the last decade'.[2]

The root objection, then, is to the failure of such reports to discriminate between Fleet Street and the local newspaper—whether the subject be content or production. Behind such protests there lies the already noted view of the provincial Press as both reliable and responsible. It was shown in chapter 1 that this view has a long ancestry, and needless to say it was frequently advanced in the context of the evidence from provincial sources to the 1947 Royal Commission. For instance, Mackie & Co. Ltd felt that for 'sound and solid editorial opinion' one must turn to the weeklies—'the

importance of which is invariably underrated in discussions on
"The Press" '.[3] Hirst, Kidd & Rennie Ltd attempted to redress this
underrating for the Commission's benefit by suggesting that 'regional
and local newspapers are the backbone of the country's Press'.[4]
Comments of this kind afford a useful insight into the local newspaper's sense of its reliable solidarity; the 'sound and solid editorial
opinion' of the weeklies is evidently seen as an index of the total
content. The implication is that some national newspapers proffer
less sound and substantial opinion, being rather more interested in
courting popularity.

National newspaper spokesmen, most of whom have had first-
hand experience of provincial Press reporting in their 'apprentice'
days, tend to view the provincials in much the same way. Thus
Arthur Christiansen of the *Daily Express* observed in his autobiography that 'national newspaper technique does not go down well
in provincial journalism. Local newspapers have a duty to be
journals of local record and it is at their peril that they neglect that
responsibility in pursuit of "bright" coverage.'[5] In other words, the
local Press acts in its own best interest if it is factual, reliable and
responsible.

Conceding, for the moment, that this is the case, it is clear that
outside those main news items that would almost uniformly be
'splashed' there is much scope for differences of emphasis—for
instance, in the prominence accorded to 'secondary' international
and national news, local crime reports, sentimental items, news from
social or cultural institutions and so on. Assumptions about readers'
interests will, of course, be a major determinant of selection and
prominence. Two further factors governing the choice of editorial
content are the editor's view of his newspaper's function and,
possibly, conscious or unconscious prejudices for or against particular subjects.

Three hypothetical editorial attitudes to the role of a local newspaper suggest themselves. First, an editor could seek to make his
paper as entertaining as possible, subject to the limitations imposed
by acknowledging family values and basic content expectations of
the community leaders and 'Mr Citizen'. This might cause him to
give relatively greater prominence to dramatic or 'human interest'
items at the expense of secondary 'institutional informative' content.
It would also influence his choice of feature material, in that he would
be less willing than more 'education-biased' equivalents to include

articles that could be construed as 'heavy'—or 'brain content', to quote one editor.

Second, an editor may see his newspaper in the role of the educator —a role in the tradition of the *Leeds Mercury* and the other leading papers of the 1820s that formed such an important sector of the 'mighty agency of the periodical press'. In this case the newspaper aspires to serve as a simplifying and judicial intermediary between the 'specialist' and the average reader. The editor of such a paper would presumably hold as a working assumption that the local Press can exercise 'considerable and beneficial influence in local government, local industrial matters and educational and philanthropic causes'.[6] This view was put to the 1947 Commission by Northcliffe Newspapers Group Ltd; a solely provincial company to share it was the Kentish District Times Co. Ltd, whose spokesman stated:

. . . I believe newspapers have some responsibility in encouraging public interest in worthwhile matters—such as the development of citizenship and its responsibilities. In this connection we have given many articles which were designed to encourage interest in local government, and on the importance of exercising the franchise (though, of course, not in any particular direction). I also feel that newspapers can do much in improving public taste, and we always devote a considerable proportion of space to cultural movements and to sincere criticism of art, music and drama.[7]

Editors who look upon their newspapers in this way are bound to give the public not only 'what it reasonably wants, but to some degree what it ought to want' (Tillotson's Newspapers Ltd).[8] They see their task as involving much more than the provision of exciting news and light reading, and 'obvious news value'[8] is a less pressing criterion for them than it is in the case of the postulated 'entertainer' editor.

A third possible position would be for an editor to try to strike a balance between entertaining content on the one hand and educational on the other. He would then hope that his newspaper was sufficiently informative to interest the more serious-minded readers and at the same time sufficiently balanced by popular material (e.g. secondary 'drama' or 'human interest' stories) to draw in the rest of his potential readership. A compromise of this kind may well come very close to the majority of readers' preferences *vis-à-vis* their local newspaper; those who take a 'quality' daily would enjoy the contrast of a somewhat lighter touch in their evening or weekly paper, while regular readers of one of the popular nationals may welcome

the relatively higher proportion of 'hard' news and features in the
community Press. This third approach, then, aims at striking a
balance between the serious and the popular; as an approach, it was
recommended by Westminster Press Provincial Newspapers Ltd in
their evidence to the 1947 Commission: 'A balance has to be struck
between news and articles on matters of international, national and
local importance and those having a more popular appeal.'[9]

The three possible positions are therefore (1) to attach major
importance to the role of entertainer, (2) to aim as much as possible
at an overall seriousness of content and (3) to try and reconcile both
these possibilities in terms of a viable compromise. In practice, one
finds little evidence that the first position is taken up by provincial
editors; the presence of the 'intelligent minority' and community
leaders works against its wholesale adoption. When local newspapers are suspected of overplaying 'personality' news, they are
liable to be reproved by one or more members of the 'serious-
minded' sector of their readerships, as in the following letter published (to the newspaper's credit) in the *Manchester Evening News*
on 14 January 1971. This was protesting about the *News*'s choice of
main headline on 11 January: 'Absent Best banned two weeks':

I am sure everybody must be sick of reading about George Best.
Almost every newspaper has carried one story or another over the last
week blazing it in large letters. Some papers even carried two or three
articles at the same time.
The last crunch came for me on Monday night when I picked up my
News. On the front page, and in the principal headlines, was George Best
again. I absolutely fail to see how an editor can consider the tantrums of
one footballer can have more importance than the lives of eight men lost
at sea, or the well-being of a British ambassador held in hostile hands—
an article which was relegated to an almost minor position on the front
page.
I am not anti-football by any means and enjoy a game as much as
anyone else, but let us get our priorities right. If you consider that George
Best getting 14 days' suspension is important football news, and it is,
then give him headlines, but use the sports page, don't blast it across the
front page. . . .

This sort of reader is undoubtedly one of a small minority in his
concept of ideal news values, but provincial editors are likely to
concede his point to some extent—and thereby avoid seeming too
closely identified with the uninhibited personality cult of the popular
national dailies.

The second position does command some following, especially
in towns and cities where there is an unusually high level of intellectual and cultural activity. An example here is Cambridge; the
editor's aim, during the main period of survey (1964–67), was to
make the *Cambridge Evening News* 'less parochial' and more
broadly informative. In the course of commenting on his approach,
he stated: 'You may get some idea of the pattern of our coverage
from a list of my special writers. In addition to the reporting staff I
have specialists in University affairs, agriculture, municipal affairs,
science, the theatre, films, television, fashion and other women's
topics, crime and police work, sport, music, art and books.'[10] He
has found the space for some of this coverage by a reduction in certain kinds of local 'secondary' news (e.g. 'exhaustive reports of
magistrates' court hearings . . . columns of funerals, golden weddings,
presentations to retiring employees, etc.'); such a change would,
perhaps, have proved less tolerable had not the weekly Press been
available to fully cover the kinds of news specified. The editor of the
Cambridge Evening News felt that, on the whole, his innovations had
been welcomed: 'During the period we have introduced these
changes, some of which might be considered too serious for certain
evening paper readers, our circulation has risen steadily. I am convinced that people want to read more thoughtful articles.'

Here, then, is an instance of an editor regarding his paper as an
educative medium and shaping the pattern of its content accordingly.
But Cambridge is not a typical town in the composition of its readership, and the evidence afforded by a sample of sixteen evening newspapers (specified in the next chapter) suggests that the compromise
position claimed by Westminster Press Provincial Newspapers Ltd
is the prevalent one. Indeed, it seems fair to say that the overall
pattern of change in the evening Press since 1947 has been towards
the compromise position rather than towards that preferred by the
editor of the *Cambridge Evening News*. As an example, one might
cite the comments of one former evening newspaper editor: 'Generally our paper now has a lighter touch. Reports of most events are
shorter in length than they used to be, and we more frequently look
for the light-hearted story. Animal stories are immensely popular
and usually lend themselves to good photographic illustration. The
field of photography has assumed tremendous importance, and pictures are now bigger and bolder. The strip cartoon has become an
integral part of the newspaper. Twenty years ago this would have

PPC—C

been beneath the dignity of papers such as ours, but the success of the *Daily Mirror* in this field of journalism has led even quality papers to follow suit.'[11] A more detailed account of what is meant by 'the light-hearted story' is offered in chapter 6. This editor's comments are of interest in that they suggest a very keen awareness of the content and techniques of the popular national dailies. The items cited are precisely those that entertain without risking any affront to 'family values'; as a result they lend themselves to incorporation into any provincial newspaper seeking a more popular image. Adherence to a former concept of appropriate 'dignity' has to be abandoned in the process.

A 'lighter touch' in the form of light-hearted stories, animal stories, larger and bolder photographs and strip cartoons is not necessarily incompatible with an increasing seriousness in the rest of a newspaper, and so need not invalidate the editorial claim of this as discussed in chapter 3.

The question of role does not confront the weekly newspaper editor to quite the same extent. Most weeklies are aimed at a small sharply defined circulation area; the local institutions and community leaders will be relatively familiar to the readership. The editor's task is largely one of finding room for all the local news, and cramming so many local names into the paper that he includes some known—in either a private or a public capacity—to every reader. In contrast, the editor of the medium-sized or large circulation evening newspaper knows that, apart from the main sports news and important news from the community's principal administrative authority, fewer names will be familiar to the readership as a whole. The alternatives for such papers were usefully summarised by Scarborough and District Newspapers Ltd in their evidence to the 1947 Commission: 'Unless there is a highly efficient system of localised editions, and we do not know of many, either the perimeter of the circulation area gets nothing but news of the centre, or the whole area gets a thin veneer.'[12] In practice the news emphasis does tend to be on the urban base ('the centre') rather than on the perimeter, news of which is in any case more comprehensively covered by the weekly Press. A further effect is that 'readability' becomes a more important criterion of news value than in the smaller evening or weekly newspapers and —as will be shown—leads to an emphasis on local disorder news at the expense of 'institutional informative' reports of secondary importance. In other words, the larger the circulation area the more difficult it is for the editor to put primary emphasis on the educational function—at least so far as his local news content is concerned. In effect, then, a large circulation acts as a pressure towards the adoption of the compromise between 'education' and 'entertainment'.

Thus far it has been hypothesised that provincial newspaper content can be seen as a response to assumptions about the interests of all readers, of majorities and of minorities. There are assumptions too about readers' expectations; it is thought that local newspaper readers look on their paper as a communications medium distinguishable from the popular nationals not only by its local orientation but also by its greater reliability and accuracy. Family and institutional values are seen as central determinants of content and of the tone and style of its mediation. Content will also be affected by the editorial concept of newspaper function, to the degree that this can be acted upon given the size and nature of the circulation area.

There is one further factor that needs consideration, a factor that sometimes affords the only possible explanation for otherwise inexplicable emphases or neglects of particular items of content—prejudice. The 1947 Royal Commission attempted to assess the part played by prejudice by asking in its questionnaire to what extent 'the accurate presentation of news or the adequate expression is distorted or restricted by . . . the limitations and prejudices of journalists and editors'. Some of the fifty-nine replies from provincial companies made it clear that they interpreted this in terms of political or religious prejudice; others saw it as involving a much wider range of subjects. As a result the classification of their replies is of limited value; roughly half the companies wholly or largely disclaimed prejudices, while a third admitted that these were bound to exist—'inasmuch as journalists are human beings' (Kentish District Times Co. Ltd) and 'one man's opinion is another man's prejudice' (The Liverpool Daily Post and Echo Ltd). The companies that allowed the possibility of prejudice added that every effort was made to minimise it. At the same time, prejudice was regarded as a factor that, for the most part, journalists themselves were well able to keep at bay; East Midland Allied Press Ltd indicated why:

> Journalists and editors, being human, cannot avoid having some prejudices and failings, but the training of journalists in the provinces is on the whole good and the ethical standard of the great majority of journalists is high. These two factors give most of them the facility for genuine

impartiality. In addition the staff should be so balanced as to prevent the distortion of news and opinion.[13]

The implication of this passage is that prejudice is at most a minor influence on newspaper content; a certain amount is inevitable, 'journalists and editors being human'. It is relevant at this point to cite an American study which shows in terms of hard fact that prejudice may be an unsuspectedly significant determinant of news selection and prominence. This is David Manning White's research into the impact of the wire editor of an American morning newspaper on the use made of news received from agencies. White studied 'Mr Gates'' handling of 11,910 column inches of news received from the Press Association over a seven-day period:

It is only when we study the reasons given by Mr. Gates for rejecting almost nine-tenths of the wire copy (in his search for the one-tenth for which he has space) that we begin to understand how highly subjective, how reliant upon value-judgments based on the 'gatekeeper's' own set of experiences, attitudes and expectations the communication of 'news' really is.
. . . Thus we find him rejecting one piece of wire copy with the notation, 'He's too Red.' Another story, categorically marked 'Never use this', dealt with the Townsend Plan, and because this 'gatekeeper' feels that the merits of the Townsend Plan are highly dubious, the chances of wire news about the Plan appearing in the paper are negligible. . . . One interesting notation on a story said 'Don't care for suicides.'[14]

D. M. White found that 'Mr Gates' had a liking for political news, that crime news as such did not appeal to him, that he consistently chose the most conservative version (both politically and stylistically) of any story offered by competing press associations, and that he had 'an obvious dislike for stories that had too many figures and statistics'.

White's findings obviously need to be borne in mind in any study of the British Press. To some extent they could be said to have been anticipated, at the level of theory, by the comments of Berrow's Newspapers Ltd on the subject of prejudice (in their evidence to the 1947 Commission):

When in every daily newspaper office the sub-editorial staff receives daily from news agencies, correspondents, staff reporters and from other sources, sufficient news to fill, say eight or ten newspapers of the size permitted, there must be drastic sub-editing by condensation, summarisation and selection if a *reasonable reflection* of all news of importance is to be achieved.

A speech by the Prime Minister or by Mr. Churchill, a Government White Paper, a vital debate in the House of Commons, a Budget statement (to mention but a few examples) can rarely be given in full; a precis must often be made.

Here, obviously, the human element within the journalist has a bearing on the result. What one journalist may think of outstanding importance the next would think of minor importance. If the same White Paper were given to six journalists the probability is that no two versions would approximately reflect the same judgment of the importance of particular statements within the White Paper.

Moreover there is a duplicated process of condensation making for risks of what might be termed distortion (if by distortion is meant an inadequate reflection of any piece of news); provincial newspapers rely for national political news on news agencies, such as the Press Association. At that point of distribution there must be some sub-editing of such news (otherwise it would be impossible to get a full service of news over the private wire system in time for publication) and at the newspaper end there must again be some measure of sub-editing.[15]

This company's analysis of the impact of 'the human element' was one of the fullest and, one might add, frankest of those offered to the 1947 Commission. It admits that the double sub-editing of news stories, combined with the different valuations that any given cross-section of journalists or editors would make of a particular news item, can lead to markedly dissimilar versions of that news in the Press. Thus although many provincial companies, like the East Midland Allied Press Ltd, virtually discounted prejudice as a significant factor, the findings of D. M. White and the quoted analysis by Berrow's Newspapers Ltd must serve as a caution not to underestimate its potential effects.

Provincial newspaper content, therefore, will in part reflect an editor's assessment of, first, the interests and attitudes of the majority of his readers[16] and, second, the values and expectations of community leaders and the more important minority groups. It will also be influenced by his concept of his newspaper's function in the community it serves and, whether in major or minor ways, by any prejudices that he or his key 'gatekeepers' bring to bear upon it.

Notes

1 *Memoranda of Evidence* (1947 Royal Commission), p. 166.
2 *West Lancashire Evening Gazette*, 6 January 1967.
3 *Memoranda of Evidence*, p. 127.

4 *Memoranda of Evidence*, p. 92.
5 Arthur Christiansen, *Headlines all my life* (London: Heinemann, 1961), p. 28.
6 *Memoranda of Evidence*, p. 141.
7 *Ibid.*, p. 117.
8 *Ibid.*, p. 203.
9 *Ibid.*, p. 199.
10 Comment submitted by Keith Whetstone, editor of the *Cambridge Evening News*, in January 1966. In 1970 Mr Whetstone became editor of the *Coventry Evening Telegraph*.
11 Comment submitted in January 1966.
12 *Memoranda of Evidence*, p. 168.
13 *Ibid.*, p. 78.
14 D. M. White, 'The "gatekeeper": a case study in the selection of news', *People, Society and Mass Communications*, ed. Dexter and White, pp. 164–6.
15 *Memoranda of Evidence*, p. 44. For a fuller understanding of the sub-editor's role see James Brennan, 'The sub-editor' in *Inside Journalism*, ed. R. Bennett-England (London: Peter Owen, 1967), pp. 93–105.
16 For the results of a pilot survey of readers' content preferences, with special reference to the *West Lancashire Evening Gazette*, see Appendix.

II Analysis and illustration of content

Among the most powerful forces in national life today are the centripetal forces making for centralization and uniformity in government, in education, in amusement and in standards of taste. The National Press is one such force, but the Provincial Dailies exert an influence in the opposite direction. . . . They can stimulate an interest in local affairs and in the work of local authorities and regional bodies: provide a forum for local discussion for both local and national affairs, and formulate and express a distinctively local opinion. By fostering and reflecting diversity of character, of custom and viewpoint, they contribute to the richness of the nation's life and the toughness and stability of its institutions.

Report of the Royal Commission on the Press, 1949

The primary function of a newspaper is to give well balanced news. Other functions should include the provision of:

(1) *A correspondence column* for public discussion and for the ventilation of grievances. It should be open to every reader, irrespective of the party or section of opinion to which he or she belongs;

(2) *Regular features* and special articles to provide background information and expert opinion.

(3) *Editorial comment* on public affairs;

(4) *Criticism* of music and the arts;

(5) *Entertainment*, e.g. cross-word puzzles and some types of articles.

In a different category falls the part played by advertising in the life of the community. Apart from displayed advertisements a provincial paper is the vehicle for many government and local government announcements, while 'small' and auction advertisements are essential to agriculture and trade.

Norfolk News Co. Ltd, in written evidence to the Royal Commission on the Press, 1947–49

5 A study of three non-local news stories, with special reference to the evening Press

The provision of news, as C. P. Scott observed, is the most important function of a newspaper; its nature is 'the acid test of quality':

> The first function of a newspaper is indicated plainly in its name; it is an instrument for the collection and dissemination of news. But what news? That is a material question. All sorts of things happen in the world every day and every hour of the day. It is all a question of selection, whether of the serious or the frivolous, of the clean or the unclean, of fact or of fiction. Some people like one sort and some another, and the newspaper can usually be found to respond to each demand. Here, in the favourite phrase of President Wilson, is the acid test of quality.[1]

In examining provincial Press news, therefore (in this and the next chapter), the tasks will be to see what kinds of news are selected, and what prominence each kind is accorded. Further, it will be important to consider how the news is handled. Is there evidence of a paramount concern for truth and accuracy, and of disdain for possible modes of emotive manipulation? For truth and accuracy were seen as compelling criteria by two of the greatest editors, John Delane (of *The Times*) and C. P. Scott (of the *Manchester Guardian*). Delane saw the 'first duty of the press' as that of obtaining 'the earliest and most correct intelligence of the events of the time'[2] and then disclosing it. Scott also saw the journalist's principal task as the collation and presentation of true facts; the newspaper's 'primary office is the gathering of news. At the peril of its soul it must see that the supply is not tainted. Neither in what it gives, nor in what it does not give, nor in the mode of presentation must the unclouded face of truth suffer wrong. Comment is free, but facts are sacred.'[3] Both editors, then, assumed that their readers were above all seeking true and accurate facts.

The past editors of two popular national dailies, in contrast, have expressed their belief that the selection and presentation of news should satisfy other reader requirements; their readers are assumed to be seeking sensation and excitement, and news has to be 'projected' accordingly. This projection may 'colour' the objective facts; if so, they claim, the colouring represents a necessary evil.

Arthur Christiansen, of the *Daily Express*:

> You cannot just put things in the *Daily Express*. By and large they must be projected. We have always got to tackle the news emphatically, with boldness and confidence. . . .
> That was the technique. Make the news exciting even when it was dull. Make the news palatable by lavish presentation. Make the unreadable readable. Find the news behind the news. Find the news even before it has happened.[4]

Silvester Bolam, of the *Daily Mirror*:

> We believe in the sensational presentation of news and views, especially important news or views, as a necessary and valuable public service in these days of mass readership and democratic responsibility. We shall go on being sensational to the best of our ability.[5]

Arthur Christiansen's comments yield some useful insights into what Bolam sums up as 'sensational presentation'. Emphasis, boldness, excitement, lavish presentation—these are the desired attributes of communicated news. Bolam's assumption appears to be that the alternative is a deterring dullness; the mass reader must be courted by means of sensationalism. Otherwise, it is implied, he may not take the trouble to read 'important news or views' and will become decreasingly capable of exercising democratic responsibility.

Broadly speaking, therefore, there are two distinguishable attitudes to news. One is that news must be objective; the true facts should be allowed to speak for themselves, and their inherent interest suffice. The other is that news must be presented in a sensational manner that magnetises the reader. The contention in this chapter will be that, in general, local newspapers handle the facts of crime stories in an objective and not sensational manner. One story in particular will be studied; it concerned the discovery of a dead child's body on Cannock Chase, Staffordshire, and was reported on 13 January 1966. First, however, it will be appropriate to point out the importance of crime news as an item of newspaper content, and to indicate what kinds of valuation particular national daily newspapers put upon it.

A majority reader interest in crime reports has long been assumed and gratified by the provincial Press; it was pointed out in chapter 1 that such reports were accorded priority treatment in its earliest decades. And, as the Carlisle Conservative Newspaper Co. Ltd noted in their evidence to the 1947 Commission, crime news could still be assessed as compulsive reading matter: 'Much as we deplore it the fact remains that the public, as a whole, revels in stories of crime and the more sordid stories of human tragedy.'[6] One Northern evening newspaper editor with whom the writer discussed this topic felt that there had been 'a slight waning of interest' in it since 1947. This may be so, but crime news continues to be prominently featured by the popular national dailies and, as will be shown, by the majority of evening newspapers. Before considering the latter, it is

Table 3

Newspaper	Mitchell headline	Main headline if not re Mitchell	Total column inches on Mitchell
Daily Express	200 hunt danger man		45 (1 photo)
Daily Mail	Car hunt as axe-man flees Moor		42½ (12 photo)
Sun	Axeman breaks free for fourth time		39 (2½ photo)
Daily Telegraph	Axe man on run from Dartmoor	Rover take-over by Leyland	12 (2½ photo)
Times	Dartmoor axe man free again	Leyland in £25m. bid for Rover	8
Guardian	Axe attack prisoner escapes for third time	100 pence to £ in decimal age from 1971	7½
Birmingham Post	Escaped man will stop at nothing—police	Leyland group bids £24m. for Rover Company	15½ (1½ photo)

necessary to establish some of the characteristics of national newspaper crime reporting.

Table 3 shows how much prominence six national papers and one regional daily gave to the escape of Frank Mitchell from Dartmoor, as reported on 13 December 1966. The table shows clearly that this item of crime news had far more value for the national popular dailies (the first three listed) than for the 'qualities'—to which, on this occasion, the *Birmingham Post*—a regional morning newspaper—can be added. All the popular dailies gave their main headline to

Mitchell's escape; in contrast, the *Times* and the *Telegraph* led with the news of Leyland's take-over bid for Rover, and the *Guardian* with Mr Callaghan's proposals for currency decimalisation. The maximum space allotted by any of the 'qualities' to Mitchell's escape was the *Daily Telegraph*'s 12 column inches; this was less than a third of the space accorded by the popular newspaper giving the story least column inches—the *Sun*, with 39 column inches. The popular and quality Press therefore diverged sharply in terms of the prominence they gave to the escape; they also differed in their manner of presenting it, although by rooting its introduction in hard fact the *Mail* aligned itself with the *Times*, *Telegraph* and *Guardian*. The *Express* and *Sun* injected varying degrees of colour into their reports as a means of maximising their capacity to excite. The essential differences between the factual, objective mode of news coverage and the 'projected' approach can be gauged by comparing the first two sentences of the *Guardian*'s report with those of the *Express* and *Sun*.

> *The Guardian:* 'An "extremely dangerous" prisoner serving a life sentence for robbery with violence was at large on Dartmoor last night after escaping from an outside work party.
>
> 'More than a hundred policemen using tracker dogs joined thirty prison officers in the search for Frank Mitchell (37), who has previously escaped from both Broadmoor and Rampton mental institutions.'
>
> *The Sun:* 'Big Frank Mitchell, who is described as Britain's most violent criminal, was on the run last night after escaping from a Dartmoor working party.
>
> 'This is the fourth escape by 37-year-old Mitchell, a six-footer of almost superhuman strength who was once known as the Mad Axeman.'
>
> *Daily Express:* 'A violent giant of a man broke from Dartmoor last night. Two hundred police scaled the moor and mounted a search in a violent hailstorm.'

In its introduction the *Guardian* was content to describe Mitchell as 'extremely dangerous'—presumably quoting a police spokesman. The *Sun* and *Express* preferred to present him as a Frankenstein figure; in the former case as 'a six-footer of almost superhuman strength', in the latter as 'a violent giant of a man'. Projections of this kind appear to assume the sort of reader typified by George

Bowling's mother in Orwell's novel *Coming up for Air*: 'Murders had a terrible fascination for her, because, as she often said, she just didn't know how people could *be* so wicked. Cutting their wives' throats, burying their fathers under cement floors, throwing babies down wells! How anyone could *do* such things!' Mrs Bowling had the continual feeling that 'Jack the Ripper was hiding in Lower Binfield'.[7] The sensational presentation of this type of crime story (court reporting, of course, has to be strictly factual) attempts to arouse such feelings of awed fascination and fear, thereby involving the reader's imagination actively. It aims to link up with that mental hinterland peopled by Mr Hyde, Dr Crippen and Ian Brady. Indeed, the *Express*'s introduction would afford a good, buttonholing start to a popular crime novel. None of the 'qualities' attempted to project the story in this way; it is interesting to note that the *Guardian* gave the lower number when referring to the police search—'more than a hundred policemen' as against 'two hundred police'.

The two distinctive styles elicited, therefore, are the objective and the emotive; the former is rooted in hard fact, whereas the latter introduces colour and generalisation in order to emphasise the story's capacity to excite. It is now possible to turn to the 'second body' story referred to above and assess (*a*) how much news value it had for the sixteen evening newspapers sampled and (*b*) how it was presented.

It is, of course, important to bear in mind that local evening newspapers are, in one respect at least, more complex media to the news analyst than the national dailies. This arises from the fact that at a certain degree of significance an item of local news—perhaps a crime, an accident, a disaster or a striking community story (e.g. a sharp increase in rates)—may be judged as of sufficient news value to warrant its precedence over, or equality with, the major non-local items. Furthermore, it is apparent that there are widely differing rules of thumb on what the necessary 'degree of significance' ought to be. The comments that follow are related to the writer's assumption that, exceptional circumstances apart,[8] editors are normally in a position to allow at least one-tenth of the front page (15–18 column inches) to a non-local report considered to be newsworthy. But column inch measurements do not, of course, take into account a report's position on the page, and deductions about news values that are based on them can only be advanced in tentative terms. It is all too easy for the outsider to forget the multiplicity of claims on space, and the extreme pressures that confront editors and sub-editors as deadlines approach.

1. The 'second body' story

The 'second body' story told of the discovery of a then unidentified girl's body in a ditch on Cannock Chase, on the day after another body—that of Diane Tift, aged five—had been found. A full 'wire' report of this would be sent to all evening newspapers by the London-based Press Association—the principal agency for the gathering and distribution of home news.[9] As a story, it would be judged to afford compelling reading for the majority of readers; by means of it, parents are reminded of the fearful fate that may await their own children if vigilance is relaxed, and their recollected memories of Jack the Ripper, or other notorious murderers, are available for evocation. All the Midlands newspapers sampled that publish leading columns (those of Wolverhampton, Birmingham and Leicester) discussed the crime in their main leaders; they noted that the murders were the work of a 'killer', 'a maniac killer', 'a psychotic child-killer'. They spoke in terms of urgent admonition to Midlands parents, as in the following extract from the Wolverhampton *Express and Star*: 'Parents with young children hardly need reminding, in view of these terrible tragedies, that it is unwise to allow them to walk home from school by themselves or play alone.'

Table 4 shows how much prominence the 'second body' story was accorded by the sixteen newspapers sampled; all the main headlines for 13 January 1966 (whether relating to this story or not) are listed, as are the headlines given to this report when it was not in the main news slot. The total number of column inches taken up by each report is also given.

The eight newspapers with the largest circulations of the sixteen (all eight over 175,000 copies daily)—those of Manchester, Leeds, Birmingham, Newcastle, Nottingham, Leicester, Bristol and Wolverhampton—were amongst the twelve that gave the story their main headline. This suggests that a major crime has the most news value for the largest evening newspapers; the same eight papers came in the first ten in terms of the total space allocated (the two others were the *Lancashire Evening Post* and the *West Lancashire Evening Gazette*).

Table 4 The 'second body' story, 13 January 1966

Main headline, and 'second body' headline if not the main headline	Column inches		
	Text	Photo	Total
Birmingham Second child's body on Cannock Chase	80	88	168
Wolverhampton Another body is found	80	83	163
Preston Second girl in death ditch!	34	20	54
Newcastle Diane: second girl's body found in ditch	34	20	54
Manchester Diane: another girl dead in same ditch	32	11	43
Nottingham Diane: body of second child is found	39	3	42
Leicester Second child in ditch	25	15	40
Darlington Body of second child in ditch	31	7	38
Leeds Second body is found in ditch	30		30
Bristol Second child's body is found in ditch	29		29
Blackpool Police find second girl's body	21	8	29
Scarborough Second child's body in ditch	26		26
Huddersfield Zambia and Britain not in disagreement over time limit (main) Second child dead in ditch (back page)	15		15
Bolton M-way limit to go (main) Another child's body found in ditch (p. 1)	13		13
Oxford Rail line 'broken' (main) Second child found dead in ditch (p. 1)	13		13
Cambridge Super gang grab £7,000 in city (main) Police find body of another girl in Cannock ditch (p. 1)	$7\frac{1}{2}$		$7\frac{1}{2}$

BODY

Birmingham Evening Mail

BODY

Yorkshire Evening Post

BODY

Newcastle *Evening Chronicle*

BODY

Wolverhampton *Express and Star*

Fig. 4(a) The 'second body' story, 13 January 1966: headline sizes, with reference to the word 'body'

Police find body of another girl in Cannock ditch

The body of another child was found today in the ditch at Cannock Chase, Staffs., where a young girl. believed to be five-year-old Diane Tift, was found dead yesterday. The second child, believed also to be a girl, lay covered in mud close to where the first was found.

The body was clothed but badly decomposed. Det. Supt. Gold; of Scotland Yard, said it appeared to have been there some considerable time and had been dumped.

There would be an intensive comb-out of the surrounding area, he said, but there was no reason to believe there might be another body.

Today's discovery was made by Det. Insp. Eric Lycett, of Cannock, and P.c. Eccleshall at about 11 a.m. during a search of the area which had begun at first light.

News of the find was given by Mr. Arthur Rees, Chief Constable of Staffordshire, at an on-the-spot Press conference.

Since September

The ditch in which the two bodies lay is in a field adjoining Teddesley Road, near the Pottal Pool beauty spot.

This afternoon the first body had still not been definitely identified. A relative of five-year-old Diane Tift was being driven to Stafford to make the identification.

Also missing from the area is six-year-old Margaret Reynolds, who lived nine miles away at Aston, Birmingham, and who vanished in September while walking to school.

Fig. 4(b) The 'second body' story, 13 January 1966: the *Cambridge Evening News* report. *By courtesy of the Cambridge Evening News*

Turning to the four papers that did not give the 'second body' report their main headline, one finds that three of them had 1964 circulations of under 51,000. The fourth, the Bolton *Evening News*, had a circulation of 88,760. This paper's choice of 'M-way limit to go' might seem to hint at a 'gatekeeper' distaste for non-local crime news; such a supposition falls down, however, when one notes that the *News* was one of only six of the papers sampled to give its main headline to a follow-up report the next day: 'Diane: Died of suffocation'. (The other five were the evening newspapers of Birmingham, Wolverhampton, Leicester, Scarborough and Blackpool.)

The three small-circulation newspapers need separate consideration. The *Cambridge Evening News* revealed no objection as such to crime news; its main headline concerned a robbery from a local firm of building and civil engineering contractors—'Super gang grab £7,000 in city'. The 'second body' story was accorded the second lead position and 7½ column inches. The *Oxford Mail* also gave its main headline to local news—'Rail line "broken" '—reporting a Ministry of Transport's inquiry into a passenger train derailment at Reading. The *Mail*'s meagre 13 column inches on the 'second body' suggests that here (and at Cambridge) the news 'gatekeepers' gave this non-local story a rather lower valuation than most of their larger contemporaries. The same point could be made about the *Huddersfield Daily Examiner*, which opted to 'splash' an item of international news of an informational kind with no exciting overtones: 'Zambia and Britain not in disagreement over time limit'. The *Examiner* was the only paper of the sixteen to keep the 'second body' story off its front page, according it 13 column inches on the back page. Even so, the Huddersfield Press falls into line with the rest when a major local crime is committed; the *Examiner*'s main headline on 21 January 1966 was 'Death in surgery/Two women stabbed at Elland/Man held'—Elland being ten miles from Huddersfield. Only two other evening newspapers in the sample gave their main headlines to this murder: the *Yorkshire Evening Post* ('Yorks stabbings: two women die') and the Darlington *Evening Despatch* ('Roving killer knifes two women'). In Northern papers outside Yorkshire these stabbings received much less prominence; for instance, they were worth a mere 6 column inches in the *Lancashire Evening Post* and 6½ column inches in the Bolton *Evening News*.

On the basis of the preceding analysis, therefore, one can hypothesise that the majority of evening newspapers (and especially those with large circulations) will be likely to give their main headlines to a major non-local crime *when there is an element of the macabre, or of unusual horror, involved*; a 'straightforward' murder, however, is primarily of interest to newspapers that circulate in the region of its occurrence.

Turning to the presentation of the 'second body' story, it was apparent that apart from certain phrases in the *Lancashire Evening Post*'s account the reporting tone and style was objective, and comparable with that of the quality dailies. Of course, the Press Association ensures that its wired news stories are presented in a neutral, factual style—a style that the provincial Press finds thoroughly acceptable. In its evidence to the 1947 Commission, Berrow's Newspapers Ltd noted approvingly that agency news services at the time were 'sober and reliable'.[10] A typical introduction to the 'second body' story—probably very close to the P.A.'s wired report—was that of the Nottingham *Evening Post*:

> The body of a second girl was found on Cannock Chase today—in the same ditch as the body which is believed to be that of five-year-old Diane Tift, missing for two weeks from her home in nearby Bloxwich.
> The discovery of the body, which was badly decomposed and covered in mud, was made by police seeking clues on the Chase after yesterday's discovery. It had been there for some considerable time, they said. . . .

The only newspaper to deviate slightly from this fact-rooted style was the *Lancashire Evening Post*—interestingly, the only paper to introduce an exclamation mark into its main headline, and the only one to yoke 'death' and 'ditch' together for alliterative effect: 'Second girl in death ditch!' The *Post* differed from the rest in its inclusion of two 'projecting' adjectives; it referred to 'the gruesome double murder' and the 'grisly mystery'. But this modest injection of colour represented the extent of its stylistic deviation.

Finally, an assessment was made of the accuracy of the facts reported; twelve key items were listed, and each paper's use of them noted. In the case of eleven no discrepancies came to light, but on one of them four papers were out of step with the rest. This concerned the relative who would attempt to identify Diane Tift; the majority version, as phrased in the Nottingham *Evening Post*, was: 'One of Diane's relatives was to be driven to Stafford this afternoon to try to make the identification.' The same fact was reported by the two evening newspapers in the region; the *Birmingham Evening Mail* stated that Diane's parents were 'too distressed' to make the identification, and the Wolverhampton *Express and Star* that neither of them was 'fit enough'. The majority version was correct; the four 'deviant' newspapers failed to point out that a relative (an uncle) would try to identify Diane's body and, in varying ways, gave their readers the impression that her parents would carry out this task:

> *Manchester Evening News:* 'The parents of five-year-old Diane . . . were asked today if they could identify the body found yesterday as that of their daughter at Cannock mortuary.'
>
> Bristol *Evening Post:* 'Diane's parents were being asked later today if they could positively identify the body found yesterday.'
>
> Newcastle *Evening Chronicle:* 'Diane's parents are expected to see the first body today to see if they can identify it.'
>
> *Lancashire Evening Post:* 'Meanwhile, later today, the parents of Diane Tift were travelling to Cannock mortuary to give a positive identification of their daughter, who vanished from home two weeks ago.'

The first three papers listed above phrased their sentences so as to allow the stated mode of identification to appear as a possibility and not a *fait accompli*; the parents had been asked, or were being asked, or were expected to travel to Cannock. The sub-editors concerned can be faulted only for not bringing the report fully up to date in the manner of the majority. Only the *Lancashire Evening Post* converted speculation into asserted fact by saying that the parents 'were travelling'. This was the sole error in a total of 120 items that were checked for accuracy.

Three main conclusions emerge from this study of the way in which one murder story was reported in sixteen evening newspapers. First, this crime commanded the main headlines of three out of every four papers in the sample, and of the eight newspapers with the largest circulations. Second, the tone and style of presentation of the reports displayed a marked similarity—in terms of emphasis on fact and absence of sensationalising elements—to the 'quality dailies'. The *Lancashire Evening Post* differed slightly by introducing such evaluating adjectives as 'grisly' and 'gruesome'. Third, the reports were—apart from one incorrect fact included in the *Post*—correct in their substance.

Thus if the majority of evening newspapers value major crime news in the light of the same assumptions about their readers' interest as those held by the national mass circulation dailies, they present it in the factual and sober manner associated with the 'qualities'.

2. Mrs Gandhi's election

Mrs Gandhi's election as Prime Minister of India, announced on 19 January 1966, afforded a good opportunity to study the coverage of important—although not 'absolutely major'[11]—international order news. It would be unwise, however, to move outwards from a description of practice to speculations about any particular newspaper's position on a 'popular–quality' spectrum; pointers there may be, but extensive comparative work would be needed in order to mount firm conclusions.

Two newspapers—the Darlington *Evening Despatch* and the *West Lancashire Evening Gazette* (Blackpool) assessed this as the 'lead' story of the day and accorded it an average of 37 column inches of space. Eleven of the fifteen newspapers studied (the sixteenth, the *Leicester Mercury* 'Extra' edition, did not cover the election) put their reports on the front page and gave the story an average of 23 column inches. Four papers—the *Scarborough Evening News*, Bristol *Evening Post*, Wolverhampton *Express and Star* and *Lancashire Evening Post*—placed this news on an inside page and gave it an average of 21 column inches. The *Lancashire Evening Post* also included an evaluating feature article (15 column inches) about the election on its front page.

The fifteen reports were classified under the headings of 'considerable prominence' (defined as at least one broadsheet column on the front page, or 20 column inches), 'average prominence' (at least half a broadsheet column, or 10 column inches) and 'low prominence' (less than 10 column inches on the front page, or inside coverage of any length). The distribution that resulted follows; column inches are shown in brackets. Those marked with an asterisk (*) are tabloid-size newspapers (if the back page is taken into account, comparison with broadsheet newspapers remains valid).

(*a*) Considerable prominence:
Darlington *Evening Despatch* (44; main headline)
West Lancashire Evening Gazette (30; main headline)

Manchester Evening News (34)
Bolton *Evening News* (31)
Newcastle *Evening Chronicle* (23)
Nottingham *Evening Post* (22)
Huddersfield Daily Examiner (22)

(*b*) Average prominence:
Oxford Mail (17½)
Yorkshire Evening Post (16½)
Lancashire Evening Post (front page comment 15 and inside page report 39)

(*c*) Low prominence:
**Cambridge Evening News* (8)
Birmingham Evening Mail (7½)
*Bristol *Evening Post* (inside page, 23)
*Wolverhampton *Express and Star* (inside page, 13)
Scarborough Evening News (inside page, 9)

One's own view—that this story was worth 'considerable' front page prominence—finds justification in the fact that four newspapers regarded it as an appropriate subject for leading column comment, while six discussed it in feature articles ranging from 15 column inches to 46 column inches in length. Interestingly, five of the papers that gave the news report only average or low prominence were amongst the nine that offered leaders and/or features about it; these are listed below:

(*a*) Considerable prominence to the news report:
Darlington *Evening Despatch*; leader, 19 January.
Bolton *Evening News*; leader and feature (16½ column inches), 19 January.
Manchester Evening News; feature (23 column inches), 18 January.
Newcastle *Evening Chronicle*; feature (40 column inches), 19 January.

(*b*) Average prominence to the news report:
Yorkshire Evening Post; leader and feature (16 column inches), 19 January.
Lancashire Evening Post; feature (15 column inches), 19 January.

(*c*) Low prominence:
Birmingham Evening Mail; leader, 19 January.
Bristol *Evening Post*; leader, 19 January.

Wolverhampton *Express and Star*; two features (46 column inches), 20 January.

The question that this tabulation poses is obvious enough. Why did the last five papers listed recognise the importance of Mrs Gandhi's election by discussing it in leading columns and/or features and yet accord it only average or low prominence as news? One possible reason is that the news lacked drama; it did not have the compelling excitement that attends non-local stories of conflicts, riots, coups, assassinations, hi-jackings, etc. An invaluable series of insights into the background to the journalistic preference for disorder stories is offered by Johan Galtung and Mari Ruge in their study 'The structure of foreign news'; in this they show that 'the more negative the event in its consequences, the more probable that it will become a news item'.[12] Certainly this event would have only moderate appeal to news 'gatekeepers' who prefer to emphasise the more dramatic stories in the day's news flow. If non-local news seems generally tepid, local events come into the reckoning; in fact, all the five newspapers under discussion featured local items in their main headlines on 19 January. These were 'Don Revie rapped by soccer chiefs' (42 column inches, *Yorkshire Evening Post*); 'Miss GB plea is dismissed' (27 column inches, *Lancashire Evening Post*—a report of the outcome of a High Court case involving Morecambe corporation's bid to 'prevent Mecca, Ltd, from running a beauty contest under the title "Miss Britain" '); 'Three hurt in blast at Bristol factory' (24 column inches, *Bristol Evening Post*); 'Coroner's grim warning' (45 column inches, *Birmingham Evening Mail*) and ' "Monstrous and tragic" ' (40 column inches, Wolverhampton *Express and Star*—the last two reports being of the coroner's inquest on Diane Tift and Margaret Reynolds of the 'second body' story. Other local news items also competed for space on the Birmingham and Wolverhampton front pages. The *Mail* allotted 31 column inches to an account of a seriously delayed, unheated train ('Passengers wrap in papers to keep warm') and 18 column inches to news of regional power cuts ('Cold brings power cuts'); the *Express and Star* gave 15 column inches to the details of, and background to, the Minister of Power's report on recent equipment failures at the local Tipton gas works—'Minister: "Gas failures were avoidable" '.

All five newspapers therefore placed more stress on their function as local news communicators than on their news surveillance of the international scene—even though the claims of the latter were recognised in leaders and/or features. There would seem to have been a case here for increasing the news space devoted to an international event editorially recognised as significant. This is said fully bearing in mind the valid point made by the editor of the *Sheffield Telegraph* in oral evidence to the 1947 Commission: 'The provincial paper has a great deal of regard for local affairs which cannot be measured by normal news values.'[13] But the study of the Indian election reports has shown that some evening newspapers (e.g. the *Lancashire Evening Post*) attached more significance to local news—as front-page content—than comparable others (e.g. the *West Lancashire Evening Gazette*). The coverage of the latter was more in keeping with the general editorial view that readerships are becoming more serious-minded.[14]

Turning to the style of presentation of the Indian election, this was—in the majority of cases—in key with the evidently sober and factual Press Association version. Four newspapers' headlines were colourfully floral: 'Garlands as Mrs Gandhi wins' (Bolton *Evening News*); 'Garlands for new leader' (Nottingham *Evening Post*); 'Garlands all the way for India's Premier' (*Cambridge Evening News*) and 'Garlands for India's Premier' (*Birmingham Evening Mail*). Only the Wolverhampton *Express and Star* attempted to capitalise on the element of conflict in an election, with 'Mrs. Gandhi wins the P.M. fight'. The *Manchester Evening News*'s report (by-lined 'Peter Jackson, New Delhi') departed in places from the characteristically objective tone of the rest—a tone typified by the Newcastle *Evening Chronicle*'s opening paragraphs:

> Mrs. Indira Gandhi, daughter of the late Mr. Nehru, was elected Prime Minister of India by the Parliamentary Congress Party in New Delhi today by 355 votes out of 526.
> She becomes the only woman Prime Minister in the world and only the second in history. The first was Mrs. Bandaranaike, who was Prime Minister of Ceylon from 1960 until last year. . . .

The *Manchester Evening News* did not neglect the essential facts of this story in the body of its report, but its opening stressed the impact of the election on Mrs Gandhi's emotions and those of the attendant crowds. This emotional element was embodied in the chosen headline: 'It's Mrs. Gandhi—she weeps in her joy'; it was amplified as follows:

> Cheering crowds nearly smothered Mrs. Indira Gandhi, 48-year-old

daughter of the late Jawarhalal Nehru, with garlands of flowers after she became Prime Minister of India today.

Mrs. Gandhi was moved to tears when the vote was announced. As she left Parliament, after receiving congratulations, a huge crowd blocked her path and security men had to link arms to prevent her being knocked over.

Many excited people were pushed into empty ornamental pools . . .

The passage emphasises Mrs Gandhi's reaction (she had been 'moved to tears'), the number and the response of bystanders ('cheering crowds'; a 'huge crowd'; 'many excited people') and movement (Mrs Gandhi had been 'nearly smothered'; the crowd had 'blocked her path' and she would have been 'knocked over' had the security men not linked arms; people were being 'pushed into empty ornamental pools'). Action and emotion are impressed upon the reader insistently.

It may well be that Manchester readers were effectively button-holed by this dramatic introduction and so drawn into reading the rest of the report, which was phrased in a much more circumspect way. It may also be the case that Newcastle readers (and those of most of the newspapers sampled) would be deterred by the unemo-tional, factual style of the *Chronicle*'s typical opening. This, of course, is merely speculation; the main intention here is simply to point out the characteristics of the majority tone and style, and of any minority deviations from it. One must add, however, that a Press Association wired report need not result in a uniform account in the receiving newspapers; it remains possible for a skilled sub-editor to shape it for a particular community of readers. But only one significant instance of this was afforded by the sample, not counting the *Manchester Evening News*, which made use of additional back-ground details sent by its own correspondent. The exception was the *West Lancashire Evening Gazette*: the news editor here clearly decided to try to interest readers by initially focusing on Mrs Gandhi as a woman—a family woman with a particular appearance, a particular taste in clothes and a particular education. In these respects she was like most other women, but the *Gazette* also emphasised her uniqueness—not least in its main headline: 'Woman leads 500 million'. These aspects preceded the detailed discussion of the election itself, and were presented in six short paragraphs set off in bold type from the rest of the report:

Mrs. Indira Gandhi, 48-year-old daughter of Pandit Nehru, today became Prime Minister of India with its 500 million people.

Slim, dark-eyed, with finely cut features, Mrs. Gandhi is a widow and
mother of two sons, aged 22 and 20. Both are studying in Britain.
She is India's third Prime Minister and the world's only woman PM.
She is only the second woman in the world to hold the top political
office. Mrs. Bandaranaike of Ceylon was the first.
Her husband, Feroze Gandhi—no relation of Mahatma Gandhi—was
an Indian MP who died in 1960.
Mrs. Gandhi, who likes to wear brightly-coloured, hand-woven saris
of silk and cotton, went to school in India and Switzerland and studied
at Somerville College, Oxford. . . .

It is clear that the 'gatekeeper' concerned arranged the wire report
on the assumption that readers would be most likely to respond to
an opening emphasis on the new leader's identity; the focus is on
Mrs Gandhi throughout: 'Mrs . . . daughter . . . Mrs . . . widow and
mother . . . she . . . woman . . . woman . . . her. . . Mrs . . .' The
quoted paragraphs were given visual coverage by the careful adjacent placing of a front-of-face photograph, 4 × 2½ column inches.
This sort of conscientious preparation of the Indian election story
was outstanding amongst the newspapers sampled; one reason for
it, of course, was that this had been selected as the *Gazette*'s leading
news report.

3. George Harrison's wedding

Equally interesting was the variety of assessments of the news value
of George Harrison's (of the Beatles) wedding, as reported on 21
January 1966. The treatment of this story afforded a useful indication of the extent to which provincial editors are prepared to acknowledge public interest in the leading figures of 'pop' culture. As in the
case of the Indian election, the nature of the local news to hand would
be a factor affecting prominence.
  The reports of the 'Beatle' wedding were placed on the front page
of all the sixteen newspapers sampled. Apart from this common
denominator, wide divergences in terms of space allocation were
evident, as table 5 shows. The biggest front-page spread occurred
in the Bolton *Evening News*, with 44 column inches, including a
photograph 10 in × 5½ in. At the other extreme was the *Cambridge
Evening News*, which confined its report to a mere 2½ column inches.
The average column inch total for all sixteen papers was 27½, or

almost $1\frac{1}{2}$ broadsheet columns; this was higher than the average for the Indian election—21 column inches (including, in this case, the inside page reports). Particular newspapers might have accorded the wedding slightly more space had not newsworthy local material been available; for instance, the Yorkshire papers had a regional murder story (the *Yorkshire Evening Post*'s main headline running 'Yorks stabbings: two women die'), while the *Leicester Mercury* led with 'Mother, three children lose home in blaze'. Even so, eleven of

Table 5

Name of newspaper	Total c.i. (inc. photo)	Size of photo (in.)
Bristol *Evening Post*	66*	$8\frac{1}{4} \times 4\frac{3}{4}$ and $6\frac{1}{2} \times 5$
Bolton *Evening News*	$44\frac{1}{2}$	$10\frac{1}{2} \times 5\frac{1}{2}$
Newcastle *Evening Chronicle*	40	$7\frac{1}{2} \times 5$
Manchester *Evening News*	37	$4\frac{1}{2} \times 7$
Lancashire Evening Post	32	$6\frac{1}{2} \times 5\frac{1}{2}$
West Lancashire Evening Gazette	31	$7\frac{1}{2} \times 3\frac{1}{2}$
Scarborough Evening News	29	$7 \times 3\frac{3}{4}$
Birmingham Evening Mail	27	$7 \times 3\frac{1}{2}$
Nottingham *Evening Post*	$26\frac{1}{2}$	$5 \times 3\frac{1}{2}$
Yorkshire *Evening Post*	24	$7 \times 3\frac{1}{2}$
Darlington *Evening Despatch*	21	$7 \times 3\frac{1}{2}$
Wolverhampton *Express and Star*	19	$6\frac{1}{2} \times 3\frac{1}{3}$
Oxford Mail	16	$4\frac{1}{2} \times 3\frac{1}{4}$
Leicester Mercury	15	$3\frac{1}{2} \times 3\frac{1}{2}$
Huddersfield Daily Examiner	12	$3\frac{3}{4} \times 1\frac{3}{4}$
Cambridge Evening News	$2\frac{1}{4}$	—

* p. 1 : 38.

the sixteen newspapers gave the wedding at least one broadsheet column—but none went so far as to make it the main news of the day! If one adopts the same assessment categories as were used for the Indian election, the following distribution results: considerable prominence: eleven; average prominence: four; low prominence: one.

That 69 per cent of the newspapers sampled gave this story 'considerable prominence' suggests that, as in the case of major crime news, the assumed interests of the majority of readers are a powerful determinant of front page news values. The newspapers that gave less than 19 column inches to the 'second body' and/or Beatle wedding reports were as follows:

'Second body': *Huddersfield Daily Examiner* (15), Bolton *Evening News* (13), *Oxford Mail* (13) and *Cambridge Evening News* (7).

'Beatle wedding': *Oxford Mail* (16), *Leicester Mercury* (15), *Huddersfield Daily Examiner* (12) and *Cambridge Evening News* ($2\frac{1}{4}$).

Three newspapers—those of Huddersfield, Oxford and Cambridge—feature in both lists, and appear to have adopted a less popular set of news values than the majority of their contemporaries.

The intention in this chapter has been to illustrate the range of treatment of three widely differing news stories, and to test the influence of known reader preferences in the field of news. The overall impression that results is that most evening newspapers, in their non-local coverage, occupy the 'middle ground' between the popular and quality national dailies; they give prominence to major crimes and to the celebrities of the 'pop' world but by no means neglect more serious, less spectacular news. The Nottingham *Evening Post* is a newspaper that would serve to validate this point. In terms of tone and style, news coverage is factual, sober and restrained.

It is clear that if a sufficient number of case studies was compiled a quite accurate sense of each paper's news values could be gained. Journalists tend to talk of news values as a 'house secret'; for instance, Harold Ffoulkes, representing the Institute of Journalists before the 1947 Commission, stated:

It used to be a common complaint when I was on the North Mail that it would have a column and a half on a good, juicy murder in London on the front page, and one that had occurred locally only got half a column on the inside page. That is one of those mysterious things known as value. . . . It is simply a case of how newspapers are made up. Each is a profound mystery to the others.[15]

In fact, there needs be little mystery; in order to cope with the sheer volume of incoming material and to meet the ever-looming deadlines, each newspaper applies its own rules of thumb, its particular valuations; the published news bodies forth a newspaper's values, attitudes and, perhaps, prejudices. In the next chapter the nature and presentation of local news is discussed in detail.

Notes

1 C. P. Scott, *1846–1932: the Making of the 'Manchester Guardian'* (London: Frederick Muller, 1946), p. 165.
2 Francis Williams, *op. cit.*, p. 15.
3 Scott, *op. cit.*, p. 161.
4 Christiansen, *op. cit.*, pp. 144, 186.
5 See Hugh Cudlipp, *At your Peril* (London: Weidenfeld & Nicolson, 1962), p. 116.
6 *Memoranda of Evidence*, p. 64.
7 George Orwell, *Coming up for Air* (Harmondsworth: Penguin Books, 1963), p. 188.
8 For instance, when the entire front page is devoted to coverage of a major local disaster—as in the *West Lancashire Evening Gazette*, 6 March, 1971 ('40 ft flames rip through furniture shop'—160 column inches).
9 See *Report* (Royal Commission, 1947–49), pp. 50–1. Also George Scott, *Reporter Anonymous—the Story of the Press Association* (London: Hutchinson, 1968), chs. 9, 10, 16.
10 *Memoranda of Evidence*, p. 46.
11 See p. 38.
12 J. Galtung and M. H. Ruge, 'The structure of foreign news', *Media Sociology*, ed. Jeremy Tunstall (London: Constable, 1970), pp. 259–300.
13 *Minutes of Evidence*, 10 December 1947, p. 25.
14 See pp. 39–40.
15 *Minutes of Evidence*, 30 October 1947, p. 29.

6 Local news: some recurring themes

It was suggested in the previous chapter that except when major non-local news stories are to hand (e.g. a macabre crime, a serious industrial disorder, significant 'consumer' news, etc.) about half the evening papers sampled tend to select the leading local story for their main headlines; the rest make more use of non-local material. The bulk of the news content on other pages is local in origin, as is the entire news content of the weekly Press. The aim of this chapter is to clarify the nature of local news in terms of themes and presentation.

Analysis of the main headline subjects of a sample of 100 weekly newspapers revealed the following categories. (Five whose front pages were given over to advertising were excluded from consideration.)

1. *Community news*
   (*a*) Community (including institutions and groups) plans, appeals for progress, and reports: 35 (37 per cent); e.g. 'Plan to rid county of slum schools' (*Hereford Times*, 15 January 1965).
   (*b*) Community controversy; community groups or individuals in a contention situation: 15 (16 per cent); e.g. 'Boldmere up in arms—betting shop is opposed' (*Sutton Coldfield News*, 11 December 1964).
   (*c*) Community closures or threats of closure (e.g. of some particular amenity), or successful or intended resistance to some externally imposed decision which will affect the community: 8 (8 per cent); e.g. 'Council wins fight to stop BR coal depot plan' (*Shields Weekly News*, 4 December 1964).
   (*d*) Rates and rents: 5 (5 per cent); e.g. 'Council rents to go up' (*Selby Gazette and Herald*, 11 December 1964).
   (*e*) Unclassified: 12 (13 per cent); e.g. 'Everything is pointing to a bumper Xmas' (*Barnsley Chronicle*, 12 December 1964).

2. *Crimes, accidents, disasters*

   (*f*) Accidents, disasters: 11 (12 per cent); e.g. 'Death crash man's 10 drinks' (*Leigh Reporter*, 21 October 1965).

   (*g*) Crimes: 9 (9 per cent); e.g. 'Armed gang beat up police and steal £500 from farmer' (*New Milton Advertiser*, 12 December 1964).

One would therefore expect a typical local weekly to ring the changes on news of community progress (37 per cent), community controversy, closures or threats of closure (24 per cent), accidents and disasters (12 per cent) and crimes (9 per cent)—these categories totalling 82 per cent of all. The same categories would account for most of the local main headlines in the evening Press.

However, the distribution of main headline news cannot be regarded as a predictor of the spread of news on other pages; it affords only a partial picture. To obtain the overall picture, systematic analysis is necessary; accordingly, copies of three evening and three weekly papers were studied in detail. These were:

1. Weekly newspapers:

   Warley Courier and Smethwick Telephone, 12 August 1966.
   Buxton Advertiser, 13 May 1966.
   Cheshire Observer, 19 February 1965.

2. Evening newspapers:

   Birmingham Evening Mail, 13 January 1966.
   Leicester Mercury, 12 January 1966.
   Bolton *Evening News*, 18 January 1966.

The weeklies were chosen because they serve different types of community. The *Warley Courier and Smethwick Telephone* circulates in a densely populated and industrialised urban area; the *Buxton Advertiser* in the small resort of Buxton and outlying rural districts, which also contain such industries as quarrying, lime and cement manufacture and textiles; and the *Cheshire Observer* in the county seat and cathedral city of Chester and outlying districts. The evening newspapers were selected from the sample referred to in the two previous chapters, on the basis of their different circulation sizes; the *Birmingham Evening Mail*'s 1964 circulation was 408,539, the *Leicester Mercury*'s 'in excess of 175,000' and the Bolton *Evening News*'s 88,107.

The approach adopted was to regard news as indicative of either order or disorder, and as primarily involving either (*a*) individuals, families or *ad hoc* groups or (*b*) organisations, institutions or the community as a whole. All news reports over 10 column inches in length were classified, and the categories that follow evolved in relation to these:

1. *Aspects of order concerning individuals, families or* ad hoc *groups.* Bravery, heroism, responsible action, public service, successes, appointments, promotions, retirements at the normal age, presentations, special celebrations, birth, marriage, death at a good age, sentimental stories and most animal stories.

2. *Aspects of order concerning the local community as a whole, or local institutions, organisations, industries, etc.* Positive projects or plans, new organisations (or existing ones extended), rate rises (intended to benefit the community), church services, fund-raising, shows (e.g. musical, dramatic, agricultural), festivals, rallies (non-sporting), dinners, elections, meetings with an 'order' intention, local MP news. Also: sports news.[1]

3. *Aspects of disorder concerning individuals, families or* ad hoc *groups:*
   (*a*) Murder, sexual assault, shooting, stabbing, fracas, vandalism, theft and the resulting inquiries and court hearings.
   (*b*) Fatal and/or non-fatal accidents or disasters, untimely deaths (and any subsequent inquiries), serious illness, enforced retirement, dismissal.

4. *Aspects of disorder concerning the community as a whole, or local institutions, organisations, industries, etc.* Strikes, controversies, allegations of error, neglect or faulty procedure, intended or actual showdown, shortages, mechanical failures, natural (but preventable) or mechanical dangers, industrial decline, closures (actual or pending).

The aim of the classification was twofold. First, it would afford evidence of the general balance as between order and disorder news in the evening and weekly Press respectively. Second, it would confirm or refute the assumption that the medium-sized or large circulation evening newspaper would contain more disorder news than the typical weekly. This assumption was held on the grounds that, in theory, much order news is of interest only to the reader who knows the people concerned, and that the involvement of an evening newspaper's readership (excepting the 12 per cent of evening newspapers with circulations of below 25,000) would be most activated by an emphasis on (*a*) the main order news affecting the town or city base and (*b*) a selection of the most newsworthy disorder stories within the circulation area as a whole.

Tables 6 and 7 show how the reports were distributed amongst the four main categories, and how many column inches each category accounted for.

Table 6 Weekly newspapers

	(i) *Indiv.* *order*	(ii) *Inst.* *order*	(iii) *Indiv.* *disorder*	(iv) *Inst.* *disorder*
Buxton Advertiser				
Reports	2	12	4	1
Column inches	28	251	147½	25½
Smethwick Telephone				
Reports	5	6	1	4
Column inches	98	215	17	60
Cheshire Observer				
Reports	4	10	5	0
Column inches	51	339½	67	0

Table 7 Evening newspapers*

	(i) *Indiv.* *order*	(ii) *Inst.* *order*	(iii) *Indiv.* *disorder*	(iv) *Inst.* *disorder*
Birmingham Evening Mail				
Reports	4	3	6	6
Column inches	91½	35	271	89
Leicester Mercury				
Reports	4	4	4	3
Column inches	86	118	55	43½
Bolton *Evening News*				
Reports	0	2	4	5
Column inches	0	53	102	90

* Three non-local reports included.

Using the figures specified in tables 6 and 7, table 8 shows (*a*) the total number of reports and column inches for each paper, (*b*) the

PPC—D

total number of order and disorder reports with column inches for each category and (c) *the ratio of order to disorder reports, and order to disorder column inches.* The summary shows that the ratio of column inches of order news to disorder news in the weekly news-

Table 8

	Overall totals	Order	Disorder	Ratios
Buxton Advertiser				
Reports	19	14	5	2·8 : 1
Column inches	452	279	173	1·6 : 1
Smethwick Telephone				
Reports	16	11	5	2·2 : 1
Column inches	390	313	77	4 : 1
Cheshire Observer				
Reports	19	14	5	2·8 : 1
Column inches	457	390	67	5·8 : 1
Birmingham Evening Mail				
Reports	19	7	12	1 : 1·7
Column inches	486	126	360	1 : 2·8
Leicester Mercury				
Reports	15	8	7	1·1 : 1
Column inches	302	204	98	2 : 1
Bolton *Evening News*				
Reports	11	2	9	1 : 4·5
Column inches	245	53	192	1 : 3·6
Summary				
Weeklies:				
Reports	54	39	15	2·6 : 1
Column inches	1,299	982	317	3 : 1
Evenings:				
Reports	45	17	28	1 : 1·6
Column inches	1,033	383	650	1 : 1·7

papers was 3 : 1; in the case of the evening Press it was 1 :1·6. The ratios for the weeklies ranged from 1·6 : 1 (*Buxton Advertiser*) to 5·8 : 1 (*Cheshire Observer*), and for the evenings from 1 : 3·6 (Bolton *Evening News*) to 2 : 1 (*Leicester Mercury*). Whereas institutional order news constituted the leading category for each of the weeklies (see table 6), individual disorder news was the main one in two of the three evening newspapers (see table 7). Thus the sole exception to the general proposition that the weekly Press mirrors more order than disorder, and the evening Press more disorder than order, was the *Leicester Mercury*, whose ratios in terms of column inches were 2 : 1 and in terms of numbers of reports 1·1 : 1 (order : disorder).

A larger random sample of both types of newspaper would be necessary in order to establish valid typical ratios for each, but it is unlikely that these would differ significantly from the ratios noted in the summary of table 8. For the function of a weekly newspaper is to mirror as fully as possible all facets of local life—including a great deal of routine news from local civic, religious, social and cultural organisations. It can cover more of this routine news than the average evening newspaper (54 per cent of evening newspapers have circulations of over 50,000) because its circulation area will typically be confined to a single urban base and its immediate out-lying area, which will contain small towns or villages unable to support a weekly of their own. In contrast, the large evening news-paper may circulate in several urban bases and their outlying areas. For example, of the 402,647 daily sales of the *Birmingham Evening Mail* in 1964, 167,487 were in ten communities with their own weeklies—a figure representing 41 per cent of all sales.[2] If, therefore, the *Mail* were to include routine or secondary news emanating either from the city or from other urban areas in which it circulates, it would do so in the knowledge that such news had scant readability value for perhaps a majority of readers. Accordingly, the editorial policy of such a paper is likely to lead to an emphasis on the follow-ing types of news:

1. The main city order news, e.g. a city council debate.
2. Secondary order news if it contains particularly appealing human or animal interest.
3. The main disorder stories arising within the circulation area as a whole.
4. The leading 'institutional informative' or dramatic non-local stories.
5. Sports news.

The reason why category 3 typically takes up a higher proportion of space in the evening than the weekly Press is that, in general, dis-order news has more reader interest than order news; key disorder

words like 'blaze', 'blast', 'body', 'orgy', or 'crisis' are more likely
to attract the reader's attention than, say, 'Takings £50 up at Hay-
field's May festival'.[3] The latter headline would be unexceptionable
in the context of a weekly newspaper, which attempts to mirror all
the news of public interest—however routine and undramatic—in its
circulation area. The evening newspaper of medium or large size
(with, say, a circulation over 50,000) will be more selective, and will
take into account the 'readability value' of its news stories *vis-à-vis*
the majority of readers—especially where a 'popular' image is sought.
Exceptions may occur, in the form of order news which the 'gatekeepers' see as their duty to feature prominently; Tillotson's Newspapers Ltd pointed this out to the 1947 Commission:

> An example of the way in which we publish material which may not
> appeal to the majority of our readers is in the reporting of Town Council
> and Civic affairs. These are sometimes not of much obvious news value if
> readability is the only test . . . We feel in this matter that in the position
> we enjoy in our community we can afford not only to give the public what
> it reasonably wants, but to some degree what it ought to want.[4]

One is not implying by these comments that the weekly Press does
not emphasise the most striking local news; of course, it does. But
in general it contains a higher proportion of order news, and much
of this will be of minority interest. The ratio of order to disorder
news in the *Leicester Mercury* issue referred to above (2 : 1 column
inches) would be likely only on evenings when there was an unusual
dearth of disorder stories; then, of course, the evening Press has to
make more use of secondary order news.

The 'order–disorder' analyses of six newspapers have shown that
it would be incorrect to suppose that the 'faithful mirror'—which
provincial companies claim to hold up to community life[5]—uniformly reflects the same features. Quite apart from the effects that
result from the editorial concept of role and from the kind of community served, the nature of what is mirrored is crucially influenced
by the newspaper's type (i.e. evening or weekly) and size of circulation. It is now appropriate to cite examples of typical order and disorder news, and to discuss the function each fulfils and the nature of
its presentation.

1. Murder, sexual assault, shooting, stabbing, fracas, vandalism, theft and the resulting inquiries and court hearings

It has already been shown that major crimes, accidents and disasters will be given prominent front-page coverage if their source is local. Key words in the related main headlines include 'body', 'death', 'killer', 'murdered', 'blast', 'blaze', 'crash', 'drama', 'gang' and 'bandits'. When the facts permit one or two of these or similar words will be intermingled with other emotive 'nub' terms, for instance, from the spheres of criminal investigation, 'pop' culture or the medical world.

> *West Lancashire Evening Gazette*, 14 January 1966: 'Yard chiefs call murder talks/Hunt for killer builds up'.
> *Ibid.*, 9 March 1967: 'Pop man on drugs murdered woman/ Then he shot himself'.
> *Huddersfield Daily Examiner*, 21 January 1966: 'Death in surgery/Two women stabbed at Elland/Man held'.

Accidents or disasters can be similarly presented, as in 'Acid slip sends 7 to hospital' (Bolton *Evening News*, 19 January 1966). Headline language stresses the general subject area into which the reported event falls, and so usually deals in anonymities: 'Yard chiefs', 'Pop man', 'Two women' or 'Hospital'. These abbreviated descriptions are phrased so as to catch the reader's eye; he must read on to become acquainted with the purged particulars.

The provincial Press's treatment of 'on the spot' crime news, resulting in a collocation of objective data, reported comment and verbatim statements, was discussed in chapter 5. Its handling of local (and non-local) court cases conforms to the practice of the nationals; it sticks to hard facts and makes extensive use of direct quotation. There is no superadded colour. Sometimes the juxtaposition of the factual court reporting style and the particular form of disorder being tried produces a mildly comic effect; law and order are presented as patient and rational, while the agents of disorder may emerge as uncontrollably irrational. This effect was created by part of a *Buxton Advertiser* report, ' "Nasty free-for all" outside a Buxton club' (13 May 1966):

> . . . as P.c. Cooper was speaking to McLaughlin a fist came over the constable's shoulder and hit McLaughlin—'an inflammatory gesture' which set the whole thing going again.

Pathologist warns of delusion risks

POP MAN ON DRUGS
MURDERED WOMAN

DEATH IN SURGERY

Two women stabbed
at Elland
MAN HELD

Fig. 5 'Disorder' news: two main headlines, from the *West Lancashire Evening Gazette*, 9 March 1967 (*upper*), and the *Huddersfield Daily Examiner*, 21 February 1966 (*lower*). Reproduced two-thirds actual size. By courtesy of the *West Lancashire Evening Gazette and the Huddersfield Daily Examiner*

Constable Lamb then arrived and during the fracas lost his helmet, which, it was alleged, was picked up by McLean, who danced around the car park with it in a most aggressive manner and said he would not give it him back until the constable put his staff back, which P.c. Lamb in his wisdom had done.

The reader sees these incidents from the magistrate's standpoint; the intruding fist is assessed as an 'inflammatory gesture' and the dancing, helmet-carrying McLean is presented as a disorder figure comporting himself 'in a most aggressive manner'. Constable Lamb, in contrast, puts his staff back 'in his wisdom'. The prose is at a far remove from the fictional presentation of violence.

The drama of major trials is effectively conveyed by means of extensive reporting of verbatim statements, as the following passage from a murder trial ('Life jail for youth after a four day trial for murder', *Buxton Advertiser*, 13 May 1966) confirms:

When you pulled it out what was in your mind?—To frighten him away.
Timmis continued: 'I lost control of myself altogether. I heard someone shout something about a knife when I was more or less coming to my senses. Then I realized what I had done. I don't know what had happened to the knife. I tried to hide the fact.

Lost control

Mr. Justice Ashworth: What had you done?—I had used it. I realized I had stabbed Barnfield. I would never have used it but for seeing Buckingham come down the stairs and but for being grabbed by my hair. It was only a short time that I lost control of myself.

Re-examined by Mr. Bingham, Timmis was asked: 'What are your feelings now of having been the instrument of Barnfield's death?' To this question Timmis replied in a trembling voice: 'I cannot say how sorry I am.'

Timmis's confusion in the rapid flux of events at the time of the murder is fully conveyed by the five verbatim sentences of the second paragraph; these contain an average of nine words each and suggest the swiftness of the action. The inescapable position of the defendant in the dock is impressed upon the reader by the cluster of first person pronouns and adjectives: 'I . . . myself . . . I . . .I . . my . . . I . . . I . . . I . . . I.'

It is fair to assert that major local 'individual disorder' news— of which this is but one example—would be assessed by virtually all provincial editors as compelling content that necessitates high prominence. This report was accorded the *Advertiser*'s main headline

and 19½ column inches on page 1 and 90 column inches on page 9—
almost one quarter of the total space allocated to all the reports over
10 column inches length.

Deference to family and institutional values may result in the
exclusion of potentially offending detail from reports of cases involving certain types of sexual offence. But many forms of violence,
and their effects, are reported in the conventional style outlined;
this eschews 'colour' and relies on factual data and verbatim or
reported statements. The same reporting style will be found to characterise news of other such disorder subjects as vandalism, accidents
and disasters.

Press spokesmen habitually claim that court reporting is a public
service: the correct facts are made available, baseless rumours are
dispelled and justice is 'seen to be done'. It is, of course, also a fact
that many types of court case make for singularly readable content,
as the *News of the World* demonstrates by its faith in the 'pulling
power' of the most striking sex and/or violence trials arising in
any given week. Majority public opinion would, it seems certain,
sanction the continued publication and prominence of major crimes
and court cases; the reason offered would no doubt be the same as
the Press's—that the operation of the law is a proper concern of the
public at large. But the instinct that drew crowds to the gallows,
the appetite for violence and sensation may well be amongst the root
reasons.

The debate about the motives of newspapers and their readers in
this area is of long standing; more recently there has been a growing
concern (although it is still very much a minority concern) about the
publicising of cases where the publicity itself is open to the charge
of being harsher punishment than that inflicted by the court. For
instance, a letter in the *Manchester Evening News* on 9 July 1970—
headed 'Branded'—contained this strongly worded paragraph about
a local newspaper report:

> If people responsible for printing had the slightest conception of the
> suffering involved in filling a miserable bit of space in the paper, they
> would perhaps spare a little compassion for a young offender on the
> threshold of her career and concentrate more on the hardened type of
> criminal to whom publicity matters not one jot.

A similarly powerful appeal for selective reporting was made at the
1970 conference of the Guild of British Newspaper Editors, by Mrs
Marjorie Jones, magistrate and wife of the editor of the *Express and*

Star (Wolverhampton). Referring to 'punitive publicity', she continued:

> Do not degenerate into the jackals, or the hyenas of justice . . . can you not cease to be the hounders of humanity, at least for its minor crimes, yet still continue to watch over and record the processes of justice?
>
> . . . In no other land but our own does the press build its circulation on publicising the names of those who have also to pay the fine, or endure the treatment, imposed by a court for a minor crime [*The Guardian*, 26 September, 1970].

The traditional editorial defence when this sort of plea is made is that 'the newspaper ought never to put itself in the position of judge or advocate by deciding that in one case the penalty shall include publicity and in another it shall not' (*Sutton and Cheam Advertiser*, 6 January 1966). It is also said that to set the precedent of non-publication would strengthen the arm of any defendant (deserving or not) seeking the same dispensation.

Whether there will be any decisive move towards selective reporting in the 1970s remains to be seen; Mrs Jones's suggestion was that the names of people remanded for medical or psychiatric reports, or those who were put on probation or given a conditional discharge, should not be published.

It would be unfair to the local Press not to add that much of the publicity it gives to crime and violence is clearly in the community's best interest. It alerts householders and commercial concerns to the kinds of burglary and/or vandalism being practised at any one time; it assists the police by publishing Identikit pictures and appeals for help, and by informing the public about dangerous criminals—as did the Midlands newspapers in the 'second body' case. In general, it helps to reassure readers that the police and the law are actively helping to safeguard their persons and property. These are all positive functions, and mention of them is necessary if a proper perspective on crime and court reporting is to be held.

2. Strikes, controversies, allegations of error, neglect or faulty procedure, intended or actual showdown, shortages, mechanical failures, natural (but preventable) or mechanical dangers, industrial decline, closures (actual or pending)

This second category of disorder news may involve the community as a whole, or local institutions, organisations, etc., within the community. Many of the related reports are disclosures of the kind that imply the need for, or explicitly request—through the comments of spokesmen—remedial action; in effect they may supplement the leading column and feature article in their possible role of watchdog. This possible function was pointed out by Scarborough and District Newspapers Ltd in their written evidence to the 1947 Commission:

> We may publish, say, a strictly factual article showing that nearly half the houses in a certain town are without a bath and that no public baths exist to make good this deficiency. To preserve the proprieties we may keep our opinion on this state of affairs for a separate column. But why do we publish the factual article, except because we think that this is a matter on which there ought to be an expression of opinion?[6]

Mention of two reports that fell within the general subject area of 'allegations of error, neglect or faulty procedure' must suffice to clarify the category as a whole. The first—'Where wives get washday blues twice over'—was published in the *Warley Courier and Smethwick Telephone* on 13 January 1966. It itemised a number of complaints about the dirt and dust erupting from the chimney of Smethwick Laundry Co. Ltd. Two of these follow:

> Mrs. Marjorie Tomlin, of No. 25, said she had to do her washing again some Mondays because of the dirt and dust from the chimney.
> 'Many women have complained about this,' she added.
> Her husband, Mr. James Tomlin, plucked a black-stained rose from his garden and said: 'This is what the stuff from the chimney is doing . . . killing my flowers. I take a great pride in my garden but I am losing my best roses.' . . .

The details cohere to indict those responsible for the offending chimney; its local impact can be seen as symbolised by the black-stained rose. The facts by themselves project an unfavourable image of the laundry, whose 'spokesman' was—as is customary in this type of report—afforded the right of reply. However, 'he had received no complaints about the matter' and the owner 'could not be contacted for comment'. Even so, local residents would no doubt assume that the publicity might well prompt remedial action.

The second report appeared in the *Birmingham Evening Mail* on 13 January 1966; it implied that the city's Housing Department had paid insufficient attention to the social problems that may confront some individuals or families who are rehoused in tall blocks of flats. It focused on an elderly woman's complaint to a sympathetic councillor:

Coun. Lawler said a 65-year-old woman living alone in a multi-storey flat in Lee Bank had complained to him that her only companions were the wind and the draughts which howled through the corridors.

'She had no complaints about the flat,' he said. 'It was just that she never saw anyone from early morning until late at night.

'She had been moved away from her friends and relatives and said that now her only friend was her electric blanket.' . . .

This report, like the previous one, draws attention to an urban community problem—in this case, personal isolation. Its publication would seem to afford grounds for hope on the part of those in a similar position; first, their plight is now known about, and second, some kind of amelioration may ensue—even though the Housing Management Committee's spokesman, after citing the efforts normally made to house people 'where they want to live', added that 'as landlords we can only do so much'. Other flat-dwellers and local voluntary organisations that take an interest in welfare matters might, however, respond positively.

The report, then, is comparable to that of the *Warley Courier* in its detailed reference to one particular case which in effect dramatises the overall theme. The similarities in presentation, including both direct and reported speech, emotive particularities ('killing my flowers'/'her only friend was her electric blanket') and the right of reply, indicate that this is the conventional mode of fulfilling the watchdog role through news reporting. The news columns can therefore combine with watchdog letters, leaders and features to make a four-pronged attack on agencies of 'disorder' possible.

Amongst the values that the Press is tacitly upholding in its reporting of individual or *ad hoc* group disorder are justice, law and order, safety and security. In its reports on disorder within, or caused by, institutions, organisations or industries one or more of the following values may be upheld: safety and security, efficiency, progress and personal or group self-fulfilment. These are the positives that sanction the Press's role of watchdog.

3. Bravery, heroism, responsible action, public service. successes, appointments, promotions, retirements at the normal age, presentations, special celebrations, birth, marriage, death at a good age, sentimental stories and animal stories

(a) Bravery, heroism, responsible action, public service At the opposite pole to reports of crime or of the victims of crime, accidents and disasters are stories of some kind of heroic action; the polarity can, of course, occur within a single story. The heroes concerned are for the most part celebrated only in the provincial Press; national media, Daniel Boorstin has suggested, tend to highlight the activities of 'celebrities'—'pop' stars, show-biz 'personalities' or 'sex symbols' —well known for their well-knownness. The deeds of the genuine heroes remain largely unsung: 'In this life of illusion and quasi-illusion, the person with solid virtues who can be admired for something more substantial than his well-knownness often proves to be the unsung hero; the teacher, the nurse, the mother, the honest cop, the hard worker at lonely, underpaid, unglamorous, unpublicized jobs.'[7]

Three kinds of genuine hero are discussed below; all three will be familiar to readers of provincial or weekly newspapers. There is the hero who risks life or limb by intervening in a perilous situation; the hero by virtue of overcoming adverse personal circumstances, such as crippling illness or the total loss of material possessions; and the hero who champions some local cause against powerful odds and wins the day—the village Hampden.

The most frequently reported mode of heroism is the first, involving intervention in, say, a hold-up, act of burglary, fire or accident; connected are valorous attempts at rescue from death by drowning, floods and pot-hole or mountain perils. One report of this type appeared in the *Warley Courier* on 12 August 1966; it was headlined ' "Splendid example of good citizenship" ':

A woman who struggled with a gunman after he stole diamond rings from the Oldbury jeweller's shop where she is an assistant, has been praised by the Chief Constable of the West Midlands Police Force, Mr. N. Goodchild.

. . . Mrs. Jesson and the other assistant, Mrs. Madge Taylor, were alone in the shop when the gunman, an escaped prisoner, came in and asked to see some rings.

He demanded money, then when Mrs. Jesson refused to open the till, snatched the rings and made for the door. She struggled with him, and he dropped the rings and fled.

Bruises

In the struggle Mrs. Jesson's dress was torn and she received bruises on her arms.

In his letter to Mrs. Jesson . . . the Chief Constable praised her courage and described her action as 'a splendid example of good citizenship.'

She told the *Courier & Telephone*: 'I was surprised to receive the letter. It was my duty to protect the rings. Our customers were very sympathetic about my bruises.'

The story is, in effect, one of 'ordered disorder'; as such it has a twofold interest for the reader. There is a strong element of drama— the escaped-prisoner gunman, the struggle and the bruises—but this is resolved on a note of order and concludes happily. The heroine is conventionally modest; the chief constable's praise had been unexpected, and she assesses her action as the natural outcome of a sense of duty. These are typical ingredients in this sort of report.

The second kind of hero is the man or woman who overcomes severely adverse personal circumstances and goes on to achieve some remarkable success, whether physical, intellectual or vocational. News of such people, like that of the jeweller's assistant, implies that the reader should admire them, and suggests an ideal pattern of conduct should he encounter similar circumstances. It has inspirational value. The *Birmingham Evening Mail* of 17 June 1966 contained a report featuring this type of hero:

Richard's really champion

Wins swim title—with a broken back

Richard Bate, an 18-year-old Birmingham boy with a broken back, has become a national swimming champion.

. . . Richard . . . has won three gold medals—for the free-style, the back stroke, and the breast stroke—at the national games for the partly paralysed at Stoke Mandeville, Bucks.

Richard, a burly six-footer, was planning a university education and a teaching career before he broke his back in a motor cycle accident two years ago. His legs were useless.

Since then he has had 26 operations, taught himself to walk by balancing on artificial aids, got himself a job, and begun re-shaping his career.

. . . His father, Mr. Ronald Bate, said today: '. . . I think he has taken what has happened in a most wonderful way. He never complains and it is not easy. It is a lifetime job.'

Stories of this kind remind the reader of the human capacity to create order from disorder; Richard Bate, the unlucky victim of a crippling motor cycle accident, has courageously faced circumstances which might well have resulted in apathy and pessimism. But he 'never complains' and has shown heroic fortitude and will-power in the face of 'a lifetime job'. The local Press ensures that he is not 'an unsung hero'; this report appeared on the *Mail*'s front page and above the fold.

Provincial newspapers also sing the praises of the man or woman who organises community resistance against some internal or external institutional policy felt to be unjust or smacking of 'Big Brother'. Such heroes are the successors of Gray's 'village Hampden' who withstood 'the little tyrant of his fields'. They may be deemed heroes even if they fail against such opposition as the local council, Whitehall or the 'Beeching axe'; if they succeed, they will be feted and honoured, and become part of the local collective memory. One man who successfully marshalled his community's resistance to the 'Beeching axe' was Mr Henry Hartley, whose efforts afforded the *Buxton Advertiser* a running story during 1964; he became locally famous as the man who saved the Buxton–Manchester railway line from closure. The line's reprieve was announced in the *Advertiser* on 31 July 1964, and the official conferment of 'local hero' status on Mr Hartley was reported on 9 October 1964. A few extracts from the report, which was accorded 56 column inches, reveal the capacity of close-knit communities to present a common front and stoically oppose the edicts of what they regard as 'Big Brother' autocracies; the victorious protagonist becomes locally analogous to the Churchill of 1940. He is seen as having saved his town from decline and relative ignominy:

'Freedom' fighter honoured

Mr. Henry Hartley's 'inspiring' lead against rail threat

. . . To a full gathering of the Borough Council, and some 260 invited guests, together with members of the public, Ald. Mrs. C. Mostyn Kershaw, herself an Honorary Freeman of the Borough, proposed the following motion: 'That Henry Hartley be, and is hereby admitted an Honorary Freeman of the Borough.

'In conferring this honour upon Mr. Henry Hartley, a former Mayor of the Borough, the Council desire to convey to him the sincere thanks of his fellow citizens for the eminent services which he rendered to Buxton in leading an inspired opposition to the proposals of the British Railways Board to withdraw passenger railway services and to close ten railway stations between Buxton and Manchester (Piccadilly).

'He knew . . . that this closure would be hitting at the very heart of the town. For what town could exist, let alone prosper, when its very life-line was in jeopardy. Buxton might well have become what Oliver Goldsmith refers to as "The Deserted Village." '

. . . Responding, Mr. Hartley said . . . 'The Beeching Report was a rallying call to the town; it united all sections. When the Minister of Transport refused his consent to close the line, the town expressed its joy. The action which you, Mr. Mayor, and the members of the Council have today taken is an expression of thanks to everyone of the very many people who worked in the fight to save our railway services.'

A number of words and phrases here are images of military conflict; Mr Hartley is styled a 'fighter', and thanks all who 'worked in the fight'. The town (or Buxtonians acting collectively) had responded to Dr Beeching's 'rallying call'; once success was achieved 'the town expressed its joy'. It might have become a moribund backwater; its 'very heart' had been threatened, its 'very life-line'. But the village Hampden won the day; Buxton was not to become like Goldsmith's deserted village, the victim of 'trade's unfeeling train'.

Mr Hartley, then, as a local hero, maintained his community's status in the face of an external threat; his qualities lay in his approaching the problem 'with courage, with confidence and with a grim determination that at all costs we must win' (Ald. Mrs C. Mostyn Kershaw). He was therefore accorded his town's highest civic honour, presented with all the pomp and circumstance that communities even of Buxton's size (1964 population, 19,236) can still invoke on such occasions. Because Mr Hartley's qualities are those which the successful 'resistance' organiser needs, similar reports of heroic efforts will be found to contain many verbal parallels.

This account of three types of local hero is by no means all-embracing. It does, however, sufficiently clarify one important form of order news. The heroes concerned 'order' disorder that besets themselves, or others in the community, or the community as a whole. They may display courage, initiative, fortitude or other inspirational qualities. News of them affords the reader solid grounds for reassurance about the pattern of local life, and suggests that not all young people are vandals, nor all older ones crooks. Furthermore, it enhances the image of the community, by revealing that amongst its citizens are people who can be admired for something more substantial than synthetic well-knownness.

(b) Wedding anniversaries, Darby and Joan romances, centenarian celebrations, retirements, sentimental animal stories, lucky escapers and lucky winners As well as extolling the deeds of local heroes, provincial newspapers give consistent prominence to various types of local celebrity, both human and animal. Such news forms an appropriate contrast to the steady flow of reports of crime, accident and disaster, mirroring the 'sunny side of life' and meeting a readership need appreciated by Chaucer's Knight:

>   . . . for litel hevynesse
> Is right ynough to muche folk, I gesse.

An assumption that almost all newspapers seem to hold in common is that readers not only have a 'soft spot' themselves—ready to manifest itself in admiration for courage or in strains of humanitarian sentiment—but like to sense that their newspaper has one too. As a result, when 'soft spot' news arises it is often quite prominently featured and accompanied by photographic illustration. The intention is to evoke the reader's Pickwickian self, and give him cause for optimistic buoyancy.

Wedding anniversary reports are a staple item of both evening and weekly newspaper content, and a form of news that is essentially local in its appeal. Characteristic headlines—'Their happy 60 years',[8] '60 years wed: "no regrets" ',[9] 'Queen's message on their Diamond day'[10]—are invariably accompanied by a photograph of two smiling faces. The reports usually contain an account of how the couple first met, where they married, where they have lived and worked, their hobbies and sometimes their attitude to marriage. One or two examples of attitudes frequently expressed show how such reports assume a reader curiosity about the relationships of others, and meet any need for reassurance that the basic human values and institutions (e.g. the loyalties and the security of marriage) are being carried on:

Warley Courier and Smethwick Telephone, 11 March 1966:
'. . . When asked who was the "boss", Mr. Fletcher said without
hesitation: "The missus."
    'Both agreed that their 60 years together had been very happy
ones.'
    Dewsbury Reporter and District News, 23 October 1965: '. . .
"We have had a comfortable life," they said, this week, "and it
has not been without its ups and downs, or its arguments. We
have never come to blows, but a marriage cannot go on without
some arguments." '
    Brighton and Hove Gazette, 22 October 1965: '. . . And how
has their marriage lasted all these years? Both agreed: "A little
bit of give and take." '

The men concerned had worked in a winding shop, as a long-
distance lorry driver and with a dairies combine. It seems to be a
convention that local journalists do not attempt to elicit the attitudes to marriage of, say, professional people; only the so-called
'man in the street' is expected to volunteer the information that 'the
missus' is the boss, or that marriage needs 'a little bit of give and
take'. In reports which dig, however shallowly, into people's private
experience the Press assumes something of the gossip's role. Occasionally a journalist will draw out vivid observations on social
change, like these from a retired Burnley tram driver (presented in
the context of a Golden Wedding report):

    . . . 'The early days were hard in Burnley,' they say. They are pleased to
see the new more modern-looking town rising from the industrial grime of
the town of their childhood. Both aged 74, they say they want to forget
the days when hungry youngsters roamed the centre of the town barefoot
begging for scraps of food.
    'I was a tram driver in those days. I worked 55 hours a week for sixpence
an hour, and although it was not a big wage, at least it was regular. We
had to fight to keep our jobs in those days,' says Mr. Walters.[11]

This sort of reminiscence must necessarily set off a train of recollec-
tion in the minds of older readers; it conveys, too, a real sense of
the time that the couple have spent together, and of the hardships
they have surmounted.
    Another and associated type of report is that of the 'Darby and
Joan' romance; its appeal is to the reader's sentimental self. The
extract that follows is from a *Birmingham Evening Mail* report

(8 July 1966) headlined 'Holiday hotel romance at 83/Now it's con-
fetti and rice for city couple':

> . . . Mr. Birchley said: 'We got talking and in no time at all I asked her
> to marry me.
> 'Living alone can be very lonely. I have plenty to occupy me during the
> day, but when I sit down at night there are just the four walls and me.
> Now all that is over and we shall be very happy. . . .'

Such a report implies that age need not be a barrier to 'romance';
life may begin again at eighty-three, having—in the popular saw—
begun once at forty. It also offers a number of reassurances. It gives
the reader grounds for hoping that old age, which may seem to offer
only the prospect of loneliness ('just the four walls and me') and fond
memories, need not be a time of inevitable brooding or solitude.
Readers' fears of ultimate isolation and gradually immobilising
senility may also be to some degree mollified by the recurring news
of seemingly dynamic centenarians—the 'long livers' who, in the
majority of reported cases, appear to enjoy good health and an
active life. Accounts of them (again, almost always accompanied by
a photograph) are a further instance of 'soft spot' news material;
'isn't that nice' is the assumed reader response. Reporters conventionally try to elicit the 'secret' or formula for attaining great age;
as in both the following passages. The first is from the *Birmingham
Evening Mail*, 30 July 1965:

Old? Not me, says Mrs. Jones, 100

> . . . On Monday, she will have a family party with friends and some of
> her nine children, seven step-children, 14 grand-children, 24 great-grand-
> children and four great-great-grandchildren.
> Mrs. MacDonald said: 'She is amazing. She still enjoys listening to the
> radio and hearing a good joke. We keep forgetting she is so old.'
> Mrs. Jones interrupted: 'I'm not that old. No one should feel their age
> if they are happy and contented—that's the secret.'
> She looked round her cosy living room and added: 'I intend to live for
> years yet. I've just had new curtains and the room redecorated. I'm going
> to be around until they are worn out.'

This report presents an ideal for the reader's old age. Mrs Jones is
seemingly immortal; she enjoys the use of her faculties and is
regarded by Mrs MacDonald (a daughter) as 'indestructible'. She
is not cut off from kith and kin in some distant, isolating flat, but
is the senior and revered member of a small urban clan and
has four great-great-grandchildren. She testifies to the truth of the

popular saw that 'you're as old as you feel'. The reader is admitted
to a consoling secret: 'no one should feel their age if they are happy
and contented'. In the second example, reported in the *West Lancashire Evening Gazette*, 30 March 1965, the 'secret' again consists of a
popular saying—that the 'busy life is a happy one'. In some towns
centenarian celebrations are an occasion for a mayoral visit; this
was the case at Blackpool:

Bispham woman (up at 7 as usual) 101 today

. . . The Mayoress (Mrs. A. Ashworth) arrived with greetings, a kiss and
a spray of spring flowers.
. . . 'I've always been busy'—That is Mrs. Tomlinson's reply to those
who ask her the recipe for old age.
Today she has been preparing a chicken lunch and refreshments for
friends she will invite in tonight.
Although her hearing is not what it used to be Mrs. Tomlinson enjoys
television.
'I like "Criss Cross Quiz" and "University Challenge",' she declared.

Aspects of the busy, vigorous life that such centenarians lead are
stressed through details like 'I've just had new curtains' and 'today
she has been preparing a chicken lunch'. It is implied that the
pattern of life described will continue: 'Mrs. Tomlinson . . . was up
at seven this morning—as usual.'
 News of this kind is essentially 'soft', but it has an important and
permanent place in the news content of provincial newspapers. It
affords the reader grounds for hope and optimism, and reminds him
that the local institutions (the church or town council, for example)
recognise longevity as an achievement of note, justifying 'a kiss and
a spray of spring flowers' from a mayoress.
 A further way in which the 'man in the street' can become news
in the provincial Press without involvement in any dramatic event
is as the result of long and faithful service for a local institution or
company. He (or she) may have worked, or be intending to work,
well past the normal age for retirement. The related reports enable
the local Press to underscore and 'glamorise' the solid virtues of
work, service and loyalty which may often be enjoined in leading
column comment. One example from the *Birmingham Evening Mail*
(6 May 1967) will serve to illustrate this type of news; it concerned
three married women who had worked together for the same firm
for fifty years, and afforded the reporter the opportunity to elicit

comments on working conditions in a period becoming dim in the
collective memory:

Now, 50 years later, they are still together

When Mrs. Jennie Dareham, Mrs. Lily King, and Mrs. Emma Loone
first started work their workshop was a bedroom and their only lighting
in the winter months was a candle.
Now, 50 years later, they are still working at the same place—although
the premises have greatly expanded.
. . . the management of Crane's Screw and Colgryp Castor Co. Ltd.,
of Floodgate Street, Birmingham, have presented a cheque to each of the
ladies.
Only Mrs. Dareham is retiring.

Spirit

Mrs. Loone said: 'There have been times when we did not have a
penny in our pockets, but we have sung from morning till night, keeping
our spirits up.'
All three women remember the days when they worked in a bedroom.
The premises were then three terraced houses with adjoining walls
demolished for easy access.
'We used to work long hours then, often until our eyes became tired
from the strain of the candlelight,' said Mrs. King . . .

This is a typical retirement report in its allusions to changes in the
place of work, to the length of the employees' service, to the presentation recognising this, and to the recollections of times past—the
'long hours' and the 'strain of candlelight'. Crane's Screw and
Colgryp Castor Co. Ltd are portrayed as benevolent employers; two
of the ladies have no intention of retiring from their jobs, cheque or
no cheque.
    The most obviously sentimental kind of order news is that which
evokes the reader's assumed affection for nature—especially birds
or animals. Many animal stories are brought to the local newspaper's attention through routine calls to local branches of such
organisations as the RSPCA and PDSA; others are sent in by
'penny a line' news-gatherers living in small communities within the
circulation area. Stories of outstanding freakishness or sentimentality
will be eagerly seized on and 'splashed' by the national popular Press.
An instance would be The People's 'Freddie's at home in his local!',[12]
a report (with photograph) of a six-week-old fawn fond of stout.
All the national dailies recognise the appeal of animal photographs;
details follow of the attention that a sample of four dailies paid to

Chi-Chi's (London Zoo's giant panda) installation in an air-conditioned house:

> *The Times:* 'Chi-Chi moves to her new quarters' (88 column inches).
> *Daily Telegraph:* 'New home with room for a guest' (42 column inches).
> *Daily Express:* 'Chi-Chi's cosy love nest' (30 column inches).
> *The Guardian:* no caption; 15 column inches.

These four visual reports were published on 14 April 1967; the distinctions made above between the crime reporting styles of the national 'populars' and 'qualities' can also be made between the Chi-Chi captions. *The Times* alludes factually and objectively to 'new quarters'; the *Daily Express* 'projects' these as a 'cosy love nest'.

Detailed comment on provincial newspaper animal reports must be confined to three of the recurring categories: the bird or animal that is humanely cared for after being orphaned, rejected or maimed (the appeal of Danny Kaye's 'ugly duckling' song is often present here); unusual animal friendships and straightforward 'freak' occurrences. The first category concerns the injured or isolated bird or animal that is given some sort of compensatory care or habitat through human intervention. The *Buxton Advertiser* of 23 April 1965, contained a report of a local family that had adopted a fox cub:

A fox cub joins the family

Although their pet dog and cat didn't seem quite so keen, Mr. and Mrs. John Hill, of Western Lane, Buxworth, have really fallen for Bruno the fox.

Just two weeks ago Mr. Hill adopted the tiny, motherless cub after hearing that it had been seen in a field close to the village.

The little animal, scarcely a month old, 'was on its last legs,' Mr. Hill told the *Advertiser*. Now it is in fine fettle—in fact he has his work cut out to catch it again!

. . . Already Bruno is a tame, trusting pet, and both recognises and makes a fuss of the couple as soon as they enter the home.

There is a distinct relaxation of the customary factual style of provincial reporting in this extract, a relaxation that often accompanies 'soft' order news. A colloquial note attaches to such comments as that Bruno's owners 'have really fallen' for him, and that Mr. Hill 'has his work cut out' to catch the cub. The fox cub is repeatedly described in emotive terms: 'the tiny, motherless cub', 'the little animal' and 'tame, trusting pet'. The reader's 'soft spot' is being assailed; the assumption is that the first family reader will respond with 'listen to this about a little fox at Buxworth'. Affection for birds and animals is evidently perceived as both universal and deep-seated, in spite of the sort of partly contradicting evidence afforded by such a headline as the *Birmingham Evening Mail*'s 'Heartbreak . . . To see 7,000 animals "put to sleep" in one year' (29 April, 1967).

A second recurring category is that of the bizarre animal friendship—often involving a large and ferocious animal caring for or refusing to part from a smaller, more delicate and fragile one. This is not quite the case in the following passage from a *Lancashire Evening Post* report (21 July 1966), but the friendship described is certainly singular:

Joey and Jennifer are good friends

Joey and Jennifer are inseparable. They live together, eat together and lean over the same five-barred gate.

And they have been good friends for a year now.

They are an unusual pair. Joey is a 17-hand hunter, with almost palamino colouring, and Jennifer is a tiny white donkey with enormous ears.

They became friends as soon as they saw each other, and now they have to have a field to themselves because four-year-old Joey has strong protective instincts about little Jennifer and won't allow any of the other horses near her.

. . . 'I wouldn't dream of separating them now,' says Mr. Heaton, 'and I don't think Joey would stand for it anyway. If any of the other horses do get near Jennifer he chases them off straight away.'

The language here parallels that of the previous extract; the adjectives 'tiny' and 'little' recur and a colloquial note is present in Mr. Heaton's comment on the animals' possible separation: 'I don't think Joey would stand for it anyway.' The animals are humanised; they became 'friends' a year ago and Joey has 'strong protective instincts'. This is the world of the children's story, of Eeyore and Mr Toad; in it animals are invested with human characteristics and sentiments, and often seem to have appealing names like Bruno or Joey.

A third type of animal story is the straightforward 'freak' occurrence of the kind reported in the *Buxton Advertiser*, 17 July 1966:

'Milly-moke' kept it all so quiet

Mr. and Mrs. M. Orme, of Whitehough, near Chinley, had a surprise last week when they woke up to find they had an extra donkey in their field.

During the night, their four-year-old jenny donkey had given birth to a foal without having given any previous sign of this happy event.

. . . The family have owned Milly-moke for about 12 months now and during this time she has not been in contact with any other donkey. She has been regularly ridden in recent weeks by Rachel, and gave no sign at all of her condition.

The sudden appearance of the foal is handled with euphemistic tact; an 'extra donkey' appeared, as it were, miraculously, and Milly is exonerated from any possible culpability for 'contact' while in the care of Mr. and Mrs. Orme.

These, then, have been examples of a recurring pattern of animal stories; as with the wedding anniversaries and centenarian celebrations, they are usually accompanied by photographs. Crimes, accidents and disasters may multiply and cause anxiety, but the animal kingdom and the human life cycle—especially birth, long marriage and working service, and survival to a ripe old age—continue to afford an important staple of news balance for the local Press.

Two final types of light-hearted order news remain to be discussed. One concerns the 'lucky escaper'—the man or woman who emerges unscathed, or nearly so, from some perilous situation; the other focuses on the lucky winner of the football pool, bingo or 'spot the ball' competition.

The lucky escaper is a 'celebrity' rather than a hero; all he does is survive an incident fraught with danger. He evades the grasp of fate in its malignant aspect, and is the 'one that got away'. A typical report appeared on the front page of the *Birmingham Evening Mail* on 18 June 1966; it took up $34\frac{1}{2}$ column inches, including an 18 column inch photograph:

Struck by lightning . . .
. . . but Robert escapes with burns and shock

Thirteen-year-old Robert Williamson was struck by lightning in a heavy storm at Wolverhampton—and lived.

Today, Robert . . . was resting at his home, at 65, Birches Barn Road, Wolverhampton, after being treated at the town's Royal Hospital for shock and burns.

The lightning, which also knocked a chimney pot off a nearby house, struck him, while he was cycling in Goldthorn Hill.

His sister, Judy Williamson, said: 'He was hit on the hand and his watch was blasted off. His cycle was also damaged.

'He was knocked unconscious and did not remember anything when he woke up in hospital.' . . .

The opening sentence here is the important one; Robert was struck by lightning—'and lived'. Confronted by an elemental hazard which often results in serious injury or death (the toppled chimney pot reminds the reader of the undiscriminating violence of lightning), he nevertheless survived. Order news of this kind, implying that Alfred Doolittle's 'little bit of luck' can work wonders, is clearly regarded by the Press as of high news value; it has all the drama of disorder news and yet is full of consolation for the reader, who can deduce that even in dire circumstances he will still have a chance if luck is on his side.

News of local lucky winners is a further recurring type. The customary ingredients are a photograph of a smiling face (or faces), an indication of how the win enables some long-standing ambition to be fulfilled, and the recipient's expression of wonderment and lingering disbelief. These were apparent in a *Birmingham Evening Mail* report headed 'Wife wins £3,500 in *Mail* contest' (19 March 1966):

Mr. James Weston and his wife, Margaret, were hoping to sell their Barton-under-Needwood bungalow and move back to Birmingham.

Now that hope may be realised because Mrs. Weston is this week's outright winner of the *Evening Mail's* Place the Ball competition.

She will shortly be receiving a cheque for the top prize of £3,500.

. . . 'When my husband told me we had won £3,500 I just wouldn't believe him. We have been entering the competition every week since we came to live here about two years ago, but I never dreamed we would win' . . .

Reports of this kind no doubt help to promote the belief—on the part of those who enjoy a 'flutter'—that one day the jackpot will shower onto the front door mat and solve all material problems; they imply that a regular competition entry is justified—a smile from Dame Fortune being all that is needed to create a lucky winner.

Lucky escapers and winners are not the only recipients of good fortune to feature prominently in provincial Press news columns. but they are among the most regular. They merge with the wedding anniversary couples, centenarians, long-serving workers, sentiment-evoking birds and animals, and genuine heroes as a silver lining to the black cloud of crime, accident and disaster. Happy news, as well

as disturbing news, can be good news for both the Press and its
readers at the local level.

**4. Positive projects or plans, new organisations (or existing ones
extended), rate rises (intended to benefit the community), church
services, fund-raising, shows (e.g. agricultural, musical, dramatic),
festivals, rallies (non-sporting), dinners, elections, meetings with an
'order' intention, local MP news**

In the previous section ways in which individuals become part of
the local Press's order news content were analysed; to complete
the account of order news, it is necessary to consider the contribution of local institutions and organisations (whether commerical,
social, cultural or religious).

(a) Local government news Spokesmen for the provincial Press
regard the communication of local government news as in many
ways its prime function; Mr W. G. Ridd, a former Director of the
Newspaper Society, when pointing to the *raison d'être* for regional
weekly newspapers, commented: 'There are 10 million regular
weekly readers, according to estimate, who rely upon their local
weekly paper for news of the sporting, religious and myriad of other
purely local interests and, perhaps most important of all, the news
of and from their local government.'[13]
It has already been noted that both evening and weekly newspapers regard major local government plans and decisions as sometimes worthy of main headline prominence. In general, local government news falls into two categories: first, the reports of individual
and corporate activities other than council debates; second, reports
of plans, policies, decisions and the committee or full council discussions thereon. The analyses that follow show how both types of
report often contain assessments of a given community's 'image',
and reveal a desire to enhance the community's status in relation
to the image of it held. Both local government officers and individual
councillors, like the local Press itself, believe that 'the good of the
community' as a whole ought to be their paramount consideration.
The exact nature of this 'good', of course, is open to a number of
possibly conflicting interpretations.

Leaving aside the mayor's role at council debates, mayoral activities as a whole belong to the first category specified. Newspaper coverage includes reports of visits to centenarians, Senior Citizens' Homes, hospitals and other institutions, and attendance at church on Mayoral Sunday, Armistice Day and so on. The implication of such reports is of ordered, constructive activity—a series of positive contributions to local community life. One annually recurring report in most provincial newspapers concerns the ceremony of mayor-making, or the installation of the chairman in the case of the smaller urban or rural district councils. This type of report invariably yields insights into the commonly shared ideals and aspirations of councillors, and into the personal qualities they most esteem. The passage that follows appeared in the *West Lancashire Evening Gazette*, 23 May 1966:

Preesall is the friendly place

The friendliness of Preesall people and the way in which they made new residents welcome was commented on by Coun. Frank Edward Milward when he was installed as Preesall Urban District Council's new Chairman at the annual meeting last night.

'Newcomers to Preesall are given a great reception. Strangers are made welcome and there is an atmosphere of neighbourliness which breaks down the barriers of loneliness to be found in larger communities,' he said.

... Coun. Milward was proposed as Chairman by Coun. H. C. Trippier, who said, 'He is a graduate of the university of life with a deep religious belief, tolerance and understanding of human nature.' ...

The chairman-elect, then, sees Preesall in terms of its friendliness and community spirit; his proposer extols him as a tolerant and perceptive man, and therefore as one likely to perpetuate the claimed 'image' of the community. Municipal mayors and chairmen, at least on the day they assume office, are accorded the status of Chaucer's paragon guildsmen:

> Everich, for the wisdom that he kan,
> Was shaply for to been an alderman ...

The ceremonial over, elected civic figureheads can proceed to relish the trappings of office—the chain and mace, the mayoral car and attendant—as well as to fulfil its duties. A less obvious trapping is the detailed coverage of the ceremony (and of subsequent public mayoral activities) in the local Press.

Although there is little or no evidence of dissent about the nature

of any given community's ideal image on mayor-making day, reports
of council debates—the main kind of local government news recurring throughout the municipal year—often reveal conflicting views
about proposals that some see as likely to modify this image. For
example, a division of opinion will invariably be apparent whenever
some particular scheme is seen by its opponents as potentially harm-
ful to their community's moral *status quo*; this was the case in a
debate reported in the *West Lancashire Evening Gazette*, 9 July 1965:

Women wrestlers banned—at Fleetwood

. . . The promoters should leave well alone, said Ald. Shaw. 'I think that
without doubt it is degrading to their sex.'

Coun. A. Greenwood thought that it would attract the wrong type of
publicity.

Fleetwood had always prided itself on being a family resort. But
wrestling by women was hardly in that tradition and would scare more
people away than it would attract.

Coun. H. Chippendale said that for the committee to adopt a Mrs.
Grundy attitude was entirely wrong. They should let people see and judge
for themselves whether it was degrading. 'Don't let us try to make up
people's minds up for them,' he added . . .

Here the allusion to Fleetwood's image as a family resort points to
the family values that the provincial Press itself claims to endorse;
the concept of these values (again paralleling the Press) is of a fixed
and acknowledged code which the passage of time, or manifest social
change, must not erode. So, even in this permissive age, it can still
be assumed as an unexaggerated possibility that the presentation of
women wrestlers at Fleetwood might 'scare away more people than
it would attract'. This argument is unacceptable to Councillor Chippendale, who sees the prospect of refused permission as an authori-
tarian action stemming from a 'Mrs Grundy attitude'.

It can be seen that a concept of the town's image acts as an important reference point; readers of the full report are enabled to
judge whether the assumptions that lie behind decisions affecting
them are ones that they share or whether they conflict with their own
ideals for the community they inhabit. Local newspapers, through
their detailed coverage of council debates, are fulfilling a crucially
important communications function—it may be, as Mr W. G.
Ridd suggested, their most important function. Provincial newspaper editors themselves feel that there is a growing interest in
civic news; at the same time, this interest is still regarded as a
minority one. Accordingly, the practice of 'angling' municipal news

(i.e. the 'snappy' headline and bright 'intro.'), although sometimes
resented by particular councillors who feel that this distorts the
overall account, can be justified as 'bait' to attract the less civic-
minded reader.

Although in general the working relationship between the local
Press and the town council is co-operative, a few instances of a
breakdown in relations do occur—a recent one being at Rugeley,
Staffs. The leader of the controlling Labour party accused the
weekly *Rugeley Times* of continuing 'acts of distortion'; the editor-
in-chief, while admitting to 'some errors in the past', stated that he
would have welcomed a Press Council inquiry and felt that 'the
Labour Party is using us as a whipping-boy because what was once
a 100 per cent Socialist council has been whittled down to a majority
of one' (*U.K. Press Gazette*, 17 August 1970). In August 1970 the
council voted to withdraw statutory advertising and to stop sending
notices of meetings, agendas and committee reports; officials of the
council would refuse comment on council news stories. The editor-
in-chief replied vigorously: 'We are not going to be bullied. We shall
continue to give an honest appreciation of the news to local readers.
We have saturation circulation in Rugeley and we are not worried
by this ban. We shall still get, and print, the news.' Two months later
the position had eased only slightly, and was some way from
resolution.

This sort of estrangement is unusual; more frequent are the ten-
sions that arise when a local newspaper is refused access to council
committee discussions—a state of affairs that provoked the *Lancashire Evening Post*, in a front-page comment of 29 January 1971, into
referring to Fulwood urban council as 'Fulwood's Secret Service'.
This is particularly a handicap for the Press where its informal
relationships with the council are tenuous; in some communities,
like Blackpool, cordial personal contacts between the Press and local
government do much to mitigate the effects of barring reporters
from committee meetings. When councils debate this issue the key
arguments advanced are invariably along the following lines (the
extracts are taken from *West Lancashire Evening Gazette* reports of
23 June and 14 July 1970 and refer to Lytham St Annes town council):

For Press admission:

I submit we have much to gain by honest reporting, by improving our
lines of communication with the residents of this borough, by bringing

our reasoned arguments into the open and avoiding public misunder-
standing which in turn may lead to witchhunting.

We should trust the Press. They have high commercial and professional
standards to maintain.

Against Press admission:

Discussion on certain topics would be stifled, and there would be the
risk of being quoted out of context.

This will mean that the Press will know decisions of committees before
councillors. It is unfair.

I think we are doing a perfectly good job. I think the Press are being
fully advised.

At Lytham St Annes the arguments against Press admission to certain committees won the day—the decision running counter to the
recommendations of the Maud and Skeffington reports. But the
number of such councils is diminishing, albeit very slowly, and there
is ample evidence that once the Press is granted access—sometimes
for a trial period—there are few complaints from councillors and the
new system works well. Even so, only about 300 councils (out of
1,400) open to the public and press committees other than those
statutorily open.

If what one may refer to as 'primary' institutional order news lacks
majority appeal, this is even more the case with secondary order
news from religious, social or cultural institutions. It has already
been suggested that such news takes up the largest proportion of
space in newspapers whose readers' institutional loyalties are most
likely to be shared, that is, in the weekly and small- or medium-
sized evening newspapers. The nature of secondary order news of
this type can be indicated by considering the reporting of church
activities.

(b) **Church news** The mirror that local newspapers hold up to the
Churches predominantly reflects ordered and constructive progress.
The general run of reports deal with the appointments and retirements of clergy; with fund-raising activities; with vicars who are
taking a positive stand in respect of some local or national debate;
or with new developments in some particular parish—perhaps a
proposed replacement for the old Sunday school, or an attempted
revival of a youth club. Characteristic headlines, therefore, are:

'New Catholic church is opened' (*Croydon Advertiser*, 11 December 1964).

'Baptist church's new minister takes over' (*Woodford and Wanstead Guardian*, 11 December 1964).

'Chelford vicar returns to open fair' (*Stockport Advertiser*, 11 December 1964).

'Local minister off to Sierra Leone/Taking family and his dog, Trusty, too' (*Crawley Advertiser*, 22 October 1965).

'Keep a tidy parish, says vicar' (*Erdington News*, 22 October 1965).

Very frequently, the related reports will be accompanied by photographic illustration; the inclusion of one or more 'vicar visuals' is quite usual in the weekly Press. The smaller evening newspapers share the same characteristic to a lesser extent. Of course, some disorder items do occur sporadically, as the following headlines remind one:

'Opposition to vicar's church hall plan' (*Lincolnshire Chronicle*, 11 December 1964).

'Curate's pulpit denial of "doubts about his faith" ' (*Stockport Advertiser*, 10 December 1964).

Such news forms only a small part of the total. In this respect the mirror that the popular national dailies hold up to the Churches is very different. Secondary order news has no news value whatever outside the local context; the popular dailies are primarily interested in major items of institutional disorder news—apart, that is, from some kinds of lightweight tittle-tattle item noted below. Most of these dailies' Church news can be assigned to one of two categories. The first consists of 'straight' disorder news that puts the minister and/or his Church in a bad light. Two headlines from the *Daily Mirror* will serve to clarify this point:

'I did it for love, says vicar who quit' (42 column inches, 22 November 1965).

'Feuding rector sacked by his bishop' (34 column inches, 17 July 1965).

The first of these reports opened in this way: 'A Vicar who left his family and resigned his living said yesterday: "I have done all this for love." And he put his arm around the shoulders of Mrs Elinor Moverly, a vivacious 40-year-old mother of two. . . .' The description 'vivacious' represents an attempt to maximise the story's titillating potential.

The second category employs the technique of incongruous juxtaposition. The Church, or the clergy, or some member of a minister's family, may be the subject, but the underlying tactic is the same—to place the Church sharply against some secular leisure 'style'. An instance of this was afforded by the *Daily Mirror* on 14 March 1966: 'Vicar is ref for girl wrestlers'. The report opened as follows: 'If Jenny Lee and "Sugar Pie" Harlem are allowed to wrestle each other, the ref. will be—a vicar.'

The two categories sometimes merge; on 20 April 1967 the popular dailies contained a report about a former nun who had recorded a song praising the Pill. The *Daily Mirror* headlined its version 'Glory be to God for the Pill, sings ex-nun'; the *Daily Express*'s was 'Singing nun praises the golden Pill'. The juxtaposing of the nun, or ex-nun (in the sense that she has left the convent although, as the *Express* noted, 'she is quick to remind people that she is still a nun'), with such phenomena of the secular world as pop records and the birth pill therefore represents a familiar reporting strategy on the part of the popular national dailies. 'Juxtaposition' stories and disorder news—whether serious or lightweight—account for the bulk of the coverage of news coverage of Church and related matters in the popular Press. In contrast, Church news in local newspapers predominantly emphasises order, stability and continuity; if 'Singing nun praises the golden Pill' can be seen as an index of the spheres of interest for the popular nationals, the following headline and opening paragraphs from a *Birmingham Evening Mail* report of 11 March 1967, suggest the contrasting news spectrum of the local Press:

Singing nun, aged 91
She presents a musical half-hour at the convent

Birmingham's singing nun, Sister St. Agnes, who will be 92 next month, still plays and sings old-time favourites for the other Sisters each day.

Each evening the cloisters of St. Paul's Convent, Selly Park, echo with the sound of old favourites, hymns and classical music.

... She retired ten years ago after working in the city for nearly 60 years, teaching at several schools and doing social work. . . .

Sister St Agnes is therefore a thoroughly orthodox nun; she still lives in the convent after a lifetime of service and is no 'disc cutter'.

Her contrast to the ex-nun cited above symbolises the contrast between the institutional news emphases of the popular national and provincial Press. The intention here is not to condemn the popular daily for its emphases or for their effect on reader attitudes to the institutions concerned—an effect which will in any case largely depend on the assumptions that particular readers already hold. Rather, it is to show that local newspapers fulfil a balancing function. For if the popular daily, in seeking to entertain its readers, tends to stress aspects of deviation from institutional norms, the local Press for the most part reports news which exemplifies institutional values and shows them to be actively held.

(c) News about the immigrant community The evidence suggests that during the 1960s the immigrant community—unlike other community groups—has not enjoyed the image-boosting benefit of a higher proportion of order than disorder news about it. To take two examples, Paul Foot's censure of the weekly *Smethwick Telephone* over the period 1960–62[14] and Harold Evans' rebuke of the *Middlesex County Times*[15] were clearly valid; they concerned the degree of prominence given to unfavourable news involving immigrants who were ethnically identified—sometimes as early in a report as the headline. Harold Evans (editor of the *Sunday Times*) attacks this sort of distinctively high valuation of immigrant disorder news:

It involves the association of ethnic groups with bad news. Because much of what we call news arises from conflict, stories with an ethnic tag look more like news because they are thought to imply some conflict of interests. Many, perhaps the bulk, of ethnic-based stories are there in print not for their intrinsic news merit but for this hidden 'news value' . . .[16]

A survey of four local London weeklies, carried out by the National Committee for Commonwealth Immigrants during August 1966–January 1967, showed that of 124 front page news stories involving ethnic identification, seventy-two (or 58 per cent) were unfavourable, as against twenty (16 per cent) favourable—the rest being classed as neutral.[17] The ratio of unfavourable to favourable stories here is approximately 3·5 : 1; this contrasts sharply with the overall ratio of disorder to order news in the weekly Press, which was established as 1 : 2·6. The survey's findings validate Harold Evans' conclusion that there should be a 'conscious effort to break the pattern of seeking racial news in conflict: there is good news too'.[16] Many episodic items need more and sustained background analysis, and there should be a real attempt to seek out order news from the immigrant community with the aim of making the above ratios more compatible.

In spite of these criticisms, there is much justification for James Brennan's view that there has been a steady improvement in the coverage of immigrant news in the latter part of the 1960s. Amusingly recalling the repercussions that attended a headline he once wrote as a fledgling sub-editor—'Pole fined for assault on police'—he suggests that at least some of the grounds for complaints of ethnic discrimination may be attributable to sheer inexperience: 'Perhaps it is a lesson that all new sub-editors have to learn.'[18] His optimism is warranted; one can point to the majority rebuttal of extremist positions and the prevalence of constructive attitudes,[19] as well as the important series of feature articles on race relations published in such newspapers as the *Birmingham Evening Mail* (5–9 January 1970) and the *Leicester Mercury* (5–12 June 1970). There is a growing awareness of the ways in which the local Press can help to foster harmony between the races—an awareness that should lead to a diminishing number of complaints about ethnic discrimination.

Before moving on to a consideration of leading column comment in the provincial Press, a brief survey of two further aspects of local news content—sports news and the 'running story'—must be made.

(d) Sports news The importance of sports news for the evening and weekly Press can be gauged by the amount of space that it takes up. An analysis of the distribution of non-advertising space in the *Birmingham Evening Mail* of 13 January 1966 showed that sports news accounted for 19 per cent of the total. Local sport took up approximately 72 per cent of the sports allocation—football, greyhounds and cricket being the leading categories. Of the total coverage roughly a third concerned Association football; the 'old triumvirate' of football, horse racing and cricket commanded 53 per cent of all. The sports news was located on two pages; there were 117½ column inches—largely on horse and greyhound racing, badminton and golf—on page 12, and 196 column inches on the back page (page 20). The placing of 62 per cent of the sports news on the back page denotes its importance as news—ranking second to front page content. Football news dominated the back page, and the three leading reports focused on local league teams: 'Bonus boost for

Blues' (21½ column inches), 'Hennessey in Forest side to face Villa' (18 column inches) and 'Walsall again injury-hit' (7 column inches). Football was the leading sports news category, taking up 31 per cent of the total sports allocation.

A weekly newspaper was also selected for analysis—the *Buxton Advertiser* of 13 May 1966. Here, as in the *Mail*, the back page was given over entirely to sports items, but there was no sports coverage on any other page; sport accounted for 10·5 per cent of non-advertising space. Football (50 per cent) and cricket were responsible for 69·5 per cent of the *Advertiser*'s sports content, as compared with 41 per cent of the *Mail*'s—the latter allocating approximately 33 per cent of its sports space to horse and greyhound racing.

One finds, therefore, that football news is accorded more space than any other sport in both newspapers. Apart from match reports, much of the news consists of information about team changes, injuries, players bought or sold, weather conditions and so on. This will be eagerly read, probably by the majority of male readers, and especially when a local team is 'in form'. One Northern evening newspaper editor has commented that 'a winning football team can boost sales considerably', and the sales of Saturday sports editions ('The Pink', 'The Buff', etc.) show discernible rises or falls in relation to the degree of success.

A systematic and detailed account of the provincial football reporting style would take up a disproportionate amount of space, and it must suffice to suggest its main features. Its strength lies in its detail; the local newspaper can justify coverage of a length that would be unwarranted in a national daily or Sunday. Generally speaking, one finds neither the idiosyncratic stylishness of an Eric Todd (of *The Guardian*), the often brilliant, lucid fluency of a Brian Glanville (*Sunday Times*) nor the hyperbolical flights of fancy of a Desmond Hackett (of the *Express*) in the provincial Press. Orthodox descriptions, fairly standard images and, usually, an undemonstrative tone are the typical elements; a passage that has the provincial 'feel' follows. It was part of a report on a Division 2 match in which Bury beat Leyton Orient 3–0, from *The Buff* (Bolton), 15 January 1966:

... The Bury keeper was barged by Flatt who forced the ball into the net but the referee had blown for a foul. After eight minutes Bury shot into the lead with a great goal following a polished move.

BELL was the architect and the scorer. He worked the ball forward and fed Owen who found winger Kerr who immediately squared the ball to the far post and Bell was there to head it through.

Detail of this kind is what the sports news reader expects and enjoys, and what the local Press is uniquely equipped to provide with week in, week out regularity.

(e) The 'running story' Local newspapers are also, when compared with the nationals, in a unique position to nurture the 'running story' that may unfold within any given circulation area. Often these stories will be found to fall within the second of the news categories outlined above (pages 94–6): aspects of disorder concerning the community as a whole or local institutions, organisations, industries, etc., within the community. It may, for instance, be some dispute or debate that constitutes a focus for dissension both within a town council and the community at large, and lasts for months or even years. If so, it will afford the local Press a series of news reports, letters to the editor, and, perhaps, occasions for leading column comment or feature articles. Such a story ('The Crescent pigeons') ran in the weekly *Buxton Advertiser* from 30 October 1964 to 18 June 1965; it began with a Health Committee resolution to thin out the number of feral pigeons in Buxton Crescent, and subsequently involved the town council's ratification after debate, a public petition ('Save the pigeons'), a further debate and, finally, the death of twenty-six pigeons. In seven months this community controversy prompted nine reports, on separate occasions, totalling 145 column inches; seventeen letters (twelve for the pigeons, five against) in thirteen separate issues, totalling 77 column inches, and one town diary assessment (6 column inches). The report headlines moved from 'Crescent pigeons may be killed' (30 October 1964) to '26 pigeons die in operation at 5 a.m.' (11 June 1965).

As 2,400 local adults signed the petition, representing an estimated eighth of the population, it can be assumed that this 'running story' had very high news value for the *Advertiser*'s readership. Whereas a national newspaper would be able to allot at most only two 'snippet' summaries of the issue at its critical stages, the local Press can go into great detail, covering every twist and turn, and affording space for the expression of every shade of opinion. In doing so, it may be said to fulfil four functions. It sets the debate in motion and keeps it alive; it acts as the principal communicating intermediary between local government and the readership; it identifies itself with local saga and the local collective memory; and it offers the only full and permanent record of community affairs. Local radio may be able to carry out the first three functions, but must, by its nature, be too selective (even snappy) to compete as a recorder. The newspaper can be highly detailed and comprehensive, and can record the carefully considered view of the correspondent as well as the sort of 'instant' comment prompted in the context of an oral situation.

The running news story, therefore, constitutes a telling sales factor when the issue at the heart of it involves strongly held local attitudes and opinions. It should be differentiated from the purely episodic item—the moment of an isolated tragedy, the unrepeatable anniversary, the freakish occurrence. It can, as Sir Linton Andrews has aptly put it, 'go bouncing on like a Chinese cracker'.[20]

In spite of the fact that a column inch ratio of 1·7 (disorder news) to 1 (order news) was established for the three evening newspapers sampled at the beginning of this chapter, the weight of subsequent comment has been on the nature and presentation of individual and institutional order news. In part, this is due to the sheer range and variety of order news, which necessitates methodical and detailed discussion. It can also be attributed to the aim of clarifying, as exactly as possible, the nature of the positive forces in community life that the Press discerns, and which contrast with the unabating flow of crimes, accidents, disasters and institutional disorders. It has been suggested that local heroes (whether in terms of bravery, resistance to adversity or community leadership), long-service workers, community-conscious councillors and other institutional leaders (e.g. the clergy) are amongst the most frequently recurring 'order' figures. The attention they receive fulfils a 'booster' function, by pointing to stability, progress, achievement or valour. Combined with the types of light-hearted, or sentimental, story outlined above, they may enable the reader to feel sufficiently reassured about his own locale to face the depressing implications of much disorder news —responding to it with critical positivity rather than apathy or dejection. Wherever this is the case, the local Press is performing no merely short-term or exclusively factual function in its recording of local news.

Notes

1 Sports news was not included for the purposes of this classification, but is considered briefly in section 4(*d*).
2 See Evening Newspaper Advertising Bureau, *Where* (an analysis of regional evening newspaper sales), London, 1964.
3 *Buxton Advertiser*, 13 May 1966.
4 *Memoranda of Evidence*, p. 177.
5 *Ibid.*, p. 85.
6 *Ibid.*, p. 167.
7 Daniel J. Boorstin, *The Image* (Harmondsworth: Penguin Books, 1963), p. 85.
8 *Staffordshire Advertiser and Chronicle*, 21 October 1965.
9 *Stafford Newsletter*, 22 October 1965.
10 *Warley Courier*, 11 March 1965.
11 *Burnley Express*, 22 October 1965.
12 *The People*, 30 July 1967.
13 Letter to *The Daily Telegraph*, 18 August 1967.
14 See Paul Foot, *Immigration and Race in British Politics* (Harmondsworth: Penguin Books, 1965), pp. 32 ff.
15 See Harold Evans, *The Listener*, 16 July 1970.
   For further illustration, see M. J. Le Lohe and A. R. Goodman, 'Race in local politics: the Rochdale central ward election of 1968', *Race*, vol. X, No. 4, pp. 435–47.
16 Evans, *op. cit.*
17 See National Committee for Commonwealth Immigrants, *Survey of Four Local London Newspapers*, 1967, pp. 7, 15–16.
18 James Brennan, 'Journalists condemn discrimination', Institute of Race Relations *News Letter*, March 1966.
19 See pp. 140–4.
20 Sir Linton Andrews, *Autobiography of a Journalist* (London: Ernest Benn, 1964), p. 150.

7 The functions of the editorial column

The evening Press leader

As a means of assessing the nature of leading column comment in the evening Press, a sample of sixteen evening newspapers was taken, covering the period 10–22 January 1966. The sample was chosen so that a variety of geographical locations and circulation sizes would be represented; it included the *Manchester Evening News, Birmingham Evening Mail, Yorkshire Evening Post, Evening Chronicle* (Newcastle on Tyne), *Express and Star* (Wolverhampton), *Evening Post* (Bristol), *Leicester Mercury, Evening Post* (Nottingham), *Lancashire Evening Post* (Preston), *Evening Despatch* (Darlington), *Evening News* (Bolton), *West Lancashire Evening Gazette* (Blackpool), *Huddersfield Daily Examiner, Oxford Mail, Cambridge Evening News* and *Scarborough Evening News*. Of these sixteen newspapers, fifteen carried a leading column; the exception was the Nottingham *Evening Post*. The column was omitted from the Saturday issues of the *Lancashire Evening Post, Manchester Evening News*, Darlington *Evening Despatch*, Newcastle *Evening Chronicle* and Bristol *Evening Post*. In these cases the omission serves to emphasise a generally lighter note, apparent in much feature material, that coincides with the reader's break from the working week. The only other deviation of interest was that the *Birmingham Evening Mail* published nine leaders (one of these on a Saturday) over the twelve days of the survey.

These facts enable one to suggest that the inclusion of a leading column is very much a convention. Of only one of the sixteen newspapers can it be speculated that comment is offered solely when comment seems called for. Almost a third refrain from the expression of opinion on Saturdays. But fourteen do include a column of editorial comment, without fail, on every other weekday. They do so whether there is an obvious need for comment or not. The space is allotted; readers are used to seeing this space filled in the customary way, and editors are used to obliging them. Furthermore, the allocations of space to leading column comment revealed a remarkable

uniformity of length as between different issues of the same newspaper. An example is afforded by the *Leicester Mercury*; on 1
January it allotted $7\frac{1}{2}$ column inches to comment on the death of
President Shastri, and on 13 January $7\frac{1}{2}$ column inches to a discussion of some unmade local roads ('Priorities of the potholes'). In
pointing this out one is not intending to imply that the first leader
deserved more space than the second, but simply to show that
editorial opinion has—except in rare and deviant instances—to be
fitted into a predetermined spatial mould. Of course, the existence of
such a mould is not peculiar to the provincial Press; the *Daily
Express*, for instance, offers a daily column length of opinion without fail.

The main differences that are apparent as between one evening
newspaper's leaders and another's can be traced principally to
differing assumptions about the column's function. One editor may
attach major importance to comment on national and international
affairs, another to the discussion of local community matters. The
discussion that follows considers the distribution of leaders into one
or other of these categories.

In the introductory chapter it was noted that the leading provincial
editors of the first half of the nineteenth century saw their newspapers
as intermediaries between the economic and political theorists and
the general public, and as articulators of the social and political
aspirations of their readers. It was also suggested that these roles
gradually became less significant in the latter half of the century,
and that local news and views assumed a compensating importance.
Since then, of course, the provincial Press has become subject to the
competition of the mass circulation dailies and television, both of
which offer the latest 'intelligence' and comment upon it. Accordingly, when local evening newspapers continue to discuss international or national affairs in their leading columns, one or both of two
reasons may underlie this. First, it may be felt that the given newspaper has a particular interpretation to offer to its particular readership. Second, comment on non-local matters may be seen as conferring a serious and respectable image that enhances the paper's
status; it then becomes part of the content that Bernard Berelson
would describe as having 'prestige value'.[1] In his article 'What
"missing the newspaper" means' Berelson suggests that 'large numbers of people' in New York City see their newspaper as a provider
of 'appropriate psychological relaxation'. He continues:

The newspaper is particularly effective in fulfilling this need for relief from the boredom and dullness of everyday life not only because of the variety and richness of its 'human interest' content or because of its inexpensive accessibility. In addition, the newspaper is a good vehicle for this purpose because it satisfies this need without much cost to the reader's conscience; the prestige value of the newspaper as an institution for 'enlightening the citizenry' carries over to buttress this and other uses of the newspapers.[1]

Many readers (and one assumes here that Berelson's study has its relevance for the British newspaper reader) may therefore appreciate an evening newspaper's 'serious' non-local content—whether in the form of news, features or leaders—as a conscience appeaser, should their real interest lie in less demanding content. Others, of course, will 'use' the ' "enlightening the citizenry" ' material to foster their own prestige; 'it enables them to appear informed in social gatherings . . . Readers not only can learn what has happened and then report it to their associates but can also find opinions and interpretations for use in discussions on public affairs.'[2] Berelson distinguishes both these types of reader (i.e. the boredom-evader and the prestige-seeker) from the 'core of readers who find the newspaper indispensable as a source of information about and interpretation of the "serious" world of public affairs'.[3] It is this function that provincial newspaper companies would cite as their primary concern, but it is clear that the newspaper's—and perhaps the reader's—prestige is also involved. For to some extent evening newspaper leaders on non-local matters will duplicate comment available in the national Press or via the broadcasting media.

Most of the leading columns sampled were readily classifiable as local or non-local, but it was found necessary to include a third category covering leaders which, although of general, as opposed to purely local, interest, did contain a local reference of some kind. Table 9 shows that the majority of the main leaders sampled fell within category D on non-local topics. These accounted for 55 per cent of the total. Of the fifteen newspapers concerned, nine offered more leaders on non-local than on local topics. Seven of these nine were amongst eight that offered leaders on the death of President Shastri (11 January 1966), suggesting that an international item of this kind is particularly favoured by evening newspapers with a marked preference for non-local topics. Table 9 contains no evidence of any correlation between size of circulation and stress on local or

Table 9

Newspaper and 1964 circulation	Main leaders				Secondary leaders			
	A	B	C	D	E	F	G	H
Manchester Evening News (474,644)	10	–	–	10	4	1	1	2
Birmingham Evening Mail (408,539)	9	5	–	4	3	–	1	2
Yorkshire Evening Post (314,343)	12	2	1	9	11	6	1	4
Newcastle Evening Chronicle (244,433)	10	8	2	–	10	9	1	–
Wolverhampton Express and Star (230,536)	12	5	3	4	25	21	2	2
Bristol Evening Post (191,330)	10	2	1	7	10	–	–	10
Leicester Mercury (175,000+)	12	3	2	7	–	–	–	–
Lancashire Evening Post (146,430)	10	1	3	6	–	–	–	–
Bolton Evening News (88,107)	11	3	–	8	7	1	–	6
West Lancashire Evening Gazette (74,263)	12	5	2	5	5	–	2	3
Huddersfield Daily Examiner (51,764)	12	1	3	8	3	–	–	3
Oxford Mail (45,210)	12	5	–	7	6	4	1	1
Cambridge Evening News (37,730)	12	6	2	4	1	1	–	–
Darlington Evening Despatch (23,002)	10	3	2	5	10	10	–	–
Scarborough Evening News (14,466)	12	3	2	7	–	–	–	–

KEY: A Total number of main leaders
     B Main leaders on local topics
     C Main leaders containing a local reference within a non-local topic
     D Main leaders on non-local topics
     E Total number of secondary leaders
     F Secondary leaders on local topics
     G Secondary leaders containing local reference within a non-local topic
     H Secondary leaders on non-local topics

non-local topics. Two of the three newspapers with the largest circulations, and the two with the smallest, assigned the majority of their
main leaders to the discussion of non-local subjects. The *Manchester
Evening News* and the *Yorkshire Evening Post* emerged as the two
evening newspapers showing the greatest preference for the non-
local: 100 per cent and 75 per cent respectively. In contrast, the
Newcastle *Evening Chronicle* did not publish a single purely non-
local leader during the period of survey; 80 per cent of its main
leaders focused on local topics. By contracting out of comment on

Table 10

Newspaper	Local	Non-local	Percentage of non-local
Manchester Evening News	4	68	94
Birmingham Evening Mail	31	32	50
Yorkshire Evening Post	33	72	68
Newcastle *Evening Chronicle*	112	10	8
Wolverhampton *Express and Star*	101	46	31
Bristol *Evening Post*	14	76	84
Leicester Mercury	22	50	69
Lancashire Evening Post	12	48	80
Bolton *Evening News*	21	66	76
West Lancashire Evening Gazette	36	51	58
Huddersfield Daily Examiner	12	69	85
Oxford Mail	43	47	52
Cambridge Evening News	43	32	53
Darlington *Evening Despatch*	52	38	42
Scarborough Evening News	22	50	69

international affairs and on national affairs except when these were
of particular interest to Tyneside, the *Chronicle* made a distinctive
use of its leading column.

In order to express the ratio of local to non-local leaders in each
newspaper in statistical terms, the following method was adopted.
All main local (i.e. category B) and non-local (D) leaders were
accorded a score of 6; in the case of main leaders which, although
largely non-local, contained some local reference a score of 4 was
added to the non-local total and 2 to the local total. All secondary
local (F) and non-local (H) leaders were accorded a score of 3; in

the case of category G (local reference within a non-local subject) a score of 2 was added to the non-local total and 1 to the local total. Table 10 shows the resulting overall scores for each of the fifteen newspapers. Using the figures in the third column of table 10 (percentage of non-local leader material), the rank order of the fifteen newspapers, from most non-local to least non-local was tabulated in table 11.

Over the period of survey, then, and on the basis of this method of assessment, ten of the fifteen newspapers sampled paid more attention to non-local than to local subjects in their leading columns, and four more attention to local than to non-local subjects. Thus the

Table 11   **Percentages of non-localness in rank order**

1 *Manchester Evening News*	94
2 *Huddersfield Daily Examiner*	85
3 Bristol *Evening Post*	84
4 *Lancashire Evening Post*	80
5 Bolton *Evening News*	76
6 *Leicester Mercury*	69
7 *Scarborough Evening News*	69
8 *Yorkshire Evening Post*	68
9 *West Lancashire Evening Gazette*	58
10 *Oxford Mail*	52
11 *Birmingham Evening Mail*	50
12 *Cambridge Evening News*	43
13 Darlington *Evening Despatch*	42
14 Wolverhampton *Express and Star*	31
15 Newcastle *Evening Chronicle*	8

majority of evening newspapers have by no means relinquished their optional role of commentator on the international and national scene, in spite of the competition of the national daily and Sunday Press, the 'serious' weeklies, TV and radio. Bernard Berelson's study of the overt and hidden functions of 'serious' content helps to account for the continuance of this role. For quite apart from the informational value of such content, it can be seen as conferring prestige upon the newspaper and thence upon its readers.

It is now appropriate to consider more fully two of the factors that bear on the choice of subject for leading columns, and on the values and attitudes evident in the treatment of these subjects, before proceeding to analyse specific functions in detail. Amongst the

factors are the type and size of the community served; the needs
and expectations of the community leaders, the intelligent minority
and the majority; editorial–proprietorial assumptions about their
newspaper's role in the community, and about its desired 'personality'; and the leader writer's own subject preferences, values and
attitudes as a key 'gatekeeper'.

Each of these factors can be seen as to some degree a variable, but
two of them may be said to act as influences of a kind that promote
some commonly held values within the provincial Press. The first is
that the provincial leader addresses a provincial community. This
means that it speaks to and for the 'provincial' as opposed to the
'metropolitan'; certain potential bogey figures, such as Dr Beeching
in his spell as the railways' overlord, or Whitehall bureaucrats, are
available as shared Aunt Sallies should their policies be resented. The
local Press tends to be suspicious of Government-sponsored questionnaires about sports and recreation facilities, allotments, housing
conditions and living standards—all of them bringing 'the feet of
snoopers, probers, quizzers and inquirers of all kinds'[4] to people's
doors. The *West Lancashire Evening Gazette*, for instance, sees such
investigations as a largely unproductive form of non-work: 'Organisational flummery, multiplication of officialdom, gobbledegook—
how this country manages to carry the burden of it all becomes a
greater miracle with every day that passes.'[4]

'Provincialism' may also manifest itself in terms of assumptions
about the stability and even the moral superiority of the provincial
community as compared with modish, 'swinging' London. Particular
newspapers will intermittently return to the theme of London's
blinkered self-adulation, and its under-estimation of the quality of
provincial life. A further excerpt from the *West Lancashire Evening
Gazette* indicates this essentially provincial valuation:

> . . . The provinces—even the North, most distant and most barbarous
> in the popular metropolitan view—are far more comfortable and cheap to
> live in than jam-packed, ruthless London and the sprawl-contaminated
> Home Counties; and mental, physical and artistic opportunities abound.
> . . . sometime, some day, these super-people of ineffable culture from
> the Great Smoke might send a few daring explorers north of Leighton
> Buzzard into what is quite clearly an unknown land to a great many of
> them.[5]

The leader from which these extracts are taken was a response to a
BBC announcer's 'puff' for a radio play depicting ' "the frustration

and poverty of life in a provincial city" '. The writer's sense of resentment at the metropolitan view of the provinces is clearly a deep-
rooted one. It is not uncommon for some regional newspapers to
express the view that their region appears to contribute far more to
the London-based Exchequer (in the form of taxes) than it receives
back in social and environmental benefits. The *Manchester Evening
News*, for instance, made the point on 9 March 1971: 'Help on the
same scale as the amount it pays in taxes is a right for the North-
west, not a benevolence.'

Fleet Street itself is perceived as in many ways a mirror of metropolitan rather than regional interests; this emerged in the course of
a radio discussion in March 1964, when Harold Evans (then editor
of the *Northern Echo*, now editor of the *Sunday Times*) commented:
'The Nationals are so divorced at the moment from life in the
country—I mean the big populars—they don't know what's going on.
They're so remote; they don't keep a continuing interest. This is
one of the big weaknesses in our country's affairs at the moment.'[6]
In provincial eyes, then, London is commonly viewed as the centre
of an often autocratic bureaucracy and as introvertedly self-
adulating. Its popular Press is seen as modish and out of touch.

The second common influence on provincial values and attitudes—
as manifested in editorial comment—arises from the importance
that the local Press attaches to the esteem of community leaders and
the institutions they represent, and from the concept of the family
readership. The provincial Press serves both to reflect and to propagate—either by mirroring or explicitly endorsing—institutional and
family values. These values are embodied in such ideals as stability,
continuity, order and the Christian ethic (whether implied or explicit).
Such ideals obviously promote newspaper content of a kind that
contrasts with the content of a popular national daily, with its
heavier emphasis on disorder news.

For a wider perspective on the characteristic values and attitudes
of the local Press, it will be helpful to refer to part of the evidence
submitted by T. Bailey Forman Ltd (the proprietors of the Nottingham *Evening Post*) to the 1947 Royal Commission; they were
answering the questions 'How is the policy of your newspaper(s)
determined? By whom and with what considerations in mind?'

Broad lines of policy of the *Nottingham Guardian* and associated newspapers follow long-established tradition, interpreted and modified in the
light of modern needs by editors and leader-writers in consultation.

Without sanctimony it may be claimed that the basis of policy is the
Christian ethic. Political and social tendencies are commonly referred to
the traditional British conception of the relationship of man to man and
Government to individual. Change for its own sake is mistrusted, but
sound progressive development is welcomed.[7]

   This rather abstract and tonally self-confident passage would, one
feels, command the assent of most provincial Press spokesmen. The
wording suggests at once how important tradition is as a yardstick;
the broad lines of policy follow 'long-established tradition' and
political and social tendencies are commonly referred to 'the traditional British conception of the relationship of man to man and
Government to individual'. 'The relationship of man to man', one
assumes, involves the sanctity of both person and property; an emphasis on this obviously links the local Press to such institutions as
the Church, the Law and the schools. Also implied, it would seem, is
the concept of 'the helping hand'—whether in the form of individual
or collective action. The 'relationship of . . . Government to individual' presumably embraces the desiderata of individual freedom and
a minimal standard of life related to the country's overall wealth.
The achievement of the latter, especially in a Welfare State, may
necessitate some curbing of individual freedom (e.g. the freedom to
accumulate capital without restrictions); the 'tradition' would be
that both ideals be fulfilled through a just and sensible compromise.
But there will inevitably be differing assessments as to where the
compromise lies, as the result of divergent social and political attitudes. T. Bailey Forman Ltd claim that their policies and attitudes
are a response to their interpretation of 'the Christian ethic'; in
other words, a rigid political platform is not the determinant of their
reaction to change, and 'sound progressive development' is welcomed,
whoever initiates it. This is the alternative to 'change for its own
sake', which is 'mistrusted'. The position can be summarised as
cautiously progressive conservatism, informed by Christian principles.
   It has been suggested, then, that the provincial Press tends to be
antipathetic towards some aspects of metropolitan life and influence,
and perceives its values and insights as sounder, and less modish,
than those of Fleet Street's 'populars'. Further, the nature of its
conservatism is such that it is predisposed to reflect and endorse the
values of the established institutions, and family values. With these
background considerations in mind, it is possible to proceed to
analyse four specific functions of the provincial leading column:

the 'watchdog', the pump-primer, the detached evaluator and the booster.

1. The watchdog and moral guardian It was noted in the introductory chapter that readers expect the local Press to keep a wary eye on local and national institutions when these are formulating policies or making decisions, or carrying out policies and decisions which will in some way affect the quality of national, local or individual life. This reader expectation is regarded as one to which it is a duty to respond; it leads, therefore, to the role of watchdog. It is a role that is by no means confined to comment on institutions and their leaders; the actions or attitudes of the general public, or particular groups or individuals, may be judged to warrant a warning growl. Amongst those who should have been alerted by provincial newspaper leaders on 11 and 13 January 1966 were Whitehall (Newcastle *Evening Chronicle*), British Rail (*ibid.*), the Home Secretary (*West Lancashire Evening Gazette*), the Minister of Power (Wolverhampton *Express and Star*), the miners' leaders (*Yorkshire Evening Post*), Leicestershire County Council (Leicester *Mercury*), Northallerton Rural District Council (Darlington *Evening Despatch*) and the general public (Wolverhampton *Express and Star* and *Lancashire Evening Post*).

The watchdog tone ranges from the sternly decisive to the gently reproving; two brief examples of the first tone follow:

> *Yorkshire Evening Post* (13 January 1966), on absenteeism in the Yorkshire mines: 'The industry's future lies in the hands of those absentees. It is high time the miners' leaders took a fresh hand here.'

> *Lancashire Evening Post* (13 January 1966), on the part that parents can play in preventing vandalism: 'Vandalism of the kind which has arisen will not obligingly fade away of its own accord. It must be purposefully put down. Parents have their vital role in this. Let that be bluntly stated.'

The speaking voice in both instances is uncompromising and almost staccato. Immediate and vigorous action is seen as an imperative. It may be significant that both the groups being 'watched' are not of the kind that could become harmfully less co-operative as news communicators, or whose unfavourable reaction might foster an antagonistic attitude towards the local Press on the part of some

Manchester Evening News

THURSDAY SEPT 18 1969

Them and us

WHEN in July the Skeffington committee published its proposals for encouraging people to become more deeply involved in local authority work, especially planning, many council members and officials could scarcely believe their eyes. There were no fewer than 47 recommendations aimed at a hitherto undreamed-of frankness about planning proposals, with heavy emphasis on the need for consultation with the Press, radio, and television, for public meetings, exhibitions, informed publicity of all kinds.

But it was all soundly based. Communication and involvement have lagged far behind the march of planning, of development, of altering the face of Britain for generations to come. And as the Skeffington report put it, failure to communicate has meant that the preparation of a plan instead of being a bridge has become a barrier between the "them" of authority and the "us" of the public.

Lukewarm

So it is disappointing to find that a report on Skeffington to Manchester City Council virtually adds up to a look at all the reasons for not doing what was recommended. There is a lukewarm acceptance that some participation is "inevitable," but the possibility of carrying out the recommendations in full is challenged by the plea of insufficient staff and money. Of course it will make life harder for council officials, and of course it will mean expense. If people are to be better informed there will have to be machinery for doing the job, and that costs money.

Remote

Town halls never will have any money or men to spare, and if the Skeffington proposals are once slipped into a pigeon hole the odds are they will never come out again. But in the reorganisation of local government, which will certainly mean larger units, there is an obvious danger that the individual citizen will become even more remote from authority and unaware of what it has in store for him.

What Skeffington urged and was quite clearly right was that every man and woman should not only have the earliest possible explanation of any plans that might affect them but also have the chance to influence those plans. It said, "We want the paper of the plans to come to life, and to come to life in a way people want." That does not mean propaganda, it means frank discussion and debate. It means, in fact, democracy at work.

THOUGHT FOR THE DAY
No word that is profitable is bad.—Sophocles.

Fig. 6(a) A 'watchdog' editorial on local government. *By courtesy of the Manchester Evening News*

WEST LANCASHIRE EVENING

GAZETTE

FRIDAY, FEBRUARY 19, 1971

CITY OF FYLDE ON CARDS?

BLACKPOOL SOUTH'S MP, Mr Peter Blaker, considers that a City of the Fylde is still a possibility under the Government's proposals earlier this week for local government reform.

As Ministry thinking appears to be that a large town like Blackpool should gather around it some of the surrounding areas, and as the new districts are intended to be rather larger in population than Blackpool, this would appear to be the case.

So Blackpool and the Fylde will now wait with interest to hear what the new Boundary Commission has to say about the future areas of local authorities.

Obviously, much consultation lies ahead.

In view of the reduction in powers which will be vested in district councils, in Blackpool, at any rate, enthusiasm for the City of the Fylde idea must be tempered by the knowledge that however impressive such a unit may sound, much of the power over its area would be exercised from outside by the county council.

There must be local apprehension over how county control of vital functions like planning, transport and education will affect local developments.

In education Blackpool is considerably further advanced than the surrounding county area in reorganising its secondary education.

In transport, it is obvious that great difficulties would arise in arranging any sort of integrated county set-up.

Blackpool's trams, the future of which is now under debate, would obviously be doubtful runners in such an organisation.

And how well would the particular needs of our holiday resorts be catered for in a county planning context? This is worrying other resorts, like Brighton, too.

What would be the future of the Illuminations under the new system, and how would they be financed? This is another question which could arise.

On the other hand, an enthusiastic county take-over of the airport could be good for the future.

Holiday resorts have unique problems. It is to be hoped that representation at county level will be strong enough to ensure that they get an adequate hearing.

Quote for today

CHANGE

Change is not made without inconvenience.
RICHARD HOOKER
(1554-1600)

Fig. 6(b) Another 'watchdog' editorial. *By courtesy of the West Lancashire Evening Gazette*

particular section of readers. The PROs of the mining industry would be unlikely to curtail their supply of hand-outs; as for 'parents', these could easily see the *Lancashire Evening Post*'s admonition as applicable to particular parents with whom they need not identify. The tone of the leaders, therefore, can safely be assertive: 'it is high time . . .' and 'let that be bluntly stated'. It is in this sort of watchdog leader that evening newspaper editorial comment comes closest to the Cerberus posture adopted by the *Daily Express* in its stereotyped diatribes on behalf of the 'nation' or the 'people'. An instance of the *Express* in watchdog vein occurred on 4 March 1967; Mr Wilson's 'growing authoritarianism' *vis-à-vis* dissenters in his own party was the subject:

Calling the Party to Heel

. . . If they find themselves in disagreement with the dominant clique in the Government, they have a simple choice to make: Conform or get out.

There can be no mistaking the dangerous ring of this philosophy. It is totally inimical to British democracy. As such it must be resisted vigorously and relentlessly.

Having simplified the issue in terms of dissenters on the one hand and a 'dominant clique' on the other, the *Express* weighs in with a fulsome denunciation of the latter—finding its 'philosophy . . . totally inimical'. 'Totally' is a favoured assertive judgment-clincher; it appeared again, in a leader on the same theme, six days later: 'The very idea of a "Fuehrer prinzip" is totally unacceptable in this country.' The Aunt Sally is set up in an emotive manner ('clique', 'Fuehrer prinzip'); it is then knocked down with a series of rhetorical absolutes. The reader, in effect, is invited to be for or against; no reservations or qualifications are admitted.

The typical provincial evening newspaper does not press cases of an analogous kind so stridently; it will be shown that its platform manner is usually more pliant and less demagogic. This is partly because a bellowing voice in a small room would come across to the local newspaper reader as incongruously pompous—in fact, as an anachronistic return to the era of Edward Baines Jr. and Mr Pott. The *Express*'s watchdog leaders often amount to an entertainment comparable to that afforded by the Hyde Park Corner orators; further, it is able to bolster its rhetorical sallies by a corroborating use of news reports, features and cartoons. The provincial Press lacks the necessary expertise and resources to compete in this vein, even supposing that it would wish to; it must ply more restrained wares in keeping with the tone and style of its news content.

When provincial newspapers are acting as watchdogs in relation to important local institutions, or attempting to mould local opinion, their characteristic tone is one of gentle persuasion. Two examples must suffice to suggest this tone. The first involves the *Leicester Mercury* 13 January 1966) 'watching' the Leicestershire County Council in the interest of some of its rate-payers, who had lodged a further protest about the 'potholed, corrugated surface of Church Hill Road, Thurmaston, with its muddy traps for the unwary and its menace to car springs . . .' The leader ('Priorities of the potholes') concluded:

> There are worse streets even than Church Hill to put right, but it will take much more to persuade people, up to their ankles in mud, that more cannot officially be done.
> Priorities come into it, of course, and also the question of cash (although the owners in the long run foot the bill), but the County Council should ask themselves whether they could not move more in pace with the times. The potholers of Thurmaston, who probably do not appreciate the niceties of authorities, would put that more bluntly.

The *Leicester Mercury*, having pointed out in fairness to the county council that it has a number of competing claims on its available resources, puts the ball in its court equably enough; at the same time, it slips in the point that a quite different tone—a much blunter one— could have been adopted had the *Mercury* chosen to speak purely from the standpoint of the protesting rate-payers. It prefers to put their case in a wider perspective, and speaks judicially rather than assertively. In doing so, it can be seen as trying to get the best of three worlds; it suggests that the residents of Church Hill Road have a case to answer, but at the same time is sympathetic towards council and to those who live in roads in an even worse state of repair. This is a typical approach for a local newspaper, and accounts for the note of restraint and circumspection.

The second example shows a provincial newspaper (the Wolverhampton *Express and Star*) acting as an anticipatory watchdog by trying to forestall a possible public reaction, which it would regard as unhelpful, to an innovation about to be pioneered by Cannock Urban Council. Here, of course, it is the public that is being 'watched'

on the council's behalf; the tone is rooted in a tactful, reasoned
appeal to the principle of fair play:

Hostels

In response to an appeal from Lady Reading, national chairman of the
Woman's Voluntary Service, Cannock Urban Council has offered to
make over two of its council houses to the service for use as hostels for
ex-Borstal boys.

This is a bold and admirable decision which cannot have been easy to
make. The council had to balance the need of these boys to find a home in
which to make their return to society, against the deserts of the 2,000
people on Cannock's housing list.

Some controversy and criticism of the decision is only to be expected,
as Councillor E. Prime, the council's chairman, commented last night. We
hope it will not also cause bitterness, and especially not bitterness against
the very boys the scheme is designed to help. [11 January 1966]

The *Express and Star* makes its own attitude fully explicit by assessing the council's decision as 'bold and admirable'. It suggests that
the decision has not been reached without a painstaking consideration of the claims of those on the local housing list. It sees that the
proposal affords grounds for a passing gripe or grumble, but hopes
that this will not take on a note of bitterness—'and especially not
bitterness against the very boys the scheme is designed to help'.
It asks for, but does not demand, a considerate and unselfish
approach.

Thus where the watchdog function is being fulfilled in relation to
competing local interests the characteristic tone is reasoned and
equable; the phrases 'the County Council should ask themselves
whether they could not move more in pace with the times' and 'we
hope that it will not cause bitterness' evince this tone. The appeal is
to a sense of justice and fair play—to the Christian ethic, it could be
said; everyone, so the assumption runs, has some sort of a case, but
it may be that one case is more deserving than another. Of course,
when a local institution or group is judged to be patently culpable
of working against the community's best interest, the tone may become more severe.

So in spite of the fact that the typical ratio of working-class to
middle-class evening newspaper readers is in the order of 2·6 : 1,
the provincial leader writer does not adopt the distinctive stylistic
ingredients of the *Daily Mirror* in some of its watchdog leaders. It
avoids the jocular 'we're as good as you' posture from which the

Duke of Edinburgh can be presented as 'the Gabby Dook';[8] it does
not attempt the colloquial connections present in the following
excerpt from a *Mirror* leader[9] recommending debate on whether
the pound or ten shillings should be the decimal unit: 'many MPs
. . . plump for the ten bob'. The easy informality of 'ten bob' (reinforced by the choice of 'plump') is of rare occurrence in local Press
leaders. This is partly because such 'popular' elements would be
deemed unsuitable for addressing community leaders and the 'intelligent minority', and partly because the editorial column is not perceived as one where a 'mix' of the formally serious and the informally
colloquial should be attempted. Accordingly, provincial editors
prefer to play safe and thereby retain the leader's 'prestige value'.

Returning to the passage from the Wolverhampton *Express and
Star*, one sees here an example of the local Press working in close
conjunction with local institutions—in this case, the council, the
WVS and the prison service. Characteristically, provincial newspapers do support the work of the Church, the police, the schools
and other institutions concerned with the community's moral and
social condition. A few extracts from the *West Lancashire Evening
Gazette*'s leading column must suffice to indicate that this co-
operation may sometimes stem from what some might regard
as an uncritical acquiescence in the attitudes and judgments of
community leaders:

. . . The probation officers, with their vast experience, should know
what they are talking about. [11 October 1965]

. . . The magistrates who sit in juvenile courts are not selected hapha-
zardly. They are people with knowledge of life and of juveniles too. They
do their job well. [*Ibid.*]

. . . we have an excellent police force in Blackpool, and the magistrates
are increasing penalties satisfactorily.
A little sunshine, bringing rather better temper all round, might do as
much good as anything.
Plus a touch of the birch, as the chairman of the local bench has been
saying. [26 July 1965]

The custodians of local law are presented as paragons; they have
'vast experience' or 'knowledge of life and of juveniles too'. The
magistrates 'do their job well' and the police force is 'excellent'. In
1966 a leader in the local weekly implied agreement with the chief
constable's opinion that we are 'too soft with offenders'.[10] It is not

surprising, therefore, that it should favour bringing back the birch and the restoration of capital punishment.[11] Comment on these attitudes as such must be deferred to the concluding chapter; the present aim is to clarify the nature of the watchdog role. One should, however, add that the *Gazette*, by including the above encomia in the context of watchdog leaders on crime and punishment, expressed its esteem of community leaders more explicitly than the typical provincial newspaper. The latter would reveal co-operative intentions and, usually, conservative attitudes; but it would be rather more sparing in its professions of esteem.

In their surveillance of the moral health of the local community served, it is apparent that some provincial newspaper companies adopt a more paternalistic stance than others; even so, there seems to be a high degree of consensus about the values and attitudes to be inculcated. Allegiance to the Christian ethic in the context of the family and community settings is the central tenet. Thus, referring to a police search which found a party of teenagers in possession of purple hearts and contraceptives, the *West Lancashire Evening Gazette* called for a 'moral revolution'—one which must start in the home, and which must represent a return to 'the old, simple virtues':

> . . . More and more it becomes clear that the main responsibility rests on the parents.
> . . . What it boils down to is that this nation is in need of a great moral revolution; a return to the old simple virtues, among which discipline, respect, obedience and honesty are not the least.
> And that revolution must start in the home.[12]

The family unit, therefore, is the one within which 'discipline, respect, obedience and honesty' should be fostered; to these could be added the values invoked by the *Gazette* in an adversely critical appraisal of the James Bond novels: 'gentleness, virtue, chastity, domesticity'.[13] Families are urged to absorb and be motivated by these values; they should not be deterred by the fact that 'modern moralists'[14] might assess some of them as of diminishing relevance.

It must be stressed that particular provincial newspapers are more active in their role of moral guardian than others; the *West Lancashire Evening Gazette* is clearly amongst the most active. But the vast majority exercise a regular 'watch' over the individual's relation to the community, and attempt to define what, ideally, his role should be within it. They urge, on appropriate occasions, pride in one's town, region and country. They recommend voluntary service within the community as well as a 'fair day's work for a fair day's pay' at work. And, as in the news columns, they give prominence to acts of selfless courage.

The watchdog function, therefore, is not confined to an appraisal of the politics or actions of local or national institutions. It may be extended to a paternalistic nurturing of family values and to defining, in terms of ideals, the reader's relationship with the community at large or to a particular section of the community.

One of the most challenging areas in which public attitudes have to be 'watched', and a working ideal established, is that of the relationship between the indigenous majority and the immigrant minority. For in this area the local Press has felt disposed to champion a minority cause in the face of antipathetic, even hostile, majority attitudes. After Mr Powell's Birmingham speech of 20 April 1968 (in which he referred to the 'grinning piccaninnies' shouting 'racialist') the Wolverhampton *Express and Star* received 5,000 letters supporting Mr Powell and 300 against him. A subsequent postcard poll conducted by the *Express and Star* resulted in over 35,000 votes in Mr Powell's favour, with hardly any against.[15] In the light of this sort of evidence, John Dodge (then Director of the National Council for the Training of Journalists) drew the following conclusion in a paper presented at Strasbourg:

> The race issue has presented British editors—and particularly provincial editors—with a pressing moral problem. It is an accepted part of an editor's job to campaign against injustice and incompetence and in this he can normally assume that he is battling for the majority of his readers against the tyranny of overbearing authority. The race issue is different; as the Wolverhampton experience shows, in areas with large coloured populations an editor who takes a liberal line is often at odds with the bulk of his readership.[15]

The 'liberal line' would be that the coloured community is here to stay, and that every effort must be made to improve race relations and immigrants' social conditions. Hence emotive attacks on immigrants are seen as a catastrophic retarding influence, and the encouragement of repatriation as a thoroughly negative solution. This summary corresponds very closely in content to the *Guardian*'s leader ('Mr Enoch Powell dismissed') on 22 April 1968. The *Guardian* felt 'sad' that a man of Mr Powell's 'strength and intelligence' had to be dismissed, but Mr Heath had acted 'promptly and properly'

in this respect. It concluded: 'The social problems caused by immigration are real and, for many people, immediate. But they will not
be solved by rhetoric.'

Before considering provincial opinion, it is important to note
that the anti-liberal attitude to which John Dodge referred was
largely assented to by the *Daily Telegraph* and *Daily Express* (also
on 22 April 1968). The logic in their leaders ran as follows:

(a) Mr Powell's rhetoric was open to adverse criticism

However unwise and intemperate Mr. Powell's speech may have
been . . . [*Daily Express*]

. . . whatever the deficiencies of his statistics and the exaggerations
of his language . . . [*Daily Telegraph*]

(b) But he spoke for the mass of the people

[He] reflected the feelings of a vast number of people [*Daily
Express*]

he was expressing anxieties felt by millions of people . . . [*Daily
Telegraph*]

(c) His dismissal was an error

Mr. Powell may have been impolitic. Mr. Heath has been foolish.
[*Daily Express*]

His congenital disposition to push an argument to its logical and
linguistic extremes was not sufficient ground for dismissing him
abruptly from the Conservative Shadow Cabinet. [*Daily Telegraph*]

The two newspapers, therefore, argued along very similar lines, and
their position can fairly be described—in this respect—as 'right-
wing'. For, as the *Guardian* pointed out, Mr Powell's re-emigration
remedy went 'quite contrary to the official policy of the Conservative Party'.

Since there was widespread agreement (allowing for differing
strengths and slants) in the national Press on the unfortunate style of
Mr Powell's speech, and since editors (provincial and national)
would be aware of the speech's likely popular appeal, a crucial point
to examine in the regional Press is whether or not his dismissal was
approved. It is in relation to this that the description 'liberal' or
'right-wing' will usually prove to be appropriate.

The newspapers studied were those in the library files of the
Institute of Race Relations. Ten English evening newspapers that
commented at length on Mr Powell's speech—all on 22 April 1968—

were the *Birmingham Evening Mail,* Wolverhampton *Express and Star,* Stoke *Evening Sentinel,* Sheffield *Star, Yorkshire Evening Post, Doncaster Evening Post,* Bradford *Telegraph and Argus,* Bolton *Evening News, Oldham Evening Chronicle* and Ipswich *Evening Star.* Of these, six assessed the speech from a 'liberal' standpoint; three made rather more concession to Mr Powell, and one adopted the position of 'detached evaluator'.

The six newspapers with a liberal approach had in common explicit (in five cases) or implied assent to Mr Heath's dismissal of Mr Powell. The parts of editorials commenting on Mr Powell's language and on Mr Heath's action are cited below:

Birmingham Evening Mail

. . . the inflammatory nature of the speech . . .

[Mr Heath] really had to dismiss Mr. Powell from the Shadow Cabinet.

Express and Star (Wolverhampton)

. . . in dealing with the general impracticability of the proposed legislation, Mr. Powell was unnecessarily extravagant in his language. It is always possible to damage a cause by overstatement and this in our opinion is what Mr. Powell has done.

[Mr Powell had] rightly been removed from the Shadow Cabinet.

Evening Sentinel (Stoke on Trent)

Both in tone and content it seemed to go far beyond the letter and spirit of official Conservative policy. There was a melodramatic prophecy about 'the River Tiber flowing with much blood', for instance, which was quite outrageous at a time when politicians of all sides are seeking to lower racial tension.

Mr. Heath . . . was clearly right to dismiss Mr. Powell from the Front Bench.

Ipswich Evening Star

Mr. Powell queered his pitch by the language he used.

Mr. Heath had no option but to dismiss him.

Telegraph and Argus (Bradford)

. . . when (utterances) are wrapped up in phrases about rivers flowing with blood, Mr. Heath could take no other course than he did.

Yorkshire Evening Post

Mr. Powell's inflammatory Birmingham speech on immigration was basically arrant nonsense. What he advocates is a bar on immigrants and

virtual deporting of those already here . . . his dramatic and intemperate
speech . . .

It should be stressed that Mr Powell's role as 'voice of the people'
was not unappreciated by the Birmingham, Bradford, Stoke on Trent
and Wolverhampton evening Press. In the words of the *Birmingham
Evening Mail*: 'It must also be admitted that he may have done a
service in calling the attention of the rest of the country to the
feelings that undoubtedly exist in areas under social pressures.' The
Express and Star (Wolverhampton) felt that if Mr Powell had used
'moderate language' his speech 'would have been justified'. But he
did not, and the *Ipswich Evening Star* commented:

If a few more people of the standing of Mr. Powell were to make speeches
as inflammatory as he did, then not only would racial integration become
an impossibility but in a short time this country would be heading for the
very disaster he wants to avoid—race riots.

Three newspapers, in varying ways, took up the middle ground
between the right wing and liberal positions. The *Doncaster Evening
Post* felt that 'Mr. Powell's inflammatory Birmingham speech held
a great deal of common sense. It was the way he said it, which whilst
typical of the man, was anything but statesmanlike.' The *Bolton
Evening News*, while conceding that the speech was 'inaccurate and
inflammatory', stood by the view that it 'reflected what a great
many people in this country really think . . .' No political party, it
suggested, should ignore popular feeling—and Mr Powell's dismissal
could turn out to be 'a blunder'. 'What is needed now,' the *News*
added, 'is a little moderation to restore the balance. And that moderation must come from the left as well as from the right.' The *Oldham
Evening Chronicle* (a Liberal newspaper) also referred to the likelihood of Mr Powell's speech finding 'an answering echo in the
hearts of many uneasy people'. It proceeded to take the blame off
Mr Powell and put it on 'the protagonists of the dangerous and
unhealthy Race Relations Bill. Their over-activity is forcing moderate
and liberal-minded people into an attitude of counter-attack.'
    It is difficult to locate a common stance on the part of these three
newspapers, except to say that they seemed to be recommending a
position that mediated between the extreme left and extreme right—
roughly equivalent to the official Conservative platform. They differed from the previous six either in not commenting on, or not

approving of, Mr Powell's dismissal from the Shadow Cabinet—attaching decisive significance to his role as 'voice of the people'.

Finally, *The Star* (Sheffield) took up the largely descriptive position of the detached evaluator—noting Mr Powell's 'unfortunate practice of couching what might have passed for fair comment in the most inflammatory terms' and observing that reactions to his speech would be 'wide and varied'.

This brief analysis of provincial approaches to Mr Powell's speech bears out the conclusion reached by a team of researchers reporting on a wider sample embracing all the British morning and evening regional newspapers that published related editorials—as reported in the *Institute of Race Relations News Letter*, April–May 1968:

... up to two-thirds were wholeheartedly critical of the Powell speech's contents, tone and timing, while the remainder, while criticising the extreme tone, were inclined to agree that it reflected certain public opinions and attitudes that had gone unrepresented.

The important point for this discussion is that the majority of editorials adopted an approach that ran counter to an assumed popular attitude. The interests of the immigrant community and good race relations were put first—a response that John Dodge assessed as 'highly praiseworthy'. He singled out Clement Jones, editor of the *Express and Star* (Wolverhampton) as particularly deserving of credit: 'Clement Jones immediately attacked Powell's views in editorial after editorial, although he knew that the overwhelming majority of his readers were against him. . . . Strongly backed by his proprietor . . . and with the full support of his editorial staff—though not the rest of the newspaper's staff—he stood by his principles. It was an act of great personal courage which many other British editors may be called on to emulate in the future.'[15]

The provincial leaders published in response to Mr Powell's 1970 election speeches evinced a marked antipathy. Five newspapers that commented on his speculations as to whether the Foreign Office was 'the only department of State into which enemies of this country were infiltrated' were the *West Lancashire Evening Gazette*, *Halifax Evening Courier and Guardian*, Bradford *Telegraph and Argus*, *Shropshire Star* and *Oxford Mail*, in editorials published on 12 June 1970. The infiltration theory was assessed as 'the language of mania' (*Oxford Mail*) and 'carrying things too far' (Bradford *Telegraph and*

Argus); the *West Lancashire Evening Gazette* saw it as a pity that 'his words are so aggressive . . . he could have said the same thing in less inflammatory terms'. The *Halifax Evening Courier*'s view of the theory was that 'if it were not so tragic it would be funny'. This last newspaper's leader ('Politics and Mr. Powell') contained a paragraph that can fairly be said to sum up the general line on Mr Powell in the provincial Press:

Why, given our firm control policies, cannot Mr. Powell accept that most immigrants came here by choice and will not leave except under unthinkable duress? In other words, why doesn't he face the facts? The only fair and reasonable way to tackle our 'colour problem' is by imaginative policies for better race relations and general social improvements. The longer Mr. Powell denies this, the longer he will go on doing grave disservice to the many people who sincerely share his fears—and the more pointed will become the suspicion of his political motives.

The appeal to the criteria of fair-mindedness, reasonableness and constructive thinking is what one would expect from the local Press in the light of the analysis of the watchdog role. In the case of race relations, it is sustaining these criteria in the face of a substantial degree of support for harsher, uncompromising attitudes. As a result, the newspapers concerned deserve credit—even from those who disagree with their liberal principles.

2. Priming the pump A second function of the provincial newspaper leading column is to 'prime the pump'—to make suggestions for the improvement of the community in some way. These suggestions may arise from the writer's own (or the editor's or colleagues' or readers') thinking or, quite frequently, they may be inspired by hearing of schemes or policies which are known to have worked successfully elsewhere. Two examples follow; the first (Darlington *Evening Despatch*, 11 January 1966) is offered as the newspaper's own idea, while the second (*Oxford Mail*, 13 January 1966) endorses a local councillor's proposal:

[1]   *But why not an Arts centre?*

. . . A year ago—almost to the day—the *Northern Despatch**** called for the formation of a Friends of the Civic group, the appointment of a professional manager for the theatre, and a more positive, constructive and generous approach to the problem from the Town Council. We have had all these things in the past year.

---

* The name of this newspaper was changed to *Evening Despatch* in 1969.

But now we need to go further. It is time the Council gave serious consideration to buying the Civic Theatre block. Grants would be available for turning it into a thriving arts centre—a meeting place for everyone interested in the theatre, music, painting, discussion; a workshop for imaginative leisure.

[2]   *Looking ahead*

When rates are going up all the time, it is vital that councils should use the most modern techniques to get the best value for their spending.

At Oxford's next council meeting Coun. Alan Wilson, an economist, is asking the Finance Committee to report on what steps would be necessary to introduce a five-year forecast for its spending. It would be a 'rolling' programme, revised each year for five years ahead. We hope the council will endorse this idea. . . .

In both cases the local Press is putting forward constructive proposals which it thinks will benefit the community. By doing so, it suggests that it is progressive and enterprising, and not merely content to comment on changes only when they have been ratified or rejected by the councils concerned. It invites the community as a whole—not just its leaders—to look critically at some aspects of the *status quo* in the light of proposals thought to be viable. This is obviously an important function, and the extract from the *Evening Despatch* indicates that positive results may ensue.

3. The detached evaluator Whereas watchdog leaders sound an admonitory, cautionary note, a third type—the detached evaluator— remains content with a descriptive account of events or trends. This is very much the function of the chorus in Greek tragedy— clarifying and interpreting the action, with reference to the past, the present or the future, for the audience. It is a role characteristically adopted when international events are being discussed, and is therefore regularly apparent in evening newspapers that publish a high proportion of leaders on non-local issues and events (see table 11 above). The mood, of course, is determined by the subject; the tone is essentially reflective. The examples that follow are of a contrasting kind; the first is part of a *Huddersfield Daily Examiner* leader on President Shastri's death, and the second an extract from a *Scarborough Evening News* editorial on the decision of a local cinema management to switch from films to bingo. Both were published on 11 January 1966.

Mr. Shastri was almost unknown—outside India at any rate—when he was called to fill the gap caused by the unexpected death of Nehru in 1964.

Many friends of India feared for the future when Nehru was removed. The problems ahead were so great and there seemed so few men who could be measured against them, but Shastri once in office seemed to grow in stature as the problems about him grew darker.

. . . the Gaiety remains as a place for entertainment and a much-needed 'umbrella' for visitors on bad days. And if and when bingo loses its popularity, the Gaiety will no doubt still be there to revert to films or whatever form of entertainment is attracting the public then.

In both leaders the writers were marking events and formulating assessments of them, i.e., that Shastri was, in the final analysis, a worthy successor to Nehru, or that the switch from films to bingo may not, all things considered, have been a change for the worse. The tone is reasoned and reflective.

4. The booster The fourth function that emerged from a study of the leaders for 11 and 13 January 1966 was that of the local booster. This involves the celebration of some local person's or group's or community's achievement. 'Local', in this case, need not necesssarily refer to the circulation area alone; it may embrace assumed loyalties to a county or even wider region. The booster leader, in theory, permits the reader to identify with the achievement and feel that he is living in a locale that affords grounds for pride. If the implication of the content of the *Daily Express* is that the provinces are a place to escape from—one is thinking here of Arthur Christiansen's professed intention to get people 'away from the back streets of Derby'[16] and his view that 'any page that looks as drab as Derby can be counted a dead loss'[17]—the provincial community puff is designed to have the reverse effect. Accordingly, leader writers are always ready to sound the praises of successful people with some local connection; this was apparent in four of the five second leaders on the English victory in the third Test Match at Sydney (11 January 1966). The *Yorkshire Evening Post*, the *West Lancashire Evening Gazette*, the *Manchester Evening News* and the *Birmingham Evening Mail* all took the opportunity to bask in a reflected glory. The *Yorkshire Evening Post* included special praise for Boycott, Yorkshire's opening batsman; the *Post*'s assumption seemed to be that all Yorkshiremen should feel a sense of pride:

Yorkshiremen will regret that the county had only one representative in the victorious XI. But Boycott served his country magnificently. His share in the opening stand helped set the course of the match, and he had a hand in two crucial dismissals in the Australian second innings.

The *West Lancashire Evening Gazette*, although unable to extol the
merits of any Lancashire player, was nevertheless in a position to
praise the two opening batsmen as Northerners—thereby affording
its readers a less potent but still acceptable boost:

> It must be a long time since the Australians saw a pair of opening
> batsmen like Barber and Boycott, smacking boundaries in all directions
> within minutes of arriving at the crease.
>
> Both, be it noted, are Northerners—Boycott a Yorkshireman! And it is
> a great pity that Barber is not still playing for Lancashire, with whom he
> made his name.

The implication of the exclamation mark would seem to be that
Lancastrians do not associate Yorkshiremen with such a swash-
buckling technique. Having made this little dig at Yorkshire cricket,
the writer is content to let the larger loyalty—to the North—stand
for the purpose of the boost.

The *Manchester Evening News* also paid particular attention to
Barber, the former Lancashire player; his success, the leader suggested, justified local pride:

> ... To many in the North there will be pride that a key man in the
> match was Bob Barber, for although he no longer plays for the county
> he is a Lancashire man.
>
> Indeed, there will be many Lancashire supporters wistfully thinking:
> 'Won't you come home, Bob Barber?'

Interestingly, Barber was also seen as an enhancer of Midlands
prestige by virtue of his playing for Warwickshire; the *Birmingham
Evening Mail* had the names of three of this county's players for
inclusion in its confident encomium:

> ... Honours all round—but Warwickshire folk will justifiably think that
> Barber's opening innings really broke Australian hearts, that Brown's
> fierce three-wicket over was the point of no return: and that Smith, as
> captain, is modestly doing a great job.

As in the case of the *Yorkshire Evening Post*, the assumption is that
all 'Warwickshire folk' should derive some sense of gratification
from the local connection of these players. And although Barber
may be a Northerner by origin, the important fact for the *Mail*'s
purpose is who he now plays for.

In three of the four leaders cited the boost involves pointing to the
virtual indispensability of the local contribution: Boycott 'helped set
the course of the match', 'a key man' was Barber—and so on. The
implication is, in effect, that 'they couldn't have managed without us'.

Only the Bolton *Evening News* remained content to appeal to the further loyalty, i.e. to the English team as opposed to the Australian one; this was the aspect stressed in the opening paragraph:

So the team nobody thought good enough has gone one up in the Tests. Well done Mike Smith and his merry men. To beat Australia at all is an achievement; to do it at Sydney of all grounds, before the famous Hill critics and by more than an innings, is a triumph.

The English Test team is identified here with the underdog that succeeds and with the folk hero Robin Hood and his followers; the analogies assist the writer to tap patriotic attitudes. But this approach to the subject was an exception; the characteristic tactic was to develop the local angle. Readers are thereby invited to take pride in the region that produces men or women who succeed in any lawful sphere of endeavour.

The preceding analysis of particular functions of the leading column has for the most part concentrated on those leaders that, wholly or partly, refer to the local communities served. The justification for this is that it is the relationship of local newspapers to their circulation areas that is the focus of this survey. Even so, the general picture should not be forgotten; the percentage figures in table 11 above indicate that non-local matters figured in 60 per cent of the total number of leaders examined. The subjects of these are similar to those of national newspaper leaders: Government policies and decisions, major reports, outstanding accidents or disasters, great achievements, industrial unrest—and so on.

The weekly Press leading column

In marked contrast to the majority of evening newspapers, leader subjects in the weekly Press are predominantly of interest to one particular circulation area only. Out of a sample of seventy-eight leading columns taken from different weekly newspapers over the period 1964–65, only ten dealt with non-local topics. Six of these were watchdog columns on subjects like the danger of lead content in toys, chemicals and synthetic ingredients in foodstuffs, and drunken drivers; the remaining four considered international or

national affairs of the kind that one associates much more with the
evening Press:

> 'Conservative policy over trade unions' (*Cheshire Observer*,
> 22 October 1965).
> 'Back bench in front for wages' (*Bucks. Herald*, 20 November
> 1964).
> 'Homes policy stagnation' (*Southport Visiter*, 5 December 1964).
> 'A new look at the Congo' (*Crosby Herald*, 4 December 1964).

The remaining leaders (sixty-eight, or 87 per cent of all) dealt with
local topics. In terms of their functions, and taking into account all
seventy-eight leaders, it was found that 65 per cent could be classed
as watchdog, 15 per cent as priming the pump, 15 per cent as
reflectors (the Greek chorus function) and 5 per cent as boosters.
The watchdog function is clearly the most important for the local
weekly Press; of the fifty-one watchdog leaders, fourteen commented
on the town council (or its committees, departments, etc.), local
institutions or services, thirteen on the local public either as a whole
or in respect of some particular group, and eleven on external
influences such as Dr Beeching or Whitehall. Ten of the twelve
pump-priming leaders offered ideas or suggestions for the consideration of the town council or local institutions.

The ideals of community progress, prestige and pride act as the
buttresses supporting critiques, ideas, eulogies or reflections. The
theoretical bases of the weekly newspaper leader, at least in their
ideal form, would run as follows. First, it seeks that degree of
environmental (i.e. physical, social and cultural) improvement that
is compatible with a reasonable rate levy, and that accords with its
sense of priorities. Second, as an intermediary between the town
council and the rate-paying public, it purports to 'watch' the council
on behalf of the rate-payer and the public on behalf of the council.
It demands integrity, fairness, efficiency and far-sightedness from
the council, and sympathy and understanding from the public.
Third, it will attempt to maintain local self-respect and buoyancy
by due celebration of any communal, institutional or individual
achievement. As instances of this last function, one finds the *Ilkeston
Pioneer* praising 'the quality of Ilkeston knitwear and underwear'
('Ilkeston industry . . . has no need to hide its light—or Ilkeston's—
under a bushel'),[18] the *Huddersfield Weekly Examiner* revelling in the
prestige of the Huddersfield Choral Society ('. . . the invitation

from Boston is a measure of the world fame now enjoyed by the Huddersfield Choral Society'),[19] and the *Woodford Express and Independent* celebrating the success of local bazaars:

The same faithful, generous customers

We live in a world of high-pressure salesmanship. Vast campaigns are launched daily, and at huge expense, with the object of convincing us of the advantage of buying a particular article.

From all points of the compass, by every conceivable modern method, we are wooed and cajoled, no longer, it seems, as individual customers, but en masse.

It is all the more refreshing, therefore, to discover that, far from declining, the small local 'effort' is still received with affection and support. There are still plenty of people prepared to walk in the rain to a small jumble sale and buy an article they probably do not want, simply to help an appeal that catches their imagination.

There are hundreds of individual examples. Let us take just one. That time-honoured institution, the church bazaar.

A dusty anachronism? Groups of middle-aged women behind trestle tables selling rock cakes and Victoria sponges? Those tempted to sneer should take the trouble to read the local Press, turn back the pages of our own editions over recent weeks. They will be surprised.

Of course, the church bazaar has moved with the times. It has widened in scope, become more highly organised, gone modern. It may be opened by a television personality or have a background of 'pop' music. But there are the same crowds of eager, faithful customers, whether the proceeds be for the church scouts, a Sunday School classroom, a new organ or a mission station in troubled Congo.

Their success, without doubt, is the personal touch, the local interest, the chat and the cup of tea.

You cannot dismiss as anachronisms functions that continue to raise individual totals ranging from £100 to £800—and these are the remarkable figures we publish week by week . . .[20]

It would be a rare occasion indeed for a national newspaper, and almost as rare for an evening newspaper, to comment on such a routine aspect of community life. The local weekly newspaper is able to do so because its news columns, emphasising community order news far more than any other type of newspaper, afford the evidence on which the leader is based; readers are in fact invited to turn back the pages of previous issues if they have any doubts. This leading column is of interest in that it contrasts the relatively impersonal world outside the community—the world of 'high-pressure sales-manship'—with the personal, homely life of the community itself;

the success of the bazaar, it is suggested, springs from 'the personal touch, the local interest, the chat and the cup of tea'. In this respect the bazaar and the local weekly newspaper have much in common, since the latter also relies on the appeal of known names, local interest, 'chat' and miscellaneous goods for sale. The boost, therefore, is for the distinctiveness of community life and its 'time-honoured' institutions.

The parish pump may well be an appropriate symbol for most of the leader content of the weekly; but it is a pump that must be contemporary and efficient, and as pride-evoking as that of any other comparable community's.

Notes

1 Bernard Berelson, 'What "missing the newspaper" means', *The Process and Effects of Mass Communication*, ed. Wilbur Schramm (New York: Harper & Brothers, 1949), p. 41.
2 *Ibid.*, p. 42.
3 *Ibid.*, p. 40.
4 *West Lancashire Evening Gazette*, 13 October 1965.
5 *Ibid.*, 24 March 1965.
6 'The provincial editor', BBC North of England Home Service discussion, 20 March 1964.
7 *Memoranda of Evidence*, p. 84.
8 *Daily Mirror*, 21 February 1967.
9 *Ibid.*, 10 March 1967.
10 *Blackpool Gazette and Herald*, 8 July 1966.
11 *West Lancashire Evening Gazette*, 22 December 1964; 26 July 1965.
12 *Ibid.*, 31 August 1965.
13 *Ibid.*, 9 April 1966.
14 *Ibid.*, 17 February 1964.
15 John Dodge, 'The British Press and race relations', Strasbourg lecture, January 1969. See also the speech delivered by Clement Jones, editor of the Wolverhampton *Express and Star*, to the Guild of British Newspaper Editors, Harrogate, 22 September 1968.
16 Arthur Christiansen, *op. cit.*, p. 166.
17 *Ibid.*, p. 163.
18 *Ilkeston Pioneer*, 22 October 1965.
19 *Huddersfield Weekly Examiner*, 23 October 1965.
20 *Woodford Express and Independent*, 11 December 1964.

8 Readers' correspondence: its nature and importance

The correspondence column is a regular and important feature of virtually all provincial newspapers. Its particular interest and uniqueness lies in the fact that it is the only part of the newspaper written by readers, many of whom feel deeply involved in the subject that prompts them to write. This involvement is apparent in the various tones and styles adopted, and accounts for the known appeal of the correspondence column. As the Manchester Guardian and Evening News Ltd noted in their written evidence to the 1947 Commission, 'it is an elementary principle of journalism that letters of criticism have "reader value"'.[1] Although this comment referred particularly to letters criticising a newspaper's political opinions, it can justifiably be said to apply to the whole range of letters of protest, some of which are specified below.

The correspondence column is seen by editors as a means of promoting reader participation and of obtaining useful guidelines about local opinion. A paragraph from a leader ('Part of the community') published in the Darlington *Evening Despatch* on the occasion of its fiftieth anniversary suggests the editorial viewpoint: 'In its columns its readers should be encouraged to express their opinions, their fears, their hopes—and, just as important, air their grievances. In short, readers should be encouraged to participate in the newspaper.'[2] The reference to grievances is one that frequently occurs when editors discuss readers' letters, as in this observation from a Midlands evening newspaper editor:

A large percentage of our letters come from women and this is something that did not happen a few years ago. These letters show that the stresses and strains of life in a highly organised society, set in a densely populated community, inevitably give rise to an endless amount of irritation and impatience and nervous upsets.

Apart from these expressions of exasperation the subject matter of letters extends over an extraordinarily wide range . . . rates, hospitals, hanging, morality, immigrants, education, expenditure, government priorities, overtime, cost of food and, of course, the motor car.

The phrase 'expressions of exasperation' is one that points succinctly to the prevailing tone of much correspondence. Exasperation is the chief motive behind the often unfulfilled intention to 'write to the paper about it'. Protests about rude bus crews, negligent dog-owners, autocratic councils and a host of similarly identifiable social groupings pour forth without respite and show every sign of continuing.

The tone of protest (usually signalled by favoured introductory words like 'disgusted', 'appalled', 'shocked', 'deplorable') is fairly well distinguishable from the tone of the local controversialist, exploring as he does the pros or cons of party political ideology, comprehensive education, fluoridation of water supplies, racialism and so on. The one rests his case on some specific, localised complaint; the other, like a Hyde Park Corner orator, is dealing with ideas in a more general manner. The particular correspondence column that is dominated by letters of protest has a quite different 'feel' to one that largely consists of controversy. One would conjecture that a reader of the *Birmingham Evening Mail*'s 'Readers' Letters' of 21 October 1967 ought to have found some, if not all, of the eight (out of thirteen published) letters of protest both topical and interesting. These concerned the effects of prostitution in Glovers Road, Small Heath; the apathy of litter louts; the inadequacy of the litter bins in Moseley; unsightly bill-posting on corporation grit bins and litter bins; the values of the Kineton petitioners seeking to reduce the frequency of church bell-ringing; the shortcomings of Birmingham's signposts and lane markings—and so on. Each letter voiced a specific complaint arising within the circulation area, and typically dealt with an alleged defect within the environment. In contrast, the weekly *Buxton Advertiser*'s letters of 10 March 1967 consisted entirely of a debate about the practice of fox hunting (three against and one for)—a long-standing subject of controversy. It had no connection with day-to-day living in the town of Buxton itself, and to many readers may have seemed like a private wrangle between two opposed minority groups. (To be fair to the *Advertiser*, its correspondence column is usually both varied and lively.) Although editors believe that such groups should have the opportunity to express their views, it is equally a tenet that they should not be allowed to take over the correspondence column. For in general the letter of protest has more 'reader value'. Indeed, it is not unusual to come across a letter complaining about the nature of some protracted controversy, especially in the weekly Press. An example follows:

A 'Hate Club' for Rochdale?

The controversy and bias on religious beliefs has gone on far too long. I suggest a change of subject, such as 'Jews', 'Freemasonry', 'Coloureds in Britain'. Anything will do as long as it strikes off hatred and bias, small-mindedness and bigotry.

. . . to judge by the letters printed in the *Observer* this last few months, there is certainly a case for a 'Hate Club' in Rochdale . . .[3]

This passage assists in understanding the background to Scarborough and District Newspapers Ltd's views on religious correspondence, in their 1947 written evidence: 'Some papers refuse to publish correspondence on religious topics. We do publish it, and have constantly to be pulling at the reins.'[4] Thus a number of filters may be applied to the correspondence a newspaper receives. Particular subject areas (e.g. religious controversy) and attitudes (e.g. anything 'against the Throne, treasonable, blasphemous or that which would give personal offence to a member of a creed or sect'[5]) may be blacklisted. Controversies or debates may be terminated ('this correspondence is now closed') once their initial interest is seen as diminishing. Further, pressure on space in itself will often necessitate selection from the letters submitted; this pressure, and the editorial belief that 'readers prefer persuasive epitomes to arguments fully extended'[6] account for opening the paragraph of 'do and don't' advice to correspondents that some newspapers include with a plea for brevity:

Contributions to 'Our Letter Bag' which, preferably, should not exceed 350 words, must be typed or written on one side of the paper only. No letter will be considered unless the name and address of the writer is supplied, not necessarily for publication. The printing of readers' letters is entirely at the Editor's discretion, and none will be returned unless a stamped, addressed envelope is enclosed. [*Huddersfield Daily Examiner*, 28 June 1967]

Thus although the correspondence column is usually referred to by newspaper spokesmen as an open platform for protest and debate, the 'editor's discretion' will in fact be variously applied. Editors will not, however, lightly risk a reputation for biased selection, if only for the reason that this would be detrimental to the newspaper's image; one evening newspaper assistant editor pointed out in discussion that the exercise of political bias could result in an undesired denunciation of the local Press in the council chamber. Even so, 'discretion' may lead to the exclusion of some topics from the letter columns, and does lead to the rejection of letters that might be construed as libellous. When 'fair' criticism of some local institution, organisation or service is published, the convention of the 'right to simultaneous reply' is often exercised by spokesmen; an example from the *West Lancashire Evening Gazette* follows:

Summer dress for postmen

Whatever has happened to our postmen's uniform?
Is it not standardised any longer? Nowadays there seems to be no uniformity at all. They wear an assortment of coats and usually no hat.

OBSERVANT

* A Post Office spokesman says, 'Postmen are allowed not to wear hats in the summer. They are also permitted to wear open-neck shirts and lightweight jackets. This relaxation of dress regulations is to cater for the weather.'

[*West Lancashire Evening Gazette*, 12 August, 1967]

This convention ensures that the reader of the criticism will be unlikely to miss reading the official reply, as he might were it to be deferred to a subsequent issue.

Before moving on to the more detailed discussion of some types of correspondence, it is necessary to consider the letter columns of a sample of weekly and evening newspapers with the following questions in mind: (1) How much space does the column take up? (2) How many letters does it contain? (3) How many of these are signed with *noms de plume*? The resulting average figures will help to suggest the norms in these respects for each type of newspaper. Table 12 overleaf refers to the weekly Press.

In the case of a sample of weekly newspapers with an average 1964 circulation of 32,736, all published in the week ending 23 October 1965, one finds that the average correspondence column takes up 72 column inches (roughly three broadsheet columns), contains eleven letters and that 16 per cent of these are signed with *noms de plume*. There is also a general pattern of decreasing space as circulation figures decrease; this pattern is broken only by the *Hereford Times*, much of whose correspondence will be 'taken over' by its fellow newspaper, the *Hereford Evening News*. Some familiar *noms de plume* occurred within this sample: 'Fair and Square' and 'Angry

Table 12

Newspaper, size of circulation and publication date	Total of letters	Noms de plume	Total of column inches
Surrey Advertiser (57,972) 23 October 1965	13	1	100
Rochdale Observer (37,497) 23 October 1965	17	6	100
Hereford Times (32,024) 22 October 1965	3	0	15
Cheshire Observer (28,220) 22 October 1965	16	2	97
Mid-Devon Advertiser (7,970) 23 October 1965	7	0	49

Rochdalian' (*Rochdale Observer*), 'O.A.P.' (*Cheshire Observer*) and 'Disgusted Guildford Resident' (*Surrey Advertiser*).

Table 13 shows the comparative figures for a sample of evening newspapers published on Wednesday 28 June 1967. The tabulation shows that the correspondence column is roughly similar in size in

Table 13

Newspaper and 1964 circulation	Total of letters	Noms de plume	Total of column inches
Yorkshire Evening Post (314,343)	6	3	25
Newcastle *Evening Chronicle* (244,433)	6	1	27
Nottingham *Evening Post* (not available)	14	4*	58
Bolton *Evening News* (88,107)	6	0	36
Cambridge Evening News (37,730)	5	3	36

* Not including two letters signed with initials.

large, medium and small evening newspapers; the only exception was the Nottingham *Evening Post*. In the case of the four other papers the column is located on the leader page—a placing that indicates the high degree of reader interest it is assumed to command as well as its importance, in the editor's view, as content. This leader page location results in a necessary limitation of space for readers' letters —a consideration that does not apply to the Nottingham *Evening Post*, which, on the day selected, used two separate pages for correspondence.

The average number of letters published in the evening newspaper sample was seven (compared with eleven for the weeklies); these took up an average of 36 column inches (compared with 72 column inches in the weeklies). Three reasons which would account for the differences here are: (1) the greater pressure on space in the case of the typical evening newspaper, as explained above, (2) the greater tolerance shown to lengthy letters and protracted debate shown by the weekly Press and (3) the evening newspaper's higher frequency of publication.

The proportion of writers using *noms de plume* was higher, on average, in the evening than in the weekly Press—30 per cent as against 16 per cent. The convention of anonymity appears to be more acceptable in large than in small communities; signed letters in the weekly Press not infrequently accuse anonymous protesters or controversialists of moral cowardice. An instance of this occurred in the weekly *Buxton Advertiser* in 1966, when a correspondent noted his 'distaste for the sort of person who writes anonymous letters to the Press'. He continued:

> Such a practice may be the result of 'moral cowardice,' but when the cover of a pen name is used to launch personal attacks and to hand out gratuitous abuse in the manner of 'Anti-Caucus' (February 18) then I feel that for such conduct, the term 'moral cowardice' is too kindly a description . . .[7]

But in spite of this evidence (and many more examples could be cited) of preference for signed letters, the majority of editors are clearly prepared to accept, and many correspondents continue to use, *noms de plume*. This convention will certainly continue; no evening newspaper editor would lightly risk the loss of as much as a third of his correspondence through its rejection. Accordingly, such *noms de plume* as 'A Very Angry Mum' and 'Puzzled' (*Cambridge Evening News*), 'Ratepayer' (Newcastle *Evening Chronicle*), 'Bird

Lover' (*Yorkshire Evening Post*) and 'Livan Letliv' (Nottingham *Evening Post*), all of which appeared in the issues specified in Table 13, will go on enjoying currency. In this respect the provincial newspaper correspondence column differs from that of the national 'quality' dailies, where the use of *noms de plume* is rare. There are, of course, other obvious differences; there is the common bond of local reference in many of the letters in a provincial column, and more emphasis on specific complaints than on general theoretical contention. But there is an important similarity, in that in both types of newspaper the bulk of the correspondence is serious as opposed to frivolous, and appears to result from genuine feelings or convictions. The provincial column is not yoked to the chatty, anecdotal image sought by the *Sunday Express* and *The People*—the latter paying a guinea for every published letter, and dividing the correspondence into such categories as 'Life', 'Lesson' and 'Laughter'.[8] Typically, local Press letter columns are given a straightforward title like 'Letters to the editor' or 'Our letter bag'; there is nothing comparable to the *Daily Mirror*'s 'Live Letters conducted by the Old Codgers'. The *Leicester Mercury* is the only provincial newspaper known to the writer that has attempted to popularise the column by means of presentational techniques. It is headed 'Your page four' and one letter is selected for illustration in the form of a bold, eye-arresting cartoon; in the issue of 28 June 1967 the cartoon accounted for 12 of the 46 column inches allotted to the correspondence section. But the *Mercury* is exceptional; the vast majority of provincial editors rely on the intrinsic appeal of the letters themselves—an appeal that correspondents like 'Not So Bold' point out from time to time: 'Readers' letters, in my opinion, are the most entertaining part of any newspaper. . . .'[9]

In the sections that follow, the nature of the letter of protest and the letter of argument is clarified in detail. The function of the correspondence column is not, of course, limited to these categories; it also acts as a platform for making appeals, expressing thanks, recollecting past events, effecting corrections, disseminating information, praise—and so on. But protest and argument certainly predominate, and it is appropriate that they should receive most consideration.

Letters of protest

The letter of protest, or expression of exasperation, arises from a sense of grievance towards some local or national group that is perceived as carrying the main responsibility for inadequacies in the environment, defects in services felt to be essential, or unwanted inroads into the weekly wage packet. The phrasing of such letters into terms suitable for publication must often sorely tax the unpractised writer even though he will have pondered his subject inwardly; an oral version, perhaps earthy, perhaps not, is unlikely to be suitable for direct transcription. Even so, the provision of concrete detail—however dressed up—makes many letters of protest highly interesting to local communities. Their readers can in any case translate obvious circumlocutions back into the colloquial idiom they would privately adopt.

From the letters of protest both newspaper staff and the readership become familiar with the nature and extent of specific local grievances. A preponderance of such letters in the correspondence column will result in an overall tone identifiable with the gripe, grouse and grumble. From time to time one comes across a reader protesting about the heavy quota of protest, as in this extract from a letter to the *Leicester Mercury*:

> . . . Are Leicester people (and I am one born and bred) so obsessed with grumbles and grouses that no one wishes to record the pleasant things done by others that happen in life?
>
> Could not Page Four in 1966 be devoted, say, once a fortnight, to reporting the happier side of people's dealings with each other—or is it still true that good news is no news . . .?[10]

An editorial footnote to this letter served to validate the correspondent's impression: '. . . Nothing delights us more than that rarity, a cheerful, optimistic, glad-to-be-alive letter but, all too often, it's the grumbles and groans that occupy most space in our postbags. . . .' The chatty, matey tone here combines with the daily cartoon already noted to confer a popular image on the column; the implication is that it is not to be thought of as an austere platform for local Polonius figures, but as—ideally—a mixture of gay and serious moods.

The subjects about which readers grumble and grouse are numerous and familiar; almost all weekly and evening newspapers intermittently publish letters about transport services (perhaps buses that

"I'm going to make an example of you—no television for fourteen days!"

TOUGH IN PRISON 60 YEARS AGO

WHEN I was fifteen, working as a dray boy, my drayman took a heavy load of railway sleepers into Welford Road prison. One poor thin fellow there couldn't lift his end and he received a swipe that knocked him flying.

Across the open yard I saw men wearing goggles and sitting in brick cubicles breaking stones. All they had to eat was skilly. If they didn't break enough stones they had bread and water. That was hard labour. This all happened 60 years ago, and I have always avoided those places since. Even if they wanted to pamper me I wouldn't ever want to be a prisoner there.

MR. TAYLOR,
163, Humberstone Road,
Leicester.

Treaty of Rome another D-Notice document?

FOR some months I have been endeavouring to obtain a copy of the Treaty of Rome. Eventually I found that the Confederation of British Industry had produced a copy in English, but my hopes were short lived for my bookseller reported that the publication had sold out and no reprint is contemplated.

The Treaty of Rome is not a confidential or secret document—or should not be so. It is vital that every person should know fully what the government is trying to commit the British people to, without the people being aware of its implications.

It is a source of some concern to a large section of the public that one cannot read the actual treaty, which is vastly different from a correspondent's version by reason of varying interpretation.

Why has no newspaper published the actual Treaty of Rome—even as a series? For though it may not be as spectacular as a crime report, it is certainly of greater concern to every thinking member of the public.

Or is the Treaty of Rome the subject of another D notice?
CONCERNED.

WARMER, PLEASE

SEVERAL readers have recently called attention to the faults of St. Margaret's Swimming Baths. I wonder how many people, like myself, would gladly pay a higher admission fee in return for a slightly warmer bathe? This applies to all the Leicester baths.
TROPICAL FISH.

Fig. 7 Part of the correspondence column of the *Leicester Mercury*, 29 June 1967. *By courtesy of the Leicester Mercury*

are too infrequent, or too expensive, or that fail to stop) or noise (dogs, radios, motor-cycles, aircraft, pop groups, etc.) or roads (unmade or continually being excavated) or offending sections of the community (the town council, the directors and/or manager of the local football club, price-raising hairdressers, negligent dog-owners, etc.) or money (rising rates or taxes, the cost of living, inadequate pensions, wage claims)—and so on. The list could be vastly extended, but detailed discussion must of necessity focus on one typical area of complaint; the area in question is the alleged autocracy, incompetence or negligence of local government authorities.

The local council and its officers, as decision-takers, constitute a prominent focus for the local Press correspondent. What the popular attitudes to the town council in reality are is a matter for guesswork and hunch; but a number of long-standing assumptions, such as that the council is a means of extending business or professional contacts and that those who sit on it are 'on the make', clearly enjoy wide currency. This attitude does not generally extend to the mayor or senior aldermen known—through the local Press—to have given long and conscientious service to the community. The version of local government that predominantly emerges from the correspondence column is that, as a totality, it is a sphere of 'officialdom'; it is felt to contain latent autocratic or pompous attitudes ever ready to erupt. It is seen as lacking a proper sense of priorities, so that its decisions need careful and sceptical scrutiny; these may well be misguided if not downright wrong. The council is harangued as the body that raises the rates, and 'deplored' whenever it is reported as involved in personality clashes or walk-outs. These are some of the images that cling to it, and they open up a marked contrast to the image postulated by council spokesmen in the euphoric atmosphere of mayor-making day.

The sense that many rate-payers have of officialdom (extending to income tax inspectors, traffic wardens, some kinds of PRO, and so on) is of an absence of sympathy for the particular case; the system, the general and accepted procedure, is what counts, and irregularities have to be regularised at all costs. This sense is fully conveyed in the following letter to the *Mid-Devon Advertiser*:

An Ashburton complaint

Sir,—This week, observing an overflow from an inspection cover of a drain, I went to the local council office to report same.

While in the enquiry office reporting same the local surveyor passed through to his office. I said to him: 'I thought it might be a danger to health,' and before I could finish the sentence with the words 'that is why I have come to report it,' I was told by the surveyor that was his business in a very superior tone upon which he entered his office, pulling the door behind him.

I wrote to the council complaining about the tone in which I was spoken to. My letter was taken in committee and I received from the clerk a reply as follows: 'I am directed by the council to acknowledge receipt of your letter, addressed to the chairman and members, dated the 12th instant, and to say the council have every confidence in their surveyor.'

There was no apology for a ratepayer reporting what was considered a public duty being spoken to in such a manner nor any hint of encouragement for reporting anything considered advisable.[11]

The hostile attitude evinced by this correspondent is the one that many writers assume when referring to local councils. He has a double complaint; there is the 'very superior tone' of the local surveyor, interrupting his sentence before closing the door on him, and the assent given to this tone by the clerk's 'every confidence' reply. The clerk's letter is couched in the impersonal style that lends itself to rate-payers' suspicions about their council's bureaucratic lack of sensitivity seeming confirmed. The writer himself evidently feels obliged to emulate this style; his opening sentence ('. . . I went to the local council office to report same') exactly copies the diction of a police constable giving evidence before the local Bench.

There is ample evidence that very many rate-payers hold a similarly disillusioned and testy attitude towards officialdom. This is implicit in the 'no nonsense' tone of their letters to the Press; in their invocation of significant counter-powers—the electors' votes or the hoped-for sympathy of a 'higher authority'—and in the occasional admonitory reference to a council's seemingly 'fascist' approach. The following letter to the *Rochdale Observer* adopts the hostile tone felt to be appropriate where officials or official bodies are concerned and concludes with the frequently expressed allegation that the council seems to have its priorities wrong:

Rochdale's roads

Sir,—Will you be so good as to publish a letter of complaint of inconvenience to the motoring public of this borough. I, as a ratepayer, would like to draw the attention of the appropriate authority to the appalling state of the roads of this town. Turf Hill road is appalling; potholes everywhere.

Then there is Lord Street–Blackwater Street, a total disgrace. Manholes raised 6 in to 9 in, sewer cuttings sunk and made good any old how. Cars are just brought to a stop or are swerving to miss bad potholes, causing near accidents.

. . . What with talk of increased motor taxation in the New Year let this Council stop talking of shops and market developments and let's have some of the rotten roads put right.

If the Borough Surveyor doesn't get out and about to see the state of the roads, I will meet him and give him a ride over these treacherous roads by day or night.[12]

The writer's tone and style here denote that he sees an attacking posture as necessary. Nobody is going to close a door on him if he can help it. He identifies himself ('I, as a ratepayer') with the 'motoring public of this borough'; these are the people in whose interest the 'appropriate authority' needs to act. A great deal of weight is obviously felt to attach to the word 'ratepayer'; this role is perceived —as in the previous letter—as the best credential when offering adverse criticism. He makes use of several well-worn phrases: the roads are in 'an appalling state'; one is 'a total disgrace'. 'Rotten' ('rotten roads') is a less conventional descriptive term, belonging to the colloquial list often ostracised by correspondents—many of whom clearly feel that the proprieties necessitate formality; it is reinforced by the detail and the conversational feel of 'sewer cuttings sunk and made good any old how'. His strictures relate both to the dangerous condition of the roads and to his view that the council is failing to put first things first; it should 'stop talking of shops and market developments . . . and let's have some of the rotten roads put right'. He ends, as he began, by inferring that the appropriate authority is perhaps unaware of the extent of disrepair; he adds a personal touch of humour by offering a bumpy ride to the borough surveyor.

The presence of this kind of correspondent, whom one might style the no-nonsense, down-to-earth rate-payer, has some important implications for the community and its Press. Before clarifying these, it is essential to stress yet again the similarity of the stance adopted by such protesters. The following letter from the *Crawley Observer* complained about the council's neglect of an unadopted road:

State of the roads

I would like to thank Dr. Clout for his letter to your paper with regard to the appalling conditions of St. John's Road (where I live), Ifield and

Westfield Roads. It appears that an outsider has to champion our cause for, if left to elected members of the Council, nothing would be done.

It is the C.U.D.C.'s obligation to put St. John's Road in repair, for it was they who permitted the contractors to leave this road in such a state. If no action is forthcoming from the local Council, I intend to take up the condition of St. John's Road with a higher authority.

It appears that we who live in these so-called private roads have sat back too long and taken what treatment the Council hand out without a cross word. Our rates continue to rise year after year and what do we who live in houses of these unadopted roads get in return—precisely nothing.

I suggest that any moonshine ideas that this Council have be shelved until these roads are put in repair, for they are a disgrace to the Old Town —and the new. . . .[13]

This letter is rather more formal and less specific than that from the *Rochdale Observer*, but two of the traditional protest words—'appalling' ('appalling conditions') and 'disgrace' ('they are a disgrace')— are shared. These are part of the 'big stick' armoury of letters of complaint, although constant use has reduced their intended impact. Both writers allude to 'this Council'; 'this' infers their sense of exasperation, and has a 'concealed expletive' function. The Crawley writer objects to the 'treatment' that the council 'hand out'—a phrase suggesting casualness and indifference; they are, perhaps, too preoccupied with 'moonshine ideas'. The council, like the Rochdale borough surveyor, are suspected of being too remote from local realities. The rates they levy are considered entirely in terms of one neglected road; the correspondent feels that he gets 'precisely nothing' for his steadily mounting contribution. If no action is forthcoming, then the matter will be taken up with a 'higher authority'; the town's status, it is felt, is in jeopardy.

The no-nonsense rate-payer, then, adopts an uncompromising tone; he often accuses the council of having its priorities wrong. At Rochdale it was 'shops and market developments' that the council seemed to care most about; at Crawley unspecified 'moonshine ideas' command their attention. Short shrift is given to such councils, and it is fair to speculate that a hard core of intransigent rate-payer correspondents will have no small influence on council thinking in some communities. Such correspondents will also be an important determinant of a leader writer's tone and style when he is dealing with local grievances; arguments known to be antipathetic to them will need to be firmly held and preferably yoked to some attribute—

perhaps the community's concern for an even more pressing area of need—that will assist in forestalling hostile reaction.

Returning to the general image of the town council as shaped by the correspondence column, it has been seen that autocracy is frequently suspected. Sometimes the suspicion is entertained so strongly that it is asserted as a virtual reality. This was the case in a letter to the *Farnborough Chronicle* that deplored the local council chairman's statement that 'the big stick' might have to be used if elderly people living in under-occupied houses did not move voluntarily:

Sir,—I read with surprise and some disgust of Farnborough Council's 'about turn' decision to remove elderly people from their homes, because they have not had all their rooms occupied. Perhaps it would be as well if our Council looked upon their houses not as so many units, but homes with sentimental attachment for those who have occupied them for years.

The people whom they seek to evict are of the age group that endured the years of depression, served in the last war, and have little to spare for a deposit on a permanent home even if their age did not exclude them from getting a mortgage. Surely they could be left in peace, having reared a family and made a home a haven for those of the family who may fall on bad times? As for the Chairman's remark on wielding the big stick: this smacks of Fascism. I would remind him that in a democracy people who talk like this are liable to have the stick removed from their grasp.[14]

This letter (signed 'Ratepayer') is rich in its exploration of the sensed conflict between the world of the planner/administrator and the private, personal life; it contains many widely held assumptions. The council is perceived as impersonal and unfeeling, looking on houses as units to be fully occupied rather than as homes in which particular people dwell. For homes are not felt to be easily vacated, or traded in every so often like a car; elderly people especially want to stay where they have put down roots,[15] in a place 'with sentimental attachment' that will act as a 'haven' if any member of the family needs one. The word 'haven' is a focal one, signifying calm waters after the stormy sea, rest after toil. This spokesman for the older generation feels that it has earned a haven; how often letters in the provincial Press refer to the experience of the years of depression, service in the war and the tiny profit margin to show for it all.[16] 'Ratepayer' finds it paradoxical that the local council chairman should now be alluding to 'the big stick'; the reference to fascism is the one commonly made when there seem to be omens of a Big Brother autocracy. Considerable emphasis is therefore placed on the word 'democracy'—primarily signifying, in this context, the selecting power of the voter. The petty dictator's metaphorical stick is his by an assent easily withdrawn at the next election.

It has been suggested, then, that local councils are often perceived in terms of latent or manifest autocratic tendencies—typified by that blank, impersonal officialdom so aggravating to the Newton Abbot correspondent. They seem to be sheltering behind a facade of bureaucratic defensiveness and the formal diction of 'I am directed by the council to say . . .' Where a mailed municipal fist is glimpsed writers are quick to point to parallels with fascism or the police State. The positive values held within the conventional wording and tone of protest include justice, humanity, civility and social awareness. It is felt to be imperative that people should be able to call their homes their own, have sufficient money to live in warmth and comfort, and enjoy adequate basic services. This is not to say that some letters of complaint do not manifest a blinkered ignorance or an ill-disguised self-centredness. But it is clear that the grumbling rate-payer often performs a useful watchdog function in the community, and it would not be difficult to demonstrate that he is a citizen carefully heeded in the local corridors of power.

It is appropriate at this point to recall the Rochdale letter about treacherous road surfaces; this had a distinctive, personal quality evolving from the writer's full sense of his subject and a refreshing uninhibitedness. In fact the range of subjects and styles in the *Rochdale Observer*'s correspondence column is sufficiently wide to permit writers to feel free of any need to shape their observations in a restrained, formalised mould. The result of such a sense of freedom is a column containing a small proportion of letters confused in thought and syntax, and a large number as fresh and spontaneous as any to be found in the provincial Press. Taken over an adequate period of time—say three months—the reader gains the 'feel' of a particular town where the residents do freely express their opinions, hopes, fears and grievances through the medium of the local Press. They look on their community newspaper as one that will publish quite minor complaints, like the account by 'Angry Rochdalian' of how a parcel posted to him ended up by crashing onto his cellar floor. The letter that follows is a protest drawing deeply on descriptive detail; it has a poetic quality and bodies forth the full texture of a district. It was signed by seven householders, five of them housewives. Adopting the customary distant stance towards

the local council, it puts predictable emphasis on the theoretical
rights of rate-payers:

Church Street protest

Sir,—Regarding the heaps of coke dust opposite our houses, the manager
of the North Western Gas Board informs us that it is a matter that concerns the Council. So let the Council concerned do something about this
nuisance. Besides having to put up with this we have to put up with the
constant whir of machinery the whole night through. Also the people who
are working all week, and look forward to an extra hour in bed at the
weekend are wakened from about 6.30 or 7 a.m. with the automatic
shovel piling the said coke dust up.

Even people who live as far away as New Barn Lane have complained
through the *Observer* about the smell of the gas, so you can imagine what
people in this street have to put up with. The children have easy access
now to the gas works yard and it is not so long ago when one child slipped
through the gate with a couple of his friends and fell between the gaso-
meter into the liquid and ended up in hospital.

So if the Council are interested, let them pick a dry day with a bit of a
wind blowing, and see for themselves. Then maybe they will be able to
answer the question we should all like to know: 'Is this what we in Church
Street pay our rates for?' [17]

This letter might serve as a helpful footnote to some of T. S. Eliot's
urban descriptions, which also note the smells and noises of an
industrial environment, or as a gloss on L. S. Lowry's paintings of
dark chimneys and terraced houses. There is the stark visual fact
of the heaps of coke dust; the noise of the automatic shovel in the
early hours; the 'constant whir of machinery' through the night and
the smell of gas that can be sniffed as far away as the ironically rural-
sounding New Barn Lane; the impressive stoicism of the protesters
who have 'put up with' (a phrase they use three times) all this. One
starts to visualise the children as though they might not differ greatly
from those of Dickens' Coketown—slipping, amidst the noise and
smell, into the local gasworks, there to risk falling into some noxious
liquid. This cumulative detail of the industrial scene is offered to the
council on the assumption that they are far removed from close confrontation with anything similar; tucked away in their town hall
amidst the piles of minutes and the ceremonial robes, they ought, if
'interested', to pick a dry day 'with a bit of a wind blowing' and 'see
for themselves'. The Church Street scene, it is implied, will constitute
a dose of harsh reality; after its itemised description, the question
posed to the council has an air of plaintive pathos.

One derives, then, from just two of this newspaper's letters the

exact feel of some of 'the stresses and strains of life in a highly
organised society'. There are roads from which manholes project
'6 in to 9 in', the whir of machinery, the smell of gas and the taste
of coke dust. This is a partial version of the environment, certainly,
but a version well worth having; it is one that not all local newspapers
mirror so effectively. The *Rochdale Observer*'s letters of protest are
of interest both to the local reader and the outsider; they are fresh
and uninhibitedly detailed, and relatively free of the conventional
euphemisms or hyperboles that appear in many provincial newspaper
letter columns. The reasons why this newspaper's correspondence is
so lively and varied would be complex ones to resolve. But they
must relate to a continuing and concerned interest, over several
decades, of the newspaper in its readership; the *Rochdale Observer*
is clearly regarded by rate-payers 'as a means by which they can draw
attention to matters which they think want putting right'.[18] Its
correspondents are drawn from all social classes, and therefore reflect
the fact of a local 'mass' readership.

It has been shown that the characteristic tone of the letters cited
is one of assertive, uncompromising denunciation. Instances of leading columns adopting this tone do occur, but they are not typical;
their usual speaking voice is one of gentle persuasion. Yet the complaining rate-payer can exercise considerable influence, through the
correspondence column, on both the newspaper's and the local
council's attitudes. His presence would, for example, account for the
Wolverhampton *Express and Star*'s support for the creation of local
ombudsmen; part of this newspaper's argument constitutes a recognition of the validity of some at least of the protesting rate-payer's
assumptions and charges:

Watch Dogs

... Too many complaints by ratepayers are lost in the pipelines or get
bandied about in the corridors of local power. Councillors often get tired
of trivial, unjustified complaints and may fail to recognise a legitimate
one. Local authorities can be hyper-sensitive about what they regard as
bad publicity and are easily put on the defensive.
   If the errors of local authorities are comparatively small, 'they are
onerous enough to the little man who suffers them'. Local ombudsmen
would reassure the public that a local authority is not a law unto itself.[19]

The criticisms offered in the first paragraph—of the dilatoriness and
bureaucratic defensiveness of local government—are amongst the
criticisms made by the correspondents referred to above.

Letters of argument

1. The letter-writing 'regular' Although letters on current controversies—such as comprehensive education, water fluoridation, fox
hunting and so on—tend to come from a range of contributors
(worried parents, spokesmen for local or national organisations and
individual or group counter-spokesmen), much debate and argument
is found, after long-term scrutiny, to have been initiated by 'regulars'
—those correspondents who submit letters at fairly frequent inter-
vals. They attract both praise and censure—the censure being
directed very often at their tendency to handle argument with a bold,
assertive flourish that does not allow for fine discriminations. The
regular is analogous to the man who will always have his say at a
debating society, offering predictable opinions in predictable language. Such a debater is usually felt to be of value—partly as a
stimulus, partly as a foil and partly as a character in his own right.
His letter-writing equivalent shares all these attributes and may ultimately command considerable affection—the kind accorded to some
of the long-standing panel members of a radio series like 'Any
questions'. He may be a bit 'cranky' but his provocative, personal
note is felt to warrant attention.

The regular letter-writer, however, has a significance that extends
far beyond considerations of his local image. In some respects, the
majority of regulars conform to a general pattern; although often
not formally educated beyond the point of adequate literacy, they
share a deep interest in the diagnosis of society from some particular
moral standpoint. Moreover, they feel impelled to communicate
their findings; Mr Fred Fletcher (a *Buxton Advertiser* regular) has
stated that 'my main reason for writing to the papers is simply
because I have to',[20] while Mr Francis B. Willmott (a contributor to
the *Birmingham Evening Mail*) is also prompted by powerful feelings:
'I feel impelled to write on many issues of the day, just as I feel
compelled to get up and speak at meetings. . . .'[21]

Many such writers tend to hark back to the 'good old days';
they see society as a decaying organism—the sentiment orally expressed as 'I don't know what the country's coming to'. The national
Press and television are regarded as important agencies in this de-
terioration; the media as a whole are felt to be partly responsible
for the incidence of juvenile delinquency and the sensed decline
in public morals and standards. While in general endorsing the

Protestant ethic, some of them feel that the Church has lost touch with day-to-day life; they would like to see Church and State activated by fundamental religious principles. The nation's political life is perceived as increasingly ineffectual; politicians are now mere television 'personalities' or fodder for opinion polls. Sir Winston Churchill is frequently cited as a paragon against whom puny successors can be measured. Thus Mr Fletcher refers to 'the great gap torn in our public life by the passing of Sir Winston',[9] while Arthur Houghton, a frequent writer to the *Lancashire Evening Post*, has suggested that we now have no party leader who can inspire the people in the event of some national emergency: 'I cannot help wondering if we have seen the last of truly great men at Westminster. How we need a Gladstone, a Lloyd George or a Sir Winston Churchill!'[22] National prestige is seen as diminished and diminishing; there is a manifest longing for the country to be as pre-eminent in moral influence as it was felt to have been in the dark days of 1940. But the horizon seems clouded by crooks, scroungers and idle lay-abouts, as well as the more disaffected members of the younger generation; to these the regulars advise hard work and the virtues of the busy life. Like Benjamin Franklin, they advocate 'industry': 'Lose no time; be always employed in something useful; cut off all unnecessary actions.'[23]

Thus, although these correspondents may differ in political affiliation or religious attachment, they are united in their preoccupation with social diagnosis and improvement. They discern significant tendencies in their immediate localities, and base their cases on these. Some readers resent their confident, generalising assertiveness. One Buxton correspondent ('Interested') asks: 'I wonder how many of your readers, like myself, are getting a little tired of Fred Fletcher always being right, and his opponents always wrong?'[24] The *Lancashire Evening Post* 'regular' referred to has also provoked antipathy: 'Arthur Houghton, besides reading his Bible after breakfast, also writes letters to your newspaper with monotonous regularity. . . . Garstang's self-appointed dove of peace twitters unceasingly and I am heartily sick of it.'[25] But these writers also have their admirers, and slowly establish themselves as local characters; when one leaves the newspaper's circulation area, the fact of community solidarity asserts itself and even former opponents may pen a parting tribute—like this one from the *Tamworth Herald* correspondence column:

. . . It is sad to find a friend leaving the town, especially one with whom one has amicably crossed swords in your columns. Such is the case this week with Mr. G. Cleeton. Alas, we may never see his like again! . . . In the field of information as Mrs. Beeton was to Cookery, so Mr. Cleeton was to Quakery. It only remains to wish him well and a Merry Christmas— as to all good-deeders (and feeders).[26]

This extract shows how a prolific 'regular' carves a niche for himself in community life. How is one to gauge his influence? It would be unwise to dismiss such correspondents as isolated cranks or axe-grinders, even if some or all of their opinions prove unpalatable. Such descriptions would, of course, apply to the least thoughtful and most bigoted writers of their type. The 'regulars' speak particularly for the intelligent layman born before, say, 1920, and for those of any age who share their leading assumptions. It is in their representativeness of a particular sector of local life that they may exert a subtle, telling influence on the provincial newspaper; they act as a constant reminder of attitudes that tend to be overlooked in the national popular Press, with its involvement in transient fads and fancies. The perceptive 'regular', taking the long view of life that he typically does, may be unrecognisedly influential as an opinion former or—more probably—entrencher.

2. Letters of topical argument It is the correspondents who take sides in current controversies who will most attract such descriptions as axe-grinding or tub-thumping to their column. Amongst the recurring subjects to have been argued out during the period of survey are watch committee censorship, water fluoridation, comprehensive education and immigration quotas—the last two often being discussed from a party political standpoint. It is probable that local newspaper controversy of this type is taken by most readers with a large pinch of salt; the political partisans are invariably specialising 'regulars' or local party spokesmen whose views are already known and seldom significantly modified, while the opponents and proponents in many non-political or marginally political debates are often sensed to be deterringly dogmatic, insufficiently versed in the given subject, or obvious propaganda middlemen writing on behalf of some national organisation. Although a few editors (particularly of weekly newspapers) seem prepared to afford space for particular debates for months on end, others, perhaps wisely, permit a representative airing of opinion and then, umpire-wise, declare the correspondence closed.

The distinction to be made between the controversialists and the 'regular' moralists discussed above is that the former do not establish themselves as personalities, and tend to confine themselves to one or two hobby-horses. They do, however, sometimes establish a temporary debating relationship with one or more other correspondents; a political letter (11½ column inches) in the *Cheshire Observer* concluded its pro-Conservative tack by pointing to such a relationship and requesting its termination:

> ... I am a three-course man, and having now consumed, with editorial indulgence, my quota in these columns I now set aside my knife and fork, whatever tempting savoury Mr. Brown may offer me next week. It is so monotonous to dine regularly at the same place every fortnight, and the same waiter breathing down one's neck is so boring. May I have my bill, please?[27]

This letter, signed F. Essex Moorcroft, notes the risk of tedium in protracted discussions; the leisurely pace at which the dining metaphor is developed would itself not be acceptable to evening newspapers, pressed as they are for space, or to weeklies striving to project a progressive image. Letters of this rather old-fashioned kind are published in only a few weeklies, generally circulating in areas where there is a significant number of retired readers with the necessary leisure to follow them.

Most of the straightforward political letters shuffle the standard pack of dogmas and platitudes in an assertive, generalising manner. Often, some favourite Aunt Sally is set up for knocking down, as when a writer to the *Southport Visiter* looked back on the 1964 general election:

> ... Political fervour excites oratorical excesses, and Mr. Quintin Hogg's stentorian battle cry, 'Stark, staring bonkers,' will be construed in political history as the classic utterance of the twentieth century, and for himself gain an immortal place among the jesters of the world ...[28]

There is an excited, exaggerating approach to the subject here, and a fondness for sonorous adjectives: 'oratorical ... stentorian ... classic ... immortal'. The correspondent went on to refer to the Tories' 'mock indignation' when the Labour government did not increase old age pensions immediately as 'just a load of hypocritical humbug'. Demagogic tub-thumping of this kind is tediously predictable; one would expect only the most narrowly partisan readers to respond to it with any enthusiasm. The freshness and local topicality of the letter of protest and the sometimes endearing idiosyncrasies of the true 'regular' are missing; the content is essentially hackneyed.

Turning to a non-political theme, it is apparent that the profuse and widespread correspondence on water fluoridation has taken place amidst public apathy. Although most of the letters published argue against fluoridation, the campaign does not seem to have generated enthusiasm except in isolated pockets. The contentions advanced sound scary enough: 'Sodium fluoride is a caustic rat poison which accumulates in the bones of our body and often damages the kidneys and thyroid gland . . .';[29] 'Fluoridation is the beginning of a system which could allow other additives to water because a group of people think it is good for us.'[30] These seem to be the two main planks in the argument against fluoridation, with much of the factual data no doubt supplied by the National Pure Water Association. But popular trust in medical science is evidently too deep-rooted to be thus dislodged; a token oral assent may be prompted ('Quite right; they shouldn't mess about with the water'), but no arousal leading to sustained, committed campaigning. Only a tiny minority would become as perturbed as Blackpool's 'Anti-Fluoride': 'I, for one, shall leave the town if this risk to health is taken and go elsewhere, possibly to Manchester, where in their wisdom the city council has turned down this proposition.'[31] It would need some startling evidence of deleterious effects to give the anti-fluoride movement the necessary impetus for creating widespread militancy.

Other controversies will come and go as company for the perennial political debate. In spite of the obvious limitations of much of the argument conducted in the provincial Press, the correspondence column would certainly lose some of its distinctive character if the range of controversialists—including the cranks, axe-grinders and tub-thumpers—were to lay down their pens. As part (but preferably only part) of the total mix of letters, they may serve to stimulate public interest in, and debate about, particular issues. Their potentially useful function should not, therefore, be superciliously or jocularly dismissed.

The discussion of provincial newspaper correspondence has focused on three of the distinctive types of letter, namely, those submitted by protesters, moralising 'regulars' and controversialists. Their letters by no means constitute the entire range of published cor-respondence, which, as already noted, includes national and local appeals, appreciations, corrections and various kinds of information.

All the letters considered enable both the Press and the readership to keep an ear to the ground and listen in to some of the leading themes of local conversation. They learn about defects (major and minor) in the environment and public services; they are assisted in gauging the public mood towards local institutions and other com-munity groups; they obtain the long moral view of the 'regular' on social issues and changes, and the reactions to him; they learn about the extent to which current controversies are commanding local attention, and where readers' sympathies lie. The local news-paper, therefore, learns a great deal of value; moreover, its selection from incoming correspondence is known to command high reader interest. And no doubt all local newspapers are pleased to receive tributes—versified or not—like this one to the *Manchester Evening News*, published on 28 August 1970:

Farewell and hail

Before you bid Cross Street 'Adieu,'
May I enjoy last words with you?
'Tis 60 years ago, or more,
Since first I started to explore
EN's live columns, rich and rare,
In current news and sporting fare;
With you I've laughed and cried in turn,
Seen City grow and City burn;
Always you've mirrored life around,
In perspective, true and sound.
I hope that in your new-found state,
In Deansgate, sales will escalate,
So that the prestige of your paper
Will reach as high as a skyscraper:
And with experience rich and ripe
EN will always be true to type.

Notes

1 *Memoranda of Evidence*, p. 130.
2 Darlington *Evening Dispatch*, 4 September 1964.
3 *Rochdale Observer*, 11 December 1965.
4 *Memoranda of Evidence*, p. 167.
5 *Ibid.*, p. 93.

6 Sir Linton Andrews, *Problems of an Editor* (London: Oxford University Press, 1962), p. 25.
7 *Buxton Advertiser*, 25 February 1966.
8 E.g. *The People*, 22 October 1967.
9 *Buxton Advertiser*, 22 October 1965.
10 *Leicester Mercury*, 10 January 1966.
11 *Mid-Devon Advertiser*, 22 October 1965.
12 *Rochdale Observer*, 8 January 1966.
13 *Crawley and District Observer*, 11 December 1964.
14 *Farnborough Chronicle*, 4 December 1964.
15 Cf. pp. 95, 190.
16 The frequency of letters from despondent pensioners must have been a major factor behind the *Manchester Evening News*'s series of features —'Pensioner's week'—in the issues of 18–22 January 1971. In a forceful 'watchdog' leader of 22 January the *News* concluded: 'From our study this week of the plight of the pensioners, one fact stands out. The old people of Britain are in desperate trouble . . . No excuses about money we cannot afford, or the time needed to pay out, are valid . . .'
17 *Rochdale Observer*, 23 October 1965.
18 *Memoranda of Evidence*, p. 94 (the Holmesdale Press Ltd).
19 Wolverhampton *Express and Star*, 28 June 1967.
20 *Buxton Advertiser*, 18 February 1966.
21 *Birmingham Evening Mail*, 15 February 1966.
22 *Lancashire Evening Post*, 12 October 1965.
23 Benjamin Franklin, *Autobiography* (New York: Rinehart, 1956), p. 84.
24 *Buxton Advertiser*, 10 December 1965.
25 *Lancashire Evening Post*, 20 January 1964.
26 *Tamworth Herald*, 18 December 1964.
27 *Cheshire Observer*, 26 March 1965.
28 *Southport Visiter*, 5 December 1964.
29 *West Lancashire Evening Gazette*, 23 February 1966.
30 *Lancashire Evening Post*, 28 October 1965.
31 *West Lancashire Evening Gazette*, 25 February 1966.

9 Features

1. The distribution of feature space

In order to determine how much space feature articles—the 'Town Diary' excepted—take up in the provincial evening Press, and how this space is distributed into specific categories, an analysis was made of the features in eight newspapers for the week of 10–17 January 1966. These were the *Birmingham Evening Mail*, Bolton *Evening News*, Bristol *Evening Post*, *Cambridge Evening News*, *Huddersfield Daily Examiner*, *Oxford Mail*, *West Lancashire Evening Gazette* and *Yorkshire Evening Post*. They were selected because they provided a wide range of locations and circulation sizes. The total numbers of column inches taken up by features ranged from 2,541 (Bristol *Evening Post*) to 920 (*West Lancashire Evening Gazette*); the average for the eight newspapers was 1,624, which was almost the same figure as that for the *Yorkshire Evening Post*—1,620. (See fig. 8(I).)

Each newspaper's features were classified into nineteen categories. Three main ones stood out: cultural subjects, consumer interest and local life—including locally connected people and local institutions, amenities or services. Cultural subjects (i.e. discussion of television, films, theatre, music, books, art, etc.) took up an average of 24 per cent of all feature space (see fig. 8(II) (*b*)). The range was from 46 per cent of the *Oxford Mail*'s feature space to 16 per cent of the Bristol *Evening Post*'s. Features of interest to the consumer accounted for an average of 21 per cent of all feature space; the range was from 31 per cent (*Cambridge Evening News*) to 13 per cent (Bristol *Evening Post* and *Yorkshire Evening Post*), as shown in fig. 8(II) (*a*). Features about local life accounted for an average of 17 per cent of all feature space; the range was from 31 per cent (*West Lancashire Evening Gazette*) to 5 per cent (*Oxford Mail*), as shown in fig. 8(II) (*c*). The three categories took up an average of 62 per cent of the total feature space in the eight newspapers.

Although these percentages are based on a one week's issues, they do have considerable representative validity; the majority of features recur each week and command roughly constant space. Both writers and readers welcome a high degree of continuity in this as in other aspects of their newspapers. The factors that account for the different emphases apparent in fig. 8(II) are complex ones to tease out. An obvious one is the nature of the community served; hence the unusually high degree of attention to cultural subjects in the *Oxford Mail*. A second factor is the number of possible interpretations as to how far the feature content should represent a response to readers' assumed interests, and how far it should offer them what they may not want but what, in the editorial view, they ought to have. Thus a

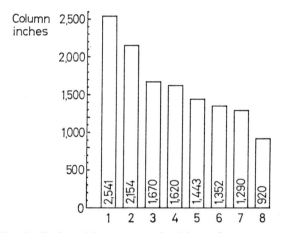

Fig. 8(I) The distribution of feature space in eight evening newspapers, 10–15 January 1966: total space taken up by features. 1 Bristol, 2 Birmingham, 3 Leeds, 4 Bolton, 5 Huddersfield, 6 Oxford, 7 Cambridge, 8 Blackpool. In order of circulation size: 2, 3, 1, 4, 8, 5, 6, 7

strong attachment to the role of educator might affect feature content as well as news values; it would account for the variations evident in fig. 8(II) (*d*) (features about national politics and/or international affairs). The 'educator' newspapers in this respect were the Bristol *Evening Post* (9 per cent of all feature space) and the *Huddersfield Daily Examiner* (7 per cent)—the only two to give this category more than 5 per cent of their features allocation. The third factor is the availability or otherwise of specialist local writers. The *West Lancashire Evening Gazette*, for instance, made good use of its assistant editor's detailed and possibly unrivalled knowledge o f loca

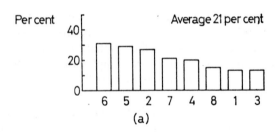

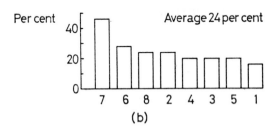

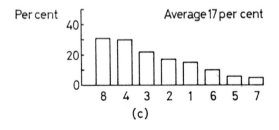

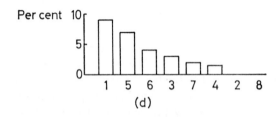

Fig. 8(II) The distribution of feature space in eight evening newspapers, 10–15 January 1966: percentage of total feature space taken up by (*a*) 'consumer interest', (*b*) cultural—TV, films, theatre, art, books, music, (*c*) local life—people, institutions, amenities, services, etc., (*d*) national political and international affairs. 1 Bristol, 2 Birmingham, 3 Leeds, 4 Bolton, 5 Huddersfield, 6 Cambridge, 7 Oxford, 8 Blackpool

rural life; his weekly feature ('In the countryside') took up almost 8 per cent of the newspaper's feature space. This was not included in the figure of 31 per cent ('local life') cited above.

Obviously, particular subject emphases (and the quality of the material offered) are bound to act as an important determinant of many readers' sense of their newspaper's 'personality'—its interests and values. If these interests and values are to a large extent shared by a reader, he or she will feel that the local newspaper is a kindred spirit. It is probable that the average percentages for the three categories (cultural subjects 24 per cent, consumer interest 21 per cent and local life 17 per cent) roughly correspond to the average

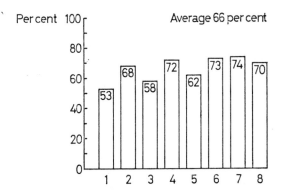

Fig. 8(III) The distribution of feature space in eight evening newspapers, 10–15 January 1966: percentage of total feature space taken up by categories (*a*)–(*d*) in fig. 8(II). 1 Bristol, 2 Birmingham, 3 Leeds, 4 Bolton, 5 Huddersfield, 6 Cambridge, 7 Oxford, 8 Blackpool

reader's preferences, although the quantity of consumer interest features will also be influenced by the Press's desire to co-operate with advertisers. The *Birmingham Evening Mail* emerges as the newspaper that comes closest to the average if all three categories are considered (cultural subjects 24 per cent, consumer interest 27 per cent and local life 17 per cent).

As the content of 'consumer interest' features is illustrated and discussed in the next chapter, it is the feature about some aspect of local life on which this chapter will primarily focus. For it is in its provision of such features—and of local news, comment and advertising—that the provincial Press fulfils its least dispensable role.

Broadly speaking, these features perform one or other of the four functions cited in the chapters on news and leading columns—the functions of reflector, booster, watchdog and pump-primer. One's immediate purpose is not to attempt to elicit the apparent functional preferences of particular newspapers, since this would necessitate a number of long-term studies; rather, it is to point out the main kinds of locally rooted feature that emerged from the sample as a whole, and so to show in some detail how local life is explored.

2. Some types of locally rooted feature article

(a) Reflector features The reflector function characterises features about local history; these may serve to sharpen a reader's sense of his community's particularity. Two historical features were published by the *West Lancashire Evening Gazette* during the period of survey—'Churches of the Fylde' and 'How it all began' (A. F. Warner). Both were part of a series.

'Churches of the Fylde' was a full tabloid page feature containing 65 column inches of visuals (e.g. 'LEFT: The vicar with the pewter flagons believed to date from 1766') and $15\frac{1}{2}$ column inches of text, not including headlines. The text opened by noting that the church might easily go unnoticed by the passer-by:

It is easy to go past St. James's Church, Stalmine, without noticing it. There is no high tower or spire to guide you and it stands back from the road partly hidden behind the high brick wall of the old hall and partly obscured by the Seven Stars Hotel . . .[1]

But the church had a long history, dating at least as far back as the thirteenth century. 'There was probably a church there when King John sealed Magna Carta in 1215—and before.' Details of the church registers (dating back to 1583), the church plate ('Notable for its three silver chalices'), a pair of pewter flagons on the steps of the modern font, and of the shaft of an old cross dated 1690 ('later made into a sundial') were included in the account. Photographs of the chalices, pewter flagons and sundial accompanied the text. The feature's appeal can be seen as multi-faceted; the reader interested in the Church of England, or in antiques, or in local history as such, would learn much of interest. In this way the term 'Fylde'—in most of which the *Gazette* circulates—is invested with additional enriching connotations.

The second feature, by the local historian A. F. Warner, was one of a series on the development of Blackpool town hall. Headlined 'Ratepayers miss a golden chance', its implications extended beyond the mere recording of fact. It lent its support to the view often advanced in provincial newspaper leaders that parsimony today may lead to even greater, and unavoidable, expenditure tomorrow. The writer had used previous files of the *Gazette*, for 1891, as his primary source; the article concerned a proposed scheme for a civic centre on a 5,000 square-yard site which was rejected by a large majority of the 2,000 rate-payers (out of the then population of 21,000) present at a meeting held at the Prince of Wales Theatre on 2 February 1891. A. F. Warner assessed this rejection as 'a great chance missed. That area now forms part of the Central Development Plan and its value today must be colossal.'[2] His account had a further implication, in that it shows how the locally held assumption that Blackpool is a progressive town and resort (the town motto is 'Progress') is one of long standing:

> The Mayor, Ald. John Bickerstaffe, who presided, described how the municipal offices were scattered throughout the town.
> He said their 'so-called Town Hall' was a disgrace to a progressive and popular place like Blackpool.
> So keen was the feeling in the town over the proposal that the speeches lasted more than six hours and filled eight columns of *The Gazette*.
> Proceedings were particularly lively, with hissing, booing and constant interruptions.[2]

The mayor's appeal to his concept of an ideal community image, however, was unable to compete with an appeal to the rate-payers' pockets—a conflict often to be found at the heart of contemporary town council debates. Thus Alderman Dr McNaughtan urged that support of the proposal would be 'to toss his money and the money of his grandchildren to the winds'.

The reader of a feature of this kind is bound to have his sense of a distinctive community identity deepened. He is made aware of the factors—the attitudes and assumptions—that have helped to shape the environment as he knows it, and he is thereby more able to appreciate leading column allusions to his town's past history and current performance. It is, of course, the permanently rooted provincial writer—whether staff or freelance—on whom the cultivation of historical awareness depends; it can hardly be adequately fostered by the mobile, Fleet Street-aiming journalist of some 'chain' circuit.

(b) Booster features For an individual to become the subject of a provincial newspaper 'booster' feature, the achievement of success or the display of notable enterprise are, in the majority of cases, necessary conditions. Most individual 'booster' features concern various types of local hero: the successful sportsman, the defeater of adverse circumstances, or the champion of some local cause. Seventeen features about individual people were published in the newspapers sampled; these were classified under seven headings:

(A) *Career women* (including voluntary workers)

1. 'She is London's traffic boss' (Bristol *Evening Post*).
2. 'Daphne Hubbard meets four women whose ambitions stretch far beyond being successful housewives' (Bristol *Evening Post*).
3. 'The helpers, No. 2. It's six days a week for Mrs Rickaby' (*Yorkshire Evening Post*).
4. 'Their helping hand to those in need' (*West Lancashire Evening Gazette*).

(B) *Career Men* (including politicians, excluding sportsmen)

1. 'A day in the life of . . . a brewery chief' (*Oxford Mail*).
2. 'Close-up: from mumbling child to TV fame' (Bolton *Evening News*).
3. 'Meeting people: Don Quixote of local politics' (*Yorkshire Evening Post*).

(C) *Local sportsmen*

1. 'Midland trio who tweaked the kangaroo's tail' (*Birmingham Evening Mail*).
2. 'Jack and Bobby' (*Yorkshire Evening Post*).

(D) *Local artists, novelists, hobby specialists*

1. 'A rival to Bond' (*Yorkshire Evening Post*).
2. 'Starting off with some old water colours . . .' (*Huddersfield Daily Examiner*).
3. 'One man's world: yes, they all have feathers' (Bolton *Evening News*).

(E) *Defeaters of adversity*

   1. 'Finger on a dish guides the spoon' (*Cambridge Evening News.* Also B3 and D2 above).

(F) *Sentimental*

   1. 'No Bridge of Sighs . . .' (Bristol *Evening Post*).

(G) *Miscellaneous*

   1. 'The incomers: No. 50—Britain gave her a surprise' (*Yorkshire Evening Post*).

   2. 'A house in California is her aim' (*West Lancashire Evening Gazette*)

   3. 'The woman of Caius praises her hosts' (*Cambridge Evening News*).

Career success or outstanding service prompted ten of the seventeen features; a further two focused on the achievements of a spare-time ornithologist (D3) and an artist (D2). Those enjoying successful careers (or in process of shaping them) including the woman chairman of the Greater London Council's Highways and Traffic committee (A1), two women who had established a theatrical agency and two others an agency for selling plays to television (A2), an active member of the WVS for eighteen years (A3), two missionaries—one based in Uganda, the other in India (A4), a brewery managing director who had risen from entry as an office junior (B1), a Granada TV interviewer (B2), a member of Leeds city council serving as chairman of its transport committee (B3), three Warwickshire test cricketers (C1), two England footballers (C2), a spy fiction writer (D1), an amateur painter (D2), and an ornithologist (D3). Thus twelve of the seventeen features listed concerned locally (or regionally in the case of B2 and D1) connected people whose significance lay in personal success or achievement—whether in a full-time or part-time capacity. To these the *Cambridge Evening News* feature about a housewife who had suddenly been afflicted by blindness and yet coped outstandingly with the adversity (E1) could be added. This results in a total of thirteen (out of seventeen) features about various kinds of 'achiever'—i.e. approximately 76 per cent of all. Such features make up a common front with leading column pleas for work and service, and with the prominent attention given to 'achievers' in provincial news columns.[3]

It is quite common to find that the individuals eulogised have

attained their success in spite of a severe physical handicap. The
Leeds city councillor (B3) had had his right leg amputated after an
accident at the age of eight; the fifty-eight-year-old Huddersfield
artist had started to paint while recovering from serious injuries
received in a road accident (D2); the blind Cambridge housewife
(founder member and chairman of the Cambridge Rehabilitation
Club for the Blind) had gone blind 'almost overnight' (E1). The feature writers habitually underscore the qualities that have enabled
individuals to overcome adversities like these. The councillor, for
instance, had 'come through' a hard childhood; he had started work
at the age of thirteen in an Otley leather works for four shillings a
week. From this inauspicious beginning he had risen to become the
current chairman of four council committees. His debating style, it
was suggested, exemplified his inner courage and kindliness:

> . . . John Rafferty is as inseparable from his crutch as was Quixote from
> his ever-ready lance. And to see him at a City Council meeting, standing
> his ground defiantly on his one leg, leaning on a prop, is a sight to
> remember.
>   It is like watching a Rugby player who has made his 'mark' and stands
> his ground while the opposing pack thunders down on him. This is
> courage. And this, as well as kindness, is the hallmark of John Rafferty.[4]

The style of this passage is rather more florid (e.g. the successive
images of Don Quixote and the courageous rugby player) and rhe-
torically emphatic ('And this . . .') than the typical provincial newspaper feature. But the tone is unmistakably genial, and shows that
localness, as a value (i.e. the councillor's citizenry of, and service to,
the city of Leeds) overrides the possible consideration that the feature might assist, however modestly, the local Labour Party—the
Yorkshire Evening Post being a strongly Conservative newspaper.
  Courage in the face of adversity was also stressed in the *Cambridge
Evening News*'s feature about a blind housewife (E1); this ended as
follows:

> Obviously she has been fortunate in her family and friends who have
> not only sympathised but encouraged her, but it is entirely owing to her
> own spirit and determination that she has conquered a tragic disability
> and in doing so not only found a new life, but a richer one.[5]

Service; courage, enterprise—these are amongst the values impressed
upon the reader in the features discussed so far. Those that deal with
local artists, writers or hobby specialists often dwell on the satis-
factions that the particular pursuit can offer, and so may influence

some readers to take it up themselves. John Butterworth, the local ornithologist subject of the Bolton *Evening News*'s 'One man's world' (D3), claimed to have seen over 100 different kinds of bird inside Radcliffe's boundary—'although it took me nearly twenty years to do it'. During 1965 he had spotted ninety-two pairs of birds of twenty-six different species in a 200 acre survey area. So the environs of Bolton are not lacking in bird life, and the writer offered a tactful hint for the interested reader:

. . . Most birdwatchers start by wanting to know the names of the birds they see near home. This leads to buying a bird-book and then wanting to see other birds which are shown in the book.
This can lead on to a search for rare birds—'tally-hunting', as it is usually called—and many excellent birdwatchers do very little else . . .[6]

A feature of this kind, in which a local man shows how the local scene affords adequate scope for the pursuit of a particular hobby, could not be adequately replaced by a national newspaper equivalent; the element of localness is essential in that it clearly demonstrates that the hobby is feasible in the area where the readers live.

The features about 'achievers' afford a useful insight into the provincial newspaper's criteria for the valuation of local people. Local government service, missionary work, sport, noteworthy attainments in the arts or hobbies, and career success are amongst the subjects that have been noted. Achievements in the spheres of commerce and industry accounted for only one of the seventeen profiles—that of the brewery chief (B1). Thus, in spite of the contributions that local commerce and industry make to a newspaper's revenue, their 'achievers' can hardly be said to take pride of place in the editorial eye. (It should, however, be noted that many of the larger evening newspapers have substantially increased their coverage of business news in recent years.) This finding is paralleled in Morris Janowitz's study of three of Chicago's community newspapers:

In contrast to the alderman, the local businessman suffers somewhat as a hero in the community newspaper. . . . Businessmen and their firms and associations seem to be less often identified with expansion and development of the community than are the alderman and the city administration.[7]

The criterion of local connection means that little or no attention is paid in provincial press features to much of the staple profile material of particular national newspapers. The royal family, leading

politicians, actors, 'pop' stars, 'showbiz' personalities and society
'names' are typically debarred from detailed consideration unless
some local link supplies the necessary justification. There is an
absence, therefore, of the sort of feature headlines that follow, from
The People and the *News of the World*:

> '20 YEARS OF ROYAL MARRIAGE—and still they chat away like
> newly-weds' (*The People*, 16 July 1967).
> 'WHEN A SEX KITTEN GETS TO 33 . . . BRIGITTE talks with startling
> frankness—about BARDOT! (*The People*, 13 August 1967).
> 'Crumbs! Fame just fell in my lap—Here it is: Twiggy's own
> story' (*News of the World*, 3 December 1967).

The desideratum of conformity to family and institutional values,
combined with the criterion of localness, leads to an at most inter-
mittent interest in the rich ore of social deviation that is regularly
mined by popular nationals like *The People*. Where deviant groups
(e.g. hippies, homosexuals, prostitutes) are discussed by local newspapers, the presentation is restrained and factual and the intention
is patently to foster an informed awareness—one instance being an
Oxford Mail feature headlined 'Finding a cure for the sex offender'.[8]
The People, in contrast, dramatises its accounts of deviants; the
related headlines and much of the text correspond to the street-
seller's cry of 'Sensation! Read all about it!':

> 'NAMED . . . men who make a fat living out of the WIFE-SWAPPERS'
> (*The People*, 13 August 1967).
> 'Would you like YOUR daughter to go to parties like this?'
> (*The People*, 30 July 1967).

The latter feature described a hippie party at the Electric Garden
Club, London; its readers were kept glued to the key-hole
throughout:

> The Hippies leapt high in the air, arms flailing—and screaming at the
> tops of their voices.
> Screaming seemed to be a social asset.
> One group walked round and round screaming in blood-curdling tones.
> Then, still screaming they writhed on the floor.
>
> Eventually the 'topless' girls and their young men, now wearing only
> the scantiest of briefs, went on stage for the 'ballet' . . .

This mode of feature writing is not practised by the provincial
Press. Nor does it, at the individual level, publish features about

local people involved in activities describable as sordid. There is no provincial equivalent to a feature in *The People* about a maker of 'nasty films', headlined 'We wouldn't touch his dollars with a barge-pole!'[9] 'Sex and sensation' are deemed to be inappropriate as content by local newspaper editors; in the words of one Midlands evening newspaper editor, 'We do not consider ourselves the right medium for this sort of thing.' The reasons for this were discussed in the introductory chapter.

The sample under consideration did not contain any 'booster' features about local institutions or amenities apart from an *Oxford Mail* advertising 'puff' on behalf of Jackson the Tailor: 'New men's wear shop opens in Oxford'.[10] Features casting a favourable light on communities as a whole were also a rarity; only the *Yorkshire Evening Post*'s 'Up the Gumption!' fell into this category. It described the way in which some leading Bradford citizens perceived Bradford's identity; their comments pointed to grounds for local pride:

> We [the non-Bradfordians] long suspected that there was something peculiar about Bradford. The trouble was knowing exactly what. Now the Headmaster of Bradford Grammar School, Mr. K. D. Robinson, has kindly placed a scholastic finger on the city's pulse and come up with a diagnosis.
> The North in general, he told an old boy's dinner at his school, has fewer people who fall into the feckless category. 'Here,' said Mr. Robinson, 'the principle is quite widely accepted that a man is what he makes himself.'
> So that is Bradford: the capital of feck folk as opposed to feckless, a place where it is Up The Gumption! . . .[11]

The style of presentation here recalls the *Post* feature cited above— 'Don Quixote of local politics'. There is the same fondness for metaphor (the 'scholastic finger on the city's pulse') and for emphasis ('So that is Bradford'). The assumption explored is that Northern people as a whole, and the citizens of Bradford pre-eminently, admire the man who pulls himself up by his own boot-straps; this attitude is judged to be so pervasive that the North can be said to have fewer feckless people than, by implication, the South. Through this feature the *Post* plays back, both to the Bradford community and the region as a whole, a highly self-congratulatory opinion that has crystallised in the former and been endorsed by a key community leader. The net effect must be to reinforce the opinion. In this way the local press is helping to foster the sense of a distinctive community identity—in this respect, rightly or wrongly, an identity affording grounds for pride.

(c) Watchdog and pump-priming features The function of watchdog, which has already been clarified in chapters 6 and 7, is also fulfilled through feature articles. These occur intermittently as and when suitable subjects suggest themselves; the fact that only two out of the eight newspapers sampled included watchdog features dealing with some aspect of community life should not, therefore, be taken as implying that the other six do not publish them.

Characteristically, watchdog features deal with topics that meet two deducible requirements. First, they should interest a sizeable body of readers, and second, they should preferably not risk alienating the good will of important advertisers or opinion leaders. Features about local transport (e.g. bus or train services, parking facilities and the road system), about urban redevelopment and its effects, about parks, playgrounds and similar recreational facilities, and about the physical environment (e.g. eyesores in the form of ugly buildings, pylons, etc.) are amongst the most frequent. The official bodies involved are therefore local government and nationalised industries; the local press 'watches' these on behalf of readers in their roles of rate-payer and tax-payer. Threats to the physical environment in the form of vandals, dumpers and litter louts, and to the security of property, are further recurring subjects. There is a high degree of overlap as between the watchdog feature and the letter of protest in terms of the predominant themes.

The two newspapers to offer watchdog features during the period of survey were the *Birmingham Evening Mail* and the Bolton *Evening News*. The *Mail* ran a series of three features about the city's bus services on 12, 13 and 14 January 1966. The first one, headlined 'The queues, crushes and chaos', considered the views of some protesting passengers. 'The Midland public,' it noted, 'is currently out of love with its buses; and it is to the *Mail* that it pours out most of its complaints.' Queue-jumping, irregularity and delay, inadequate service and discomfort were amongst the principal causes of protest. The second feature ('the lost 10,000 loads a day') showed how fares had increased and the number of passengers decreased over the previous ten years. Delays had caused growing numbers of people to use cars; the additional cars made the delays even longer—and so the vicious circle continued. The final feature, 'Time for drastic action', aired some possible remedies and was therefore carrying out the function of pump-primer; it suggested that there should be special lanes for buses, radio control, television cameras covering the busiest loading points, flat-rate fares and one-man, pay-as-you-enter buses.

On 17 January 1966 the *Mail* converted its correspondence column into a 'reader's forum' on the city's bus services. Seventeen letters, taking up 87½ column inches, were published; they included further complaints, expressions of agreement with the *Mail* and alternative suggestions. One correspondent praised the newspaper for focusing on the problem:

> Thank goodness the *Mail* has looked into the present chaotic state of bus running in the city. Do the Transport Department realise how we lag behind other cities with our public transport? Their 'Service Extra' signboards alone are a laughing point. . . .

It is probable that the majority of readers of the three features would share this writer's sense of gratitude to the local press. The 'campaign' had clearly been prompted by considerable evidence of public dissatisfaction; the *Mail* was capitalising on an already existing mood. By exploring in detail the background to this mood it identifies itself with the ideals of community progress and prestige.

In the same week the Bolton *Evening News* published three watch-dog features; one complained about the number of 'eyesore' air raid shelters still surviving in the town, and another considered the effects of vandalism and general neglect on Lever Park, a favoured local spot for walks and picnics. The third explored the problems of those who live in areas undergoing redevelopment:

'Survivors' wait in dust and dirt

Once the Vernon-st. area of Bolton rang with the laughter of children at play and echoed to the bustle of life in an everyone-knows-everyone-else 'Coronation Street' world of tight-packed terraced houses.

But most of the laughter and the teeming life have fled from this corner of West Ward.

Now the days are hideous with the endless thunder of bulldozers, the eternal bonfires of crackling, smoking timbers, the clonk of sledge-hammers and the noisy cascades of crumbling old bricks into lorry after lorry, as one by one the houses are swept away under a clearance order.

Here and there in the rows of gaunt, windowless, doorless, roofless shells that once were homes, a wisp of smoke curls from a chimney over the still-curtained windows to proclaim that someone still waits for the word to move on and begin a new life.

Seventy-nine-years-old Mrs. Mary Elizabeth Redshaw, a rheumatism-plagued widow who lives alone at 41 Ainscow-st., huddled over the fire in the black-leaded grate of her tiny home and said: 'It's disgraceful. They should never have started knocking the houses down until they had found us all somewhere else to live.

'At one time folks used to call this Coronation Street. You couldn't feel lonely in those days. Everyone was so friendly and helpful, and the place was full of life. Now it's like a graveyard.

'No one has told me when I will be leaving or where I will be going. But what's going to happen to me in the meantime if I'm suddenly taken ill? I'm the only one living on this side of the street. Once I could have knocked on the wall for help from a neighbour. Now no one would hear me.' [12]

The feature sets the old order, characterised by the 'laughter of children' and the 'bustle of life', against the new one, which has brought noise, dirt and loneliness into the lives of the remaining residents. The TV programme 'Coronation Street' serves as an illustrative referent both for the writer and for Mrs Redshaw; it is seen as portraying an intimate, friendly mode of community life—one that keeps isolation and the fear of loneliness at bay. The feature mould permits a detailed analysis of the nature and effect of demolition in a redevelopment area; it serves to validate the widow's appraisal of her plight as 'disgraceful', and her view that she should have been rehoused before the demolition started.

Traditionally, watchdog features afford the right of reply to those implicitly or explicitly criticised; this one ended with the comments of Bolton's housing committee chairman:

Housing Committee Chairman Counc. James Rigby said: 'Most of the people still living in this area have already been offered alternative accommodation, but they do not wish to move if the new home is not in the area of their choice.

'Most of them want one-bedroom homes, which are in very short supply. We will rehouse them all as soon as possible and we are going to visit them all again to see if they are now willing to move to areas where we can fix them up.'

The reader of a feature of this kind will no doubt assume that its disclosures are likely to accelerate remedial action; the newspaper identifies itself with the principle of fair play for the individual.

The two watchdog features discussed have analysed deficiencies in an essential community service (*Birmingham Evening Mail*) and the undesirable effects of redevelopment on a particular house-holder (Bolton *Evening News*). Through them the two newspapers reveal how, in certain respects, the *status quo* falls short of the ideal; they also show what the ideal is in their view. In this way they associate themselves with the desiderata of community progress and fair play for individual citizens. Such an association must enhance a newspaper's image; this would be enhanced even more if the local press were to enlarge the scope of its watch to include, for example, commercial practice.[13]

The survey that has been made of locally rooted features by no means covers the whole range; it has, however, permitted the clarification of the main functions. Reflector and community booster features can serve to sharpen the reader's sense of a distinctive community identity; it has been suggested that it is in the long-term financial interest of a local newspaper to foster such a sense. Booster features about local 'achievers' typically extol one or more of the following attributes: career success, courage and perseverance. As compared with the national popular press, there is relatively little attention to the 'celebrity'—the person whose well-knownness depends on sex appeal, commercially viable 'personality' or social deviance. Reflector and booster features enhance a community's image of itself; watchdog features fulfil a contrasting function by disclosing defects in community life. The very act of disclosure, combined with the customary inclusion of remedial proposals, assists in prompting an optimistic, as opposed to despondent, reader reaction.

The functions of reflecting and evaluating local life constitute the principal justifications for the existence of provincial newspapers. Community-rooted features are an important means of fulfilling these functions, and warrant at least the average proportion of the week's total feature space (17 per cent) in the eight evening newspapers sampled. Indeed, the above-average percentages of the *West Lancashire Evening Gazette* and Bolton *Evening News* (31 per cent and 30 per cent respectively) strike one as more appropriate for a local newspaper than the average. The newspaper that falls consistently below the average figure runs the risk of appearing insufficiently close to, and identified with, local community life. As such, it is that much less a unique communications medium, and that much less an irreplaceable socialising influence. For this reason, the steady growth —during the 1960s—of London agencies that ply the provincial Press with non-local feature material must be seen as an unhealthy development that needs checking.

3. Some further aspects of the feature and 'diversion' content of the provincial evening Press

In order to widen the account of evening newspaper features given in the previous section, a brief survey of three further categories is necessary; these are the 'town diary', the 'nature' feature and features about national politics and international affairs. Consideration is also given to the use of cartoons.

(a) The 'town diary' All the eight evening newspapers sampled included a 'town diary' on at least five of the six available evenings. Four—the *West Lancashire Evening Gazette, Cambridge Evening News, Huddersfield Daily Examiner* and *Oxford Mail*—published this feature every evening; three—the Bristol *Evening Post*, *Yorkshire Evening Post* and *Birmingham Evening Mail*—omitted it on Saturdays, while the Bolton *Evening News* omitted it on Fridays. The importance of the 'town diary' in the newspapers' view can be gauged by the fact that except in the *Cambridge Evening News* it was always placed on the same page as the leader and/or correspondence columns. The average amount of space taken up each evening was 38½ column inches—a figure almost identical to that established for the typical correspondence column (36 column inches). The title of each newspaper's diary and its average daily size are listed below:

> *Birmingham Evening Mail*: 'Day by day'—24 column inches.
> Bolton *Evening News*: 'Topics of the day'—45 column inches.
> Bristol *Evening Post*: 'Blackboy's diary'—48 column inches.
> *Cambridge Evening News*: 'Robin Goodfellow'—33 column inches.
> *Huddersfield Daily Examiner*: 'In and about, by Touchstone'—29 column inches.
> *Oxford Mail*: 'Anthony Wood'—47 column inches.
> *West Lancashire Evening Gazette*: 'Seasider's diary'—31 column inches.
> *Yorkshire Evening Post*: 'Diary of a Yorkshireman'—44 column inches.

The total number of separate diary items published on 12 January 1966 was forty-two; the average number was therefore slightly over five. When a classification of these items was made it was found that the two main categories were 'interesting achievements, assignments, appointments, resignations and visitors' (ten) and 'unusual objects, curiosities' (twelve). An example of the first category would be the *Yorkshire Evening Post's* brief profile of the new secretary of the London Society of Yorkshiremen, and of the second, a light-hearted account in the *Oxford Mail* of some mice that had gnawed through the organ bellows at Lockinge parish church, Wantage. In general, diary paragraphs lack the importance of news stories; they are analogous to casual conversational chat. The people to figure most frequently in this feature are local 'achievers' and community leaders; some sort of local connection is essential. Only a very small proportion will be known outside the immediate circulation area; for the most part they are not the people who interest the diary colum- nists of particular national newspapers. The internationally or nationally known 'names' that are judged to be of interest to readers of '*The Times* Diary' (e.g. 'Trevor-Roper in Formosa'[14] and 'De Gaulle meets Miss Bardot'[15]), and the seemingly endless gallery of society leaders and their hangers-on unflaggingly gossiped about in the *Daily Express*'s William Hickey column (e.g. 'Lord Boothby's excited in-laws'[16] and 'Lady Anne's young guest list'[16]) will feature in a provincial 'diary' only when a local angle is involved.

(b) 'Nature' features The attention that the evening Press pays to the natural world varies considerably from paper to paper. The largest single feature in the eight newspapers sampled was the *West Lan- cashire Evening Gazette*'s 'In the countryside' (68 column inches). It was presented more imaginatively than any other feature in this newspaper; the 31 column inches of text were illustrated by an artist's sketch and accompanied by a photograph of a rural scene captioned 'A corner of a country lane near Bay Horse'. The high degree of prominence and the careful presentation can in part be accounted for by the fact that the writer, R. G. Shepherd, was also the assistant editor. He comments on his observations and experiences as a gar- dener, on animals, birds, trees and flowers, on changes in the seasons and in rural customs and speech, and on the effects of technological advance on country life. On 15 January 1966 twenty-four of the thirty-one column inches of text were given over to comments on the birds that the writer had observed in or from his own country garden. The main item was an attempt to explain why blue tits would not feed at the wire mesh base of a container hung from 'the ivy-wreathed bird table on the lawn' but did so when it was hung from 'a firethorn branch close to the front window':

> . . . With the box in its new position, however, they have the shelter of the firethorn and the wall of the house to protect them: and they feel happy and safe.
>
> If you take notice, you will see that a bird in the open is always casting swift glances aloft—the legacy of thousands of years of peril from hawks (although nowadays the peril from cats below is far greater).
>
> There is no peril from above when there is a tree to shelter them and they can relax.
>
> I shall suggest to my friend that he transfers his disappointing feeder to a site under a tree, and watches what transpires. It could be interesting.

This writer attempts to establish a close relationship to his reader; he speaks as an 'I' and to a 'you' ('if you take notice . . .'). He has the specialist knowledge of a naturalist, and seeks to convey it to the sympathetic but relatively less expert reader; much of his comment is prompted by correspondence or by telephoned observations. He assumes an active or latent interest in nature, and that Washington Irving's early nineteenth-century assessment has a continuing, if possibly diminished relevance:

> The English, in fact, are strongly gifted with the rural feeling. They possess a quick sensibility to the beauties of nature, and a keen relish for the pleasures and employment of the country. This passion seems inherent in them. Even the inhabitants of cities, born and brought up among brick walls and bustling streets, enter with facility into rural habits, and evince a tact for rural occupation. . . .[17]

Such assumptions appear to be borne out by the fact that the major increases in population between 1951 and 1961 were in small towns with populations below 50,000 ($+14\cdot9$ per cent) and in rural districts ($+10\cdot7$ per cent); Mark Abrams cites these increases as part of the evidence of an 'exodus from the big cities and conurbations' and adds: 'the new settlers were people who wanted to become home-owners . . . and to enjoy a garden, fresh air and open-air physical exercise'.[18] Elsewhere he notes that in 1963 51 per cent of all adults lived in homes possessing a lawn mower, and that over 40 per cent of the English people now live in small towns and rural districts. Even so, Irving's comments have little application to the urban working class living in the 'massed proletarian areas'[19] described by Richard Hoggart:

. . . street after regular street of shoddily uniform houses intersected by a dark pattern of ginnels and snickets (alley-ways) and courts; mean, squalid, and in a permanent half-fog; a study in shades of dirty-grey, without greenness or the blueness of sky; degrees darker than the north or west of the town, than 'the better end'.[19]

For those brought up in this environment, he suggests, the country is 'an occasionally remembered backcloth, a place you sometimes visit'.[20]

Having made this proviso, it remains true that 'the rural feeling' still exists in varying ways and strengths, and is therefore available for articulation and intensification by feature writers like R. G. Shepherd. Accordingly, although all the evening newspapers sampled offered some sort of 'nature' feature, the average column inch attention (27 column inches) strikes one as unexpectedly low. The reason for this is probably the difficulty of obtaining freelance writers able to communicate their knowledge effectively; a 'journalist–naturalist' of R. G. Shepherd's calibre constitutes an asset enjoyed by few newspapers, national or provincial. But some contributors do warrant more attention in terms of space and presentation; 'F. A. L.' of the Bolton *Evening News*, for instance, communicates his interest in nature in an attractively informal way, yet on 15 January 1966 his feature ('When is a weasel not a weasel?') occupied a mere 12½ column inches; there was no visual illustration. It opened:

Two Bolton families have told me in recent weeks that they have a weasel in the garden. One of my informants seemed rather worried lest the weasel should take goldfish from his garden pond, while the other, I suspect, had fears that his weasel might use a well supplied bird table as bait.
Weasels are not uncommon around Bolton, although stoats are sometimes mistaken for weasels. I have seen more stoats than weasels locally, which is probably because I have spent more time on the moors than in people's gardens. Stoats tend to be more numerous on higher ground and weasels nearer the town . . .[21]

This sort of exploration of the natural environment deserves at least the degree of attention given by the *West Lancashire Evening Gazette*; 'the rural feeling' is still active, and warrants cultivation at the local level.

(c) Features about national politics and international affairs Fig. 8(ii) (*d*) shows that the attention given to national politics and inter-

THE blue tits and great tits and coal tits are not quite so interested in their peanut box and wire danglers as they were a month ago.

They still come dipping like flying jewels from the surrounding trees; but their natural food supply is increasing, and amorous dalliance is taking up more of their time.

The great tits utter the two wheezing notes that make up their song. It probably sounds deliriously exciting to the feminine ear of the species, even if to us it does lack something of the liquid splendour of the blackbird or the sparkling challenge of the wren.

The coal tits have a miniature version of the song, befitting their small size; the blue tits chatter softly.

I was asked the other day how it was that birds came down in flocks the instant food was put out, although previously there was not a bird of any sort in sight. My questioner wondered whether they had some sort of extrasensory perception.

Grapevine

No—the reason is that there are more birds about than we think, and that most of them know by experience where food supplies are likely to appear.

It needs only a couple of sparrows to fly down from a chimney stack, or a couple of squawking starlings from a tree, to alert all the rest. If you watch, you will see that they come in twos and threes, faster and faster as the crowd grows.

This in turn is noticed by rooks and gulls cruising in the air half a mile away, and they come drifting over the garden to reconnoitre.

Quite a number of people succeed in persuading birds to feed from their hands; particularly robins and tits. I have never managed this, but that is probably because I have not the time to spend in training them.

I suppose that if I chose a frosty day in mid-winter and stood on the lawn with the wire feeder dangling from my finger, tits would come to it if I could keep still long enough. The secret of gaining the confidence of all wild things is to make no sudden movement.

Fewer frogs

ALL the birds are here as usual, there are baby rabbits in the field beyond the garden; but there is one thing missing from the unfolding pattern of spring.

It is the crowd of frogs that come to breed in the garden pool. I have not seen a single one this year, and there is only one small cloud of spawn.

They have been dwindling in numbers for some years now, and I miss them very much; as one does miss any token of spring that fails to appear.

They used to gather from all sides, crossing many fields and roads on the way, and when they had finished their croaking and dispersed they left behind masses of the black-dotted grey-jelly spawn that in due course produced tadpoles that wriggled in all directions among the plants and under the flat-leaved lilies.

This scarcity of frogs is general. They, too, are said to be victims of the insecticides and weedkillers so freely scattered; and it probably is so.

Water-snails, water-beetles, tadpoles—what is a pond without them?

Fig. 9 Part of R. G. Shepherd's 'In the countryside' feature, *West Lancashire Evening Gazette*, 18 March 1967. *By courtesy of R. G. Shepherd, J. Selby and the West Lancashire Evening Gazette*

national affairs in features varied widely from paper to paper. Only two of the evening newspapers sampled gave these subjects more than 5 per cent of their feature space—the Bristol *Evening Post* and the *Huddersfield Daily Examiner*. The *Post* offered four features: one on the death of President Shastri, one on the future of the Commonwealth, one about local efforts on behalf of the 'Freedom from hunger' campaign, and one about the need for aid to aged and destitute refugees—perhaps through supporting a local appeal that was being organised. Of the first two it could be said that much of the content would have been available in non-local media; this was not the case with the third—'We all have a part to play', by Professor T. K. Ewer, chairman of the education committee of Bristol's 'Freedom from hunger' campaign. This referred to Bristol's raising £50,000 'to build its own Freedom from Hunger project, the Likuni Farm Institute in Central Malawi'. It described the related educational work being undertaken in Bristol's primary and secondary schools, and in the teacher-training colleges. It ended by inviting readers to participate:

> We, the sleek, well-fed ones, have this matter on our consciences.
> The bitter fact is that in some areas, men, women and children are eating even less today than they were five years ago . . .[22]

This feature is an instance of the local Press co-operating with particular community leaders whose horizons are not parochial; its aim is to involve the readership as a whole. Professor Ewer's comments represent a challenge to the mass of consumption-promoting content described in the next chapter; they point to other possible outlets for spare capital. An article of this kind, which links the non-local to the local, makes a unique use of the provincial newspaper. If all features in this category were to effect this sort of link, and so not be purely non-local, they would be well worth the 9 per cent of all feature space noted in the case of the Bristol *Evening Post*, and would make their total neglect in the *West Lancashire Evening Gazette* and *Birmingham Evening Mail* (during the period of survey) difficult to justify. But at this time the editors of these newspapers could rightly claim that many of the features in this category published elsewhere overlap considerably with material available in non-local media.

(d) Cartoon content One point of interest that emerges from a study of cartoon content is that in general the number of cartoons increases as circulation size increases; the evening newspapers with the largest circulation contain the most cartoons. Two reasons for this can be adduced. First, cartoons add to production costs, and the bigger newspapers are in a better position to pay for them—quite often, in order to brighten up a full page of advertising. Second, the local news published in newspapers serving large conurbations will for the most part seem more distant—sports news excepted—to the average reader than the news in a smaller community newspaper; as a general proposition, one might say that the smaller the newspaper the more names are likely to be familiar. The cartoon, like the 'light-

'You're right—it *is* one of mine!'

Fig. 10(a) From the *Lancashire Evening Football Post*, 1969. *By courtesy of K. Wignall and the Lancashire Evening Post*

hearted' types of story cited in chapter 6, may help to offset this sense of distance; it introduces a note of warmth and humour. If a reader becomes a 'fan' of one or more of the cartoons, he has an additional ground for purchase. Hence the newspapers in question have good reasons for dispelling any doubts that might be raised about the effect of cartoons on the newspaper's image—especially as it might appear to local readers of the national quality press.

During the period of survey the *West Lancashire Evening Gazette* (1964 circulation, 77,722) published no cartoon at all; in contrast, the *Yorkshire Evening Post* (1964 circulation, 314,809) included fourteen single cartoons and two daily 'strips'—Twick and Muffin.

The *Gazette*'s practice is typical of the small- or medium-sized evening newspaper, and the *Post*'s of newspapers serving large conurbations. There are very few staff cartoonists of the calibre of K. Wignall of the *Lancashire Evening Post*, whose regular contributions to this newspaper's Saturday sports edition have enlivened its pages since the early 1960s.

'Above all the thing we pride ourselves on most is our team spirit'

Fig. 10(b) From the *Lancashire Evening Football Post*, 1969. *By courtesy of K. Wignall and the Lancashire Evening Post*

4. Summary

This chapter has concentrated on some of the main kinds of locally rooted feature in the provincial evening Press, and shown how the functions of reflector, booster, watchdog and pump-primer are fulfilled; the effects of the controlling factors of localness and 'family values' have also been noted. The local feature can sharpen the reader's awareness of his community's particularity—whether it be his sense of its past development, its current strengths and limitations, or its future role and character.

The feature content of the weekly press usually consists of the community diary, special features for women and children, extracts from past issues of the newspaper, summaries of church, youth club and Women's Institute activities, an entertainment guide, and columns for the gardener and/or motorist. These features, some or all of which are also provided by evening newspapers, help to foster a feeling of local togetherness—a realisation of the corporate life available for sharing, and of common domestic or leisure interests. The 1947 Royal Commission was not quite doing justice to the weekly Press when describing its content as 'almost entirely advertisements and local news'.[23]

Notes

1 *West Lancashire Evening Gazette*, 15 January 1966.
2 *Ibid.*, 14 January 1966.
3 See chapter 6.
4 *Yorkshire Evening Post*, 13 January 1966.
5 *Cambridge Evening News*, 10 January 1966.
6 Bolton *Evening News*, 11 January 1966.
7 Janowitz, *op. cit.*, p. 95.
8 *Oxford Mail*, 19 January 1966.
9 *The People*, 22 August 1965.
10 *Oxford Mail*, 14 January 1966.
11 *Yorkshire Evening Post*, 10 January 1966.
12 Bolton *Evening News*, 12 January 1966.
13 See pp. 221–2, 279.
14 *The Times*, 12 December 1967.
15 *Ibid.*, 11 December 1967.
16 *Daily Express*, 22 August 1967.
17 Washington Irving, *The Sketch Book of Geoffrey Crayon, Gent* (London: J. M. Dent), pp. 55–6.
18 Mark Abrams, *The Newspaper-reading Public of Tomorrow* (London: Odhams Press, 1964), p. 17.
19 Richard Hoggart, *The Uses of Literacy* (Penguin Books edition 1962), pp. 58–9.
20 *Ibid.*, p. 26.
21 Bolton *Evening News*, 15 January 1966.
22 Bristol *Evening Post*, 11 January 1966.
23 *Report* of the 1947 Royal Commission, p. 239.

10 The nature and importance of advertising

Advertising as a source of revenue

R. M. Wiles, in his study of the earliest provincial newspapers, notes that the volume of advertising grew markedly in the period 1701–60. From the first decade 'one finds papers in which more than a quarter of the available space was occupied by advertisements', and during the years 1751–60 'there were many papers which regularly had six, seven, even eight columns out of twelve filled with advertisements. It was an extensive business'.[1] Wiles also observes that advertising soon became a crucial source of revenue; referring to a specific issue (No. 396 of the *Western Flying Post*, 27 September 1756), he concludes that 'if the net profit per copy was only a farthing, the profit on Goadby's forty-three advertisements would equal the net gain from the sale of nearly 3,100 copies. Advertising PAID.'[2]

Advertising still pays—so much so that the national newspaper that lacks either the massive circulations of the *Daily Mirror* or *Daily Express*, or the prestigious (i.e. in financial terms) readership of *The Times* or *Daily Telegraph* (thereby finding it difficult to command advertising) is liable, like the *News Chronicle*, to be taken over, or, like the *Sunday Citizen*, to be closed down. Advertising is also a crucial source of revenue for the provincial Press. Its volume is closely related to the general state of the economy; in periods of economic standstill or recession such as the 'squeeze' of 1966–67 provincial companies find it hard to maintain the profit levels of previous years characterised by buoyant expansion. Thus when the Birmingham Post and Mail Ltd's profits for 1965–66 fell short of the 1964–65 level the company's chairman, Sir Eric Clayson, ascribed the drop to the general state of the economy:

... The effects of the Squeeze are already being felt quite severely and must inevitably damage our advertising revenues during the current year, a situation not peculiar to the Birmingham area alone. The important Situations Vacant advertising in all our papers has been to some extent affected by the change in the employment position.

It would seem inevitable that, in common with many other companies, profits for the current year must be appreciably lower because of the general economic situation, from which we cannot be immune.[3]

The state of the national economy, therefore, affects the volume of advertising and thence profit margins.

Advertising is so crucially important for the financial viability of newspaper companies that great attention is paid to the methods of securing it. The editorial side seems to receive little comment in company reports, but progress in advertising is a matter for self-congratulation and detail. In his statement about the financial position of United Newspapers Ltd at the end of 1966 the chairman, Mr W. D. Barnetson, spoke of 'new procedures for the promotion of classified advertising' introduced by the *Lancashire Evening Post* in April 1966; 'the results have been highly rewarding. . . .' These procedures were 'in the process of development by the *West Lancashire Evening Gazette* at Blackpool' and 'the group's weekly newspapers are also involved in this operation'. Not that progress would rest at this: 'a new Group Marketing Department' had been established in London, 'with particular emphasis at this stage on the expansion of display advertising, local as well as national'. 'More sophisticated techniques' would be developed.[4] It is logical, therefore, that Thomson Newspapers—moving along the same lines— should advertise for 'bright young sales executives' and 'more young, energetic men' to assist its advertising expansion programme.[5]

The provincial newspaper reader who pays 8s (40p) for a private classified advertisement of ten words in the *Birmingham Evening Mail* (January 1966 rate) or 4s (20p) for twelve words in the weekly *Buxton Advertiser* (1965 rate) may well not appreciate what large total sums are contributed by classified and display advertisers. Table 14 shows what the rates were in 1964 for display advertising in four evening newspapers, and also how the rates are linked to circulation size. One implication of these figures is that newspapers with circulations over 100,000 (roughly the dividing line) make more money from a column inch of display advertising than from a column inch of classified. For instance, one notes that the *Birmingham Evening Mail* receives £44 for an 8 column inch display advertisement. For 8 column inches of classified 'Houses for sale' ads at the January 1966 rate (ten words 9s (45p) per insertion, and 4s 6d (22½p) for every additional five words or less), calculation indicates a revenue of about £26 10s 0d (£26·50). But the *West Lanca-*

shire Evening Gazette (1964 circulation 74,262) receives £9 4*s* (£9·20) for an 8 column inch display ad as against £12 3*s* (£12·15) for 8 column inches of classified trade advertising at 2*s* 3*d* (approximately 11*p*) per line (1966 rate). Of fifty-eight English provincial evening newspapers in 1964, eighteen had circulations over the 100,000 mark, forty below it. In the case of these forty, more profit will be made from a column inch of classified advertising than from a column inch of display.

The contribution that advertising can make to the total revenue on any one day is easily demonstrated. The estimates of revenue which

Table 14

Name of newspaper and 1964 circulation figure	Display advertisement rates*		
	Full page	*24 column inches*	*8 column inches*
Birmingham Evening Mail (408,539)	£1,300	£132	£44
Lancashire Evening Post (146,430)	£470 5*s*† (£470·25)	£57	£19
Bolton *Evening News* (88,107)	£250	£36	£12
Huddersfield Daily Examiner (52,558)	£160‡	£21	£7

* See *ENAB Planning Guide*, September 1964.
† Nine columns.
‡ Eight columns.

follow are based on published advertising rates; the figures were not supplied by the two newspaper companies concerned. The daily sales of the *Birmingham Evening Mail* in 1964 would bring in approximately £6,809 (not deducting any costs of commissions); this sum would be equalled by the proceeds of five full pages and two columns (approximately) of display advertising. In fact, on 2 December 1966 the *Mail* included 1,834 column inches of display ads of 8 column inches or more, value (at the 1964 rate) £10,087. These advertisements constituted only 46·1 per cent of the total space given to advertisements, notices and announcements in this issue. On the same evening the *West Lancashire Evening Gazette* published 907 column inches of display ads of 8 column inches or more. The value of these, again at the 1964 rate, was estimated at £1,043, as compared with a gross income of £1,237 from sales. The 907 column inches in question constituted 47·1 per cent of the total space given to advertisements, notices and announcements. (Ads in the two categories of 'Business notices' and 'Entertainment' were not included in the above column inch totals.)

Only approximate assessments can be made of the value of the classified advertising in these issues. The total number of classified advertising column inches (taking into account only those sections measuring 8 column inches or more) was 1,836 (46·1 per cent of all advertising space) in the *Birmingham Evening Mail* and 820 (42·5 per cent) in the *West Lancashire Evening Gazette*. The value of the former was calculated as £6,081, of the latter £1,240. If these figures are added to those for display advertising, totals of £16,168 result for the *Birmingham Evening Mail* (as compared with £6,809 from daily sales) and £2,283 for the *West Lancashire Evening Gazette* (as compared with £1,237 from daily sales). Since only 92·2 per cent of the *Mail*'s advertising, and 89·6 per cent of the *Gazette*'s, have been assessed, it is fair to hypothesise that the ratios of 2·4 (advertising revenue) : 1 (sales revenue) for the *Mail* and 1·9 : 1 for the *Gazette* over-emphasise the revenue contribution of sales.

Thus on 2 December 1966 advertising accounted for at least 70 per cent of the *Mail*'s total estimated gross revenue of £22,977 and 61 per cent of the *Gazette*'s £3,520. These percentages are close to the average of 62 per cent of total revenue attributable to advertising—for the provincial evening Press as a whole—in 1960.[6] In the case of the weekly Press in 1960, advertising contributed 79 per cent of total revenue.[6]

It is hardly surprising, therefore, that in recent years the indispensability of advertising revenue should have been recognised by the increasing sophistication of techniques for attracting it. It is now appropriate to assess how much space advertising as a whole, and the main constituent categories, take up in the two newspapers under discussion.

The space taken up by advertising, and its distribution

The two issues of the evening newspapers referred to in the previous section (the *Birmingham Evening Mail* and the *West Lancashire Evening Gazette* of 2 December 1966) were analysed in order to determine (*a*) what proportion of the total space was taken up by advertising and (*b*) how this space was distributed. These issues were selected for two reasons: first, because the volume of advertising reaches its peak on Friday as the evening before the weekend's shopping, and, second, because this particular Friday occurred at the beginning of the Christmas shopping season. Accordingly, one anticipated that the proportion of advertising would be at its highest on this day, and so would enable one to assess the spatial ratio of editorial content to advertising at a time when newspapers are receiving at least as much advertising as they can cope with.

The total number of column inches available on 2 December 1966 was 3,072 in the *West Lancashire Evening Gazette* (thirty-two pages, then tabloid size) and 5,760 in the *Birmingham Evening Mail* (twenty-four pages, broadsheet size). The number of column inches taken up by all forms of advertising (display and classified) was 1,924, or 62·6 per cent of all space (*Gazette*) and 3,982, or 69·1 per cent of all (*Mail*). If the two percentages are averaged out the proportion that emerges is almost exactly two-thirds. It has already been suggested that these percentages may well represent the highest of the year, and as a means of effecting a comparison the percentage of advertising space in three issues of the *Gazette* in January 1967 was also assessed. The resulting figures were:

> 17 January (Monday)   : 51·8 per cent
> 19 January (Wednesday) : 52·4 per cent
> 21 January (Friday)   : 58·7 per cent

The percentages confirm that the volume of advertising grows proportionately larger as the weekend approaches; the Friday figure is 4·4 per cent higher than the average of 54·3 per cent. For this newspaper, therefore, it seems that slightly more than half of the total space will normally be given over to advertising, and that the proportion rises to almost two-thirds in the context of seasonal sales campaigns.

In the two issues analysed, commercial display advertisements of eight or more column inches in length accounted for 907 (*Gazette*) and 1,834 (*Mail*) column inches respectively. These figures represented 47·1 and 46·1 per cent of all advertising space. Of the *Gazette*'s 47·1 per cent, 38·8 came from local sources, 8·3 from non-local; of the *Mail*'s 46·1 per cent, 39·6 came from local sources, 6·5 from non-local. Thus almost half the advertising space in these two issues was taken up by display advertisements over 8 column inches in size; of this space only one-sixth (*Gazette*, approximately) and one-seventh (*Mail*) respectively was non-local in origin.[7] So the predominant style (or styles) of evening newspaper display advertising is determined by local commercial concerns addressing a particular community of readers, however small or large.

The total number of column inches taken up by display advertisements over 48 column inches in size (i.e. half a tabloid page or more) was 406 (*Gazette*) and 937 (*Mail*). These constituted 21·1 and 23·5 per cent respectively of all advertising space. In the *Gazette* there were six of these large display ads, all of local origin, while in the *Mail* there were twelve, ten being of local origin. Local multiple stores, clothing, carpet and TV stores or shops accounted for fifteen of the eighteen display ads in this category. Again, therefore, one finds that the role of non-local advertisers is a modest one. This in turn suggests that the advertising priorities of provincial newspapers are still very much the same as those outlined in oral evidence to the 1947 Royal Commission by Mr W. A. McWhirter, representing Northcliffe Newspapers Group Ltd:

5379. Mr. Beaton: Are the bulk of them local or national advertisements?—We give preference rather in this order: first of all local public notices, such as notices from the Town Council or the Ministry of Health; then the classified advertisements, or what are called 'smalls.' We attach great importance to these 'smalls' because they are part of the life of the community. . . . Thirdly, we put the local display advertisements, for example, by the local draper or the furniture man. After that, and very far after it, we carry the national advertising, because we consider it our duty to give as much publicity to the local community as is possible. We have cut national advertising down, and now it is very much smaller than ever it was.[8]

Mr McWhirter puts considerable stress here on the newspaper's obligations to the community as the factor that determines the priorities. A little reflection suggests that this might not be the only or even the main reason. Advertising from local sources is the more likely to be submitted year in, year out, with unflagging regularity; national advertising is a fine-weather friend to a much greater extent, its volume being closely linked to the general state of the economy. And for perhaps as many as 69 per cent of evening newspapers local classified advertising is more profitable, per column inch, than local or non-local display advertising.

It is, therefore, commercially logical to place non-local advertising at the foot of the list of priorities. Even so, the proportion of space it does command resulted in the establishment of the Evening Newspaper Advertising Bureau, and in the issues under discussion would be worth at least £1,440 to the *Birmingham Evening Mail* and £184 to the *West Lancashire Evening Gazette*. It is clearly an important source of income for the evening newspapers with the largest circulations, but rather less so for those with, say, a circulation under 100,000.

A survey was also made of the classified advertising, again limiting analysis to sections of eight or more column inches in length. The total number of column inches taken up by such classified sections in the *Gazette* was 820 (42·5 per cent of all advertising space) and in the *Mail* 1,836 (46·1 per cent). When compared with the percentages already cited for display ads over eight column inches, these figures reveal that there is a slightly greater proportion of display (as opposed to classified) advertising in the *Gazette* (4·6 per cent more), whereas in the *Mail* the two categories balance exactly. The main kinds of classified advertising, including here 'Births, marriages and deaths' and 'Public notices', are tabulated below:

Type of advertising	Gazette	Mail
Motor cars for sale	120	419
Houses for sale	118½	415
Situations vacant	82½	353
Entertainment guide	146½	104
Miscellaneous for sale	109½	130
Births, marriages and deaths	38	58
Public notices	29½	56½
Totals (column inches)	644½	1,535½

The seven categories listed accounted for 78·6 per cent of the *Gazette*'s measured classified advertising space, and 83·6 per cent of the *Mail*'s. The four most important categories for the *Gazette*, in terms of space taken up, were (in order): 'Entertainment guide', 'Motor cars for sale', 'Houses for sale' and 'Miscellaneous for sale'. In the

Mail's case they were 'Motor cars for sale', 'Houses for sale', 'Situations vacant' and, much less important, 'Miscellaneous for sale'. Blackpool's role as a seaside resort is reflected in the prominence of the 'Entertainment guide' even in this out-of-season month. Motor cars, houses and 'Miscellaneous for sale' occur in both lists and account for 42 per cent of the *Gazette*'s measured classified advertising, 50 per cent of the *Mail*'s.

The analyses above have shown that there is a rough balance as between display and classified advertising in both newspapers. The display advertising is predominantly local and the classified ads almost entirely so. In the next section the styles of both kinds of advertisement are considered.

The presentation of display and classified advertising

A comprehensive account of display advertising styles (verbal and visual) would necessitate so much illustration that it must suffice to point out just the salient characteristics. Considering the display advertisements in the two newspapers as a whole, three broadly distinguishable styles were apparent. These were not necessarily mutually exclusive, as some advertisements made use of the appeals of all three. First there were the display ads that assumed a bargain-hunting reader; these comprised about 42 per cent of the total. A further 46 per cent consisted of ads that offered 'straight' information, i.e. details of goods available with little or no superadded appeal. Third, and very much in a minority (12 per cent), there were advertisements directed at the status seeker—in particular, the reader seeking social success or prestige.

The first kind of display ad, then, aims to appeal to the bargain hunter—the reader who is assumed to want maximum value for money. Thus T. J. Hughes (Blackpool), in a full tabloid page ad headed 'Bargains For Everyone!' included particular 'box' sections entitled 'Terrific Value Wm's Underwear' and 'Sensational Offer Electric Blankets'. The text of this last ad ran:

> The answer to cold beds this
> winter. Comply to Electrical
> Standards.

```
Single size
Usually 83/11 ...............49/6
Double size
Usually £5/8/0 ..............69/6
```

Large advertisements of this kind are given visual appeal by varieties of print size and style and also, quite frequently, by small sketches which will arrest the reader's eye more effectively than print alone; this ad contained seven such sketches.

The technique, then, is to point to a dramatic reduction in price: 'Was £39 Now £15'; 'Scoop'; 'Half price' and so on. It also involves an assortment of huckster's adjectives: 'genuine', 'smashing', 'colossal', 'terrific' or 'sensational'. The intention is to infer the 'once in a lifetime' bargain. One recalls the nineteenth-century Press historian James Grant's comment on some of the *Times*' advertisements:

> Though, as in the case of sales of haberdashery, you do not read in all cases the words 'To be sold at a tremendous sacrifice', yet that is, in effect, the burthen of what is said in relation to all the sales advertised in the *Times*, no matter of what kind. . . . Philanthropists of this class spend their strength in vain.[9]

But not, one assumes, entirely in vain; the Allied Carpet Warehouse (Birmingham) presumably recoup more than £330, or believe they do, as the result of a 60 column inch display advertisement costing this amount.

The second category (46 per cent of all display ads) relied on a straight descriptive account of the goods for sale and made no mention of price cuts or special offers. Thus W. H. Smith & Son, in a half-page ad in the *Birmingham Evening Mail*, laid out their wares in eighteen boxes (each approximately 3 in. × 2 in.); every box contained a sketch, verbal description and price. Some 'straight' ads rely more on visual effects than this one, like that of C & A Modes, whose 120 column inch ad in the *Mail* was dominated by three large sketches of models wearing party dresses ('Polyester and glitter nylon in pastel shades give these dresses a party sparkle'). The third display advertising style, involving no more than 12 per cent of the total, was adopted particularly by non-local advertisers seeking to sell luxury goods. It is a style much more in evidence in a glossy magazine like *Nova*. One example must suffice; this was for a cocktail dress sold by Richard Shops. It made use of a full-

Fig. 11 An advertisement for the bargain-seeker, *Huddersfield Daily Examiner*, 20 January 1966. The original was some 8 ins × 4 ins. *By courtesy of the Huddersfield Daily Examiner*

length photograph of a 'deb.-type' girl, and the accompanying text ran as follows:

> She was having such fun . . . whirling and
> twirling, really enjoying herself. And
> looking gorgeous. No wonder all the men
> wanted to dance with her.
> I didn't know her name but Gaby knew
> exactly where she bought her dress: Richard
> Shops. . . .
> Such clever clothes from
> RICHARD SHOPS

The ad is a straightforward enough appeal to the reader's desire to identify—to wear the five-guinea dress that is 'clever', makes a girl look gorgeous ('whirling and twirling . . .') and the men all want to dance with her. The phrasing clearly has links with the narrative style of girls' and women's magazine romance stories; the unknown 'she' is admired by an 'I', a 'Gaby' and 'all the men'. At the same time there is a conscious attempt to add a 'U' element—presumably with the model of a status-seeking suburban reader in mind. Hence the adjective 'gorgeous' and the shortened version of the very 'OK' name Gabrielle; hence too the 'superior' tonal associations of 'such clever clothes . . .' At this point the narrative ends and the key to it all is posited as Richard Shops.

The dominance of 'bargain' and 'straight' display ads—88 per cent of the total—is an indication of the social composition of the readership. Assuming that the *Birmingham Evening Mail*'s readership is almost identical to that for all Midlands evening newspapers, C2DE readers constitute 70 per cent of the total. 'Bargain' ads clearly address these readers in particular; the 'straight' ads can be seen as non-selective in their appeal, although perhaps of particular interest to C1C2 readers, who constitute 54 per cent of all. Advertising that deals in superior social status conferment has the ABC1 reader (30 per cent of all) primarily in mind.

Classified advertising: 'Property', 'Motor cars for sale', 'Situations vacant', 'Miscellaneous for sale' and 'Births, marriages and deaths'

1. Property Property advertisers draw on a long-established stock of descriptive adjectives and phrases for the purpose of persuasion

'Superior', 'select', 'charming', 'delightful' and 'splendid' are amongst
the recurring additions to the basic account of houses on offer in
detached or semi-detached suburbia; such adjectives imply that
these houses are to be distinguished from the terraced dwellings
which, row upon row, lie in the precincts of town or city centres:

Moseley. Superior new development in select residential area, houses
containing reception hall, cloakroom, lounge, dining area, fitted kitchen,
2 bedrooms, bathroom, full central heating, landscaped gardens, garages
available. From £3,400 . . .

Clitheroe Road, St. Annes. A glorious, spacious, immaculate semi detached
chalet bungalow which cries out for immediate viewing . . . At only
£5,395.

Such ads primarily address the ABC1 reader; they invite him to
acquire the social status that will, in theory, result from the purchase
of a house in some 'select residential area'. Status conferment is
ascribed in a number of related ways: 'occupying enviable position';[10] 'this much-favoured area';[11] 'this high-class area';[11] 'a
prestige development';[12] 'high-class cul-de-sac';[13] 'imposing modern
detached gentleman's residence'[13]—and so on. The *Surrey Advertiser* contained an ad for 'Georgian-style flats at Farnham, so ideal
for retired couples seeking a small home with a good address'.[14]
Many status-claiming ads allude to distinctive material benefits,
ranging from 'very charming elevation'[15] to 'full central heating' or
'mature garden with fishpond'.[14] The descriptions 'rural' and 'semi-
rural' are clearly regarded as potent sales factors; they may be used
directly, as in 'set in a quiet rural hamlet',[16] or implied: 'a most
select position with open hill views'.[17] For about £9,000 most
requirements of the status-seeker can be met:

Gentleman's Residence in the heart of South Devon and adjacent to the
Moor, also within easy reach of the sea resorts. 2 miles from golf course,
centre of hunting area. Stone built Georgian property, seven bedrooms,
four reception, two kitchens, two bathrooms, normal domestic offices.
Garden and paddock and stabling in all about 4 acres. . . .[18]

'Glorious' and 'select' are obviously inappropriate as descriptions
of much monotonous urban property, but the estate agents have
other verbal stocks-in-trade at their disposal, other postulated
advantages to command the appropriate reader's attention. Descriptions like 'well maintained', 'well built', 'modernised', 'immacu-

late' and 'conveniently situated' are frequently used to recommend older dwellings no longer classifiable as 'superior':

Walsall . . . Modernised 2-bedroomed Villa . . . £1,750.

Bearwood . . . Immaculate end terraced residence, garden side, rear, front, garage space £2,950.[19]

Coronation Street, then, can have its own particular virtues; as a last resort, a factual appeal to the bargain-hunter can be effected:

Ossett. Smaller type Terrace House in the moderate price group. Accomm. comprises—ent. hall; lounge (m. t. fp); liv. rm. (m. t. fp., s.s.s.u., cupbds.); 2 bedrms; small front gdn. Yd. to rear. Outside W.C. . . .[20]

The reader of such an advertisement could be excused for assuming that few, if any, attractive features existed—other than the actual accommodation and fittings specified.

2. Motor cars for sale A similar spectrum to that for property occurs in the case of 'Cars for sale'—running from maximum luxury to minimal adequacy. When they can, dealers like to stress the finely differentiated colour and/or gadgetry of particular vehicles. The colours, of course, emanate from the manufacturing source: Horizon Blue, Trafalgar Blue, Ambassador Blue, Pacific Blue, Meteor Blue and so on. The distinctiveness of colour is matched, especially in the ads for the more expensive saloon cars and sports models, by a careful itemisation of individuality-conferring gadgetry. An example follows:

1964 Jaguar 3·8 Saloon. Metallic maroon/beige int., overdrive, wire wheels, radio, reclining seats, genuine 28,000 miles, original paint-work. . . .[21]

Sometimes this sort of miscellany is abbreviated to the cheaper insertion 'host of extras'.

Three further desiderata urged, whenever possible, upon the potential purchaser are a car's 'one careful owner' history, its 'immaculate' condition and low mileage. The 'one local owner' attribute suggests the archetypally safe and steady 'family man' driver. Sometimes dealers embellish this standard phrase in ways assumed to enhance a car's image: 'driven only by a very careful gentleman owner';[22] 'both privately owned, one ex a reverend gentleman';[23] 'one elderly lady owner from new';[24] 'this car has been a

second car to a Rolls Royce with one lady owner'.[11] All these descriptions are designed to infer sedate and careful driving by owners
of vague but high social rank—all ladies or gentlemen. They are
therefore calculated to dispel the nagging fear that accounts for notes
like 'never used in competition'.[25] A different but connected mode of
reassurance is intended by phrases like 'sold and maintained by us' or
'regularly serviced by us and in A1 condition'.[21] The recurring
implication is that the car is a known quantity; it is not some alien
vehicle traded in by a reckless, non-local speed merchant or ever-
hustling 'rep.'

As with domestic property, indices of condition are given due
emphasis; 'immaculate' is once again a frequently used evaluation.
The intention is to suggest either that a given car might easily be
mistaken (perhaps by the neighbouring Jones family) for a new one,
or that it is remarkably younger in appearance than it is in reality.
Hence 'absolute specimen condition';[21] 'showroom condition';[21]
'absolutely mint condition';[26] 'in absolutely amazing condition for
year';[10] 'quite as new in every detail';[21] 'this incredible car is
unmarked throughout';[24] 'as good as new';[21] 'perfect in every
respect'[21] and the prestige-conferring 'chauffeur maintained'.[25]
Some of these phrases contain the same sort of huckster's adjectives
that characterise the 'big bargain' display ads referred to above, e.g.
'absolutely amazing' and 'incredible'. Obviously, if the dealers are
right, the car industry can take great pride in its products.

Details of mileage are included where they represent a telling
sales point: 'certified 2,500 miles from new';[21] 'genuine 16,000
miles'.[21] The phrasing here implies that the public is seen as suspicious of mileage claims—with some justification, in the light of the
prosecutions for false claims that have occurred since the passing of
the Trade Descriptions Act, 1968. This Act has caused some, but
by no means all firms to tone down the eulogistic aspect of motor
car description.

Colours, gadgetry and details of ownership, condition and mileage by no means exhaust the dealer's range of appeals. There is also
a range of descriptions applicable to cars below paragon standard.
'Little' is sometimes included, presumably to stimulate a protective,
affectionate response: 'excellent little car';[25] 'extremely nice little
runabout';[27] 'a little sparkler at the right price'.[28] Colour, gadgetry
and status may be non-starters as sales factors for such cars, but they
are presented as having the appealing nature of affectionate mongrel

dogs. They 'run' in their own happy, busy way as 'runners' and 'runabouts'; with careful maintenance they can look like 'little sparklers'. If the Jaguar 3·8 saloon is the car equivalent to a seven-bedroom Gentleman's Residence, the 'extremely nice little run-about' is analogous to the 'immaculate' terraced house.

3. Situations vacant The very wide range, in terms of social appeal, noted in the first two categories is slightly narrower in the case of 'Situations vacant'. Situation seekers are assumed to be primarily in the C1C2D groups; it is apparent that many AB positions are not advertised in evening or weekly newspapers. These positions are for the most part channelled into the quality nationals or specialist journals like the *Times Educational Supplement*. The main existing distinction in the provincial Press is between the salaried position and the 'job' undertaken by the wage-earner. On the one hand 'Senior Forging Technician. Salary £2,500 per annum'; on the other 'Cleaners Required . . . Rate of pay 3/6 and 5/- per hour'.[19]

Of course, many advertised situations point to the kinds of work in which a given area specialises. In the *Birmingham Evening Mail* the industrial feel of the Midlands comes across from ads for 'Die Maintenance Man for Aluminium Diecasting Toolroom', 'Tipped Tools—Reamers and Horizontal Borers'. The cotton mills of north-east Lancashire account for the quantitative prominence of advertisements for 'Female Condenser Ring Spinners', 'Male Intermediate Tenters', 'Assistant Mule Overlooker' or 'Doffers and Gaiters' in weeklies like the *Rochdale Observer*.[29]

4. 'Miscellaneous for sale' The columns of miscellaneous goods for sale hold a similar appeal to the bargain boxes of the multiple store display ad—the appeal of the bran tub lucky dip or the jumble sale. The range of goods on offer characteristically includes washing machines, sewing machines, vacuum cleaners, fur coats, golf clubs, dog baskets, tricycles, train sets and many other appliances, toys, etc. Usually there will be one or two uncommon inclusions like

Rowing machine, excellent condition, suitable slimmers, keep fit, £3 o.n.o.[19]

or the unworn dinner jacket, often sold as a consequence of the intended wearer's death:

Gentleman's Dinner Suit, never worn; chest 40 in. waist 38 in. Inside leg 27 in. Offers.[12]

Birds and animals have their own 'for sale' section, and here advertisers often introduce an emotive element in the manner of the estate
agents and car dealers. Dogs in particular are presented as animal
paragons: 'bewitching black cocker puppies';[30] 'chow chow
puppies like cuddly teddy bears'[14] or 'beautiful pug puppies'.[26]
The loss of a pet will often be brought to public notice by means of
the 'Lost and found' column; sometimes a note of pathos attaches:

Lost. Pedigree dachsund, chocolate colour; answers to name Hiendl;
children pining; lost Macclesfield Rd., Wilmslow . . .[17]

5. Births, marriages and deaths This category was the sixth largest in
the issues of the *Birmingham Evening Mail* and *West Lancashire Evening Gazette* of 2 December 1966. James Grant, the nineteenth-century
Press historian, observed that the list of births in *The Times* of his
day was so attractive to married ladies 'that it is not only the first
they peruse, but in the case of many of their number, the only part
of the paper they read'.[31] If applied to communities below, say,
the size of the major cities, one might justifiably speculate that
Grant's first comment would still have some relevance. For 'hatches,
matches and despatches' (or, as the *San Francisco News Letter* once
styled them, 'the cradle, the altar, and the tomb'[32]) are certainly
perceived as important content by provincial newspaper editors;
Harold Evans, in *The Practice of Journalism*, offers the following
advice to young reporters:

Working in a district for a weekly paper you will be very close to the
everyday life of the people, and you will find that the neighbourliness of a
small community grows from an intimate but kindly knowledge of other
people's family affairs. . . . So humble news about 'hatches, matches and
dispatches' is grist to your daily mill.[33]

Accordingly, the 'Births, marriages and deaths' column is usually
given a prominent and regular position in evening and weekly
newspapers. In the weekly *Burnley Express and News* of 31 July 1965,
this section was located on the back page and took up four full
columns (86 column inches.) The distribution of announcements was
characteristic for most periods of the year, i.e. apart from the spate
of engagements at Christmas and New Year, and marriages at
Easter. The main categories, in order of spatial prominence, were:

In memoriam: 32 column inches (forty insertions for twenty-
seven people).

Deaths: 15 column inches (twenty-two insertions for twenty-two people).

Thanks for sympathy: 10½ column inches (fifteen insertions for fifteen families),

Engagements: 7½ column inches (twenty insertions for nine couples).

Coming of age: 5½ column inches (twenty-one insertions for ten people).

Births: 2½ column inches (six insertions for six babies).

Silver Weddings: 2 column inches (six insertions for four couples).

The 130 insertions classified should be multiplied several times if the total number of family networks involved is to be assessed; this leaves out of account friends and colleagues. It is clear that the number of connected people must run into thousands, and so form a significant proportion of the paper's 32,889 readers (1964 circulation).

The phrasing of many of the announcements is standardised: 'congratulations' and/or 'best wishes' (coming of age, engagements, silver weddings); 'thanks to all concerned' (births); thanks 'for kind expressions of sympathy and floral tributes received' (thanks for sympathy). Only the 'in memoriam' column is characterised by the inclusion of rhymed verses; this issue contained twenty-seven separate insertions—most of them frank expressions of remembered love and affection:

> You meant so very much to us, there's nothing we can say,
> To tell the love that's in our hearts as we think of you each day.
> The flowers and leaves may wither, the evening sun may set,
> But the hearts that loved you dearly are the ones that never forget.

Some provincial newspapers hold a selection of verses at the advertising desk for the reader to choose from if he wishes, although this was not the case with, for instance, the *West Lancashire Evening Gazette*; the assistant editor of this newspaper informed the writer that no such selection was available. Yet the *Gazette*'s 'in memoriam' column still contains verses of the kind quoted, and one's assumption must be that many are personal expressions of affection, although to some extent modelled on those previously published. The passage of time means that most of the tributes of wives or husbands occur within a five-year period from the time of death; the average to

which the *Burnley Express*'s insertions on 31 July 1965 referred
was 1960.

It is appropriate at this point to refer to the publication of wills,
which must command considerable reader interest—especially in
small or medium-sized towns and rural areas, where there is the
greater likelihood of the deceased, or the beneficiaries, being known.
Typically, newspapers publish only details of wills over £5,000. A
list of people thought to have left more than this sum is regularly
drawn up; individuals are selected on the basis of existing staff
knowledge and of the information in obituaries. The list is then sent
to a London agency which specialises in this field; the agency returns
the itemised details once probate has been granted. Cases do occur
of an objection to publication being lodged—usually when some
item or items are regarded as embarrassing, or as likely to prompt
unwanted rumour and gossip. The editor's discretion may then be
exercised and some, or all, specific bequests omitted.

The main kinds of display and classified advertising have now been
outlined; it remains to observe that a study of church notices and
public notices of the type that announce meetings, bazaars and the
range of available entertainments (commercial and otherwise)
permits quite a full grasp of that part of a community's socio-
cultural life that is available for all to share, whether casually or
regularly. Analysis of the notices and entertainment ads in the
weekly *Keighley News* of 12 December 1964 showed how, side by
side with the traditional activities of religious, political, cultural and
social organisations, and established forms of entertainment like
pantomime, revue, old time dancing and whist, more recent modes of
diversion—'X' films (e.g. 'Flesh and the fiends'), 'pop' groups (e.g.
'Billy Atom and the Fallouts' at the R A O B club) and bingo ('£500
in Jackpots' at the Star Bingo and Social Club)—prominently claimed
the reader's attention. In terms of actual space the cinema and bingo
were the most prominent; of the total of 114 column inches of church
notices, public notices, dances and whist drives, and other entertainments, 63 column inches (or 55 per cent of all) were taken up by
these two alone. A more comprehensive analysis would serve to
validate the claim made by W. G. Hoskins in his *Local History In
England*: 'The advertisements, above all, are particularly valuable for a
detailed picture of the life of a small town during the period covered
by the newspaper.'[34]

The influence of advertisers on the local Press

The main local commercial organisations (e.g. multiple stores, supermarkets, car sales firms and the leading estate agents) make such an indispensable contribution to provincial newspaper revenue that there is a widely held belief that advertisers can and do exert an influence on editorial policy. Such influence, it is thought, would be primarily directed towards the concealment of news or the suppression of comment unfavourable to the image of the organisation concerned—whether it involved the organisation as a whole or a particular individual (or individuals) within it. Specific instances might be news of workers' dissatisfaction at conditions or some scandal or misdemeanour in which an organisational leader was concerned. No commercial, or non-commercial, institution likes to be presented in an unfavourable light by the media. Their jointly held attitude in this respect has been frankly clarified by Kenneth Wheare, rector of Exeter College, Oxford, in the 1967 Rede lecture at Cambridge:

... How different is our attitude when we are in the news or are likely to get into the news in an unfavourable light. If there is trouble on the campus our first thought is likely to be: Will the press get hold of it? Is there any chance that it may stay, or be kept out of the papers? How little can we tell the press? In this matter we are, of course, no different from many other institutions—governments, central and local, commercial undertakings, churches, or political parties. We prefer to appear in a favourable light. We are anxious to feed the press with our good news, and we are reluctant to release or to enlarge our bad news.[35]

In theory the institutions cited have means of exerting pressure in the form of modes of withdrawal. Commercial concerns can, if they so desire, withhold their advertising; other institutions can clamp down on spokesmen's comments and make it as difficult as possible for the Press to obtain even routine news. In practice, editors know that retributive strategies of this sort will, in the long run, hurt the institutions more than the Press, which is in a position to play down or even exclude the good news anxiously fed to it. And the commercial institution that withholds advertising is cutting its own financial throat, especially in the predominant monopoly situation. Its revenue will often largely depend on advertising in the local Press. Charles Fenby, editorial director of Westminster Press Provincial Newspapers, has given some telling illustrations of the power of local newspaper advertising in an article in the *Financial Times*:

... an advertisement in a northern evening paper which cost £22 sold lawn mowers to the value of £500; an advertising feature for a redesigned store published on a Wednesday evening brought in 20,000 people in three days and the doors had to be closed for a time on the Saturday; a supplement published in another northern evening brought sales in such volume that the happy store management gave every member of the staff a day off and a gift voucher. . . .[36]

In other words, the newspapers concerned prompted a demand that did not previously exist, at least on any scale; fat profits were clearly the result.

The Press, then, is in a strong position to resist pressure against disclosures; even so, an editor is still free to accede to it. One key reason why he might be reluctant to do so is that if a favour to one individual or institution is granted, and subsequently becomes known about, it will be perceived as a precedent for similar favours to others; a chain reaction may be set in motion and prove difficult, if not impossible, to contain. The newspaper therefore risks losing the lustre that attaches to its theoretical impartiality.

When provincial newspaper companies comment on the subject of advertisers as a pressure group they invariably put forward two propositions: first, that extremely few attempts to influence content occur, and, second, that when they do occur they are firmly resisted. One of the questions posed by the 1947 Royal Commission was 'To what extent if at all do you consider that the accurate presentation of news and the adequate expression of opinion is distorted or restricted by . . . the interests and influence of advertisers?' Out of fifty-eight provincial companies, fifty-six considered that the interests and influence of advertisers had no effect; two representative replies follow.

H. Jackson & Co.:

In the vast majority of newspapers any idea that advertisers have any effect on the editorial side is a myth . . .[37]

The Midland News Association Ltd:

In the experience of the editor of the *Express and Star* no attempt has ever been made to influence policy, and the few attempts to secure publicity or the omission of court cases concerning an advertiser have not been successful.[38]

Scarborough and District Newspapers Ltd also noted their rejection of attempts to secure publicity:

> In our experience all that a local paper has to contend with—and these in great volume—are attempts to get free puffs. In our case they do not succeed, but this never has any noticeable effect on their attitude towards us or to the flood of free puff material which every day clogs our waste-paper baskets . . .[39]

Thus provincial newspaper companies claim that advertising sources do not influence policy, and that attempts to exercise pressure, except in the form of unsought publicity hand-outs, are rare. It has been suggested above that the Press has much to lose and little to gain by acceding to direct pressure.

Nevertheless, a study of local newspaper content shows that the provincial Press does acknowledge the financial contribution of advertisers in two main ways. First, it can and very largely does opt out of fulfilling the role of watchdog in relation to consumer goods and linked topics like the standard of service, except in general, non-specific terms. It also refrains from anything approaching a comparative critical assessment of particular kinds of retailer; so far as one knows, the *Birmingham Evening Mail* and *West Lancashire Evening Gazette* (to take two evening newspapers with which the writer is particularly familiar) have never commented on the standard of cafes and restaurants in their circulation areas. One newspaper that has done so is the Bolton *Evening News*, in a series of articles about restaurants within a fifty-mile radius of Bolton. The article 'Eating out' (published on 20 January 1966) took up 50 column inches; there was no accompanying related advertising, and adverse criticisms, although in a minority, were lodged incisively. Thus in the course of comment on 'The Turnkey' (a Wigan cellar restaurant) the writer stated:

> With the main course we were frankly disappointed. My gammon was dry and an end slice; my companion's lamb chop was not hot enough. An apologetic Mr. Doxey afterwards said we should have returned these meals to the kitchen.
> The two young chefs have orders to cook fresh for anyone, among the 7,000 customers with whom they are now coping each month, who complains.[40]

This sort of critical analysis of a consumer service is, in the writer's experience, a rarity in the provincial Press. There is without question considerable scope for extending the watchdog function into the field of consumer goods and services. At the national level *The People* intermittently 'watches' some aspect of these in the way that local newspapers (apart from the few exceptions of the kind cited) seem studiously to avoid. In a feature article headed 'And they had the nerve to call them *bargains*' *The People* of 8 January 1967 focused on the January sales of the Lewisham store, Chiesman's, and in particular on the sales price of 'Lened' poplin macs for children. One of these bore a ticket claiming a reduction from 55s (£2·75) to 39s 11d (£1·99½). The reporter was informed by Lened's importers that the wholesale price was 27s. 6d (£1·37½); the article continued:

> I then contacted Mr. G. Summers Sladden, general manager of Chiesman's Ltd.
> I asked him if his firm had bought the macs at 27s 6d each.
> He replied: 'As a matter of fact, we paid considerably less than that—but I will not tell you how much.'
> I asked Mr. Sladden if, considering the wholesale price ,he thought the alleged price of 55s was very high.
> He replied: 'No. My buyer marked them at that price—it seems reasonable to me.'
> But what about a profit approaching 100 per cent. on the sale price of 39s 11d—was not that unduly high?
> 'No,' said Mr. Sladden, 'we sell articles at what we can get for them.'
> . . .

This sort of probing into commercial undertakings is not pursued by the overwhelming majority of evening and weekly newspapers; nor do they pass on the detailed findings of national or local consumer research organisations. The scientific tone and factual assessments of the latter are shunned; one would deduce that the provincial Press is concerned to promote an unquestioning acceptance, on its readers' part, that local commerce is beyond reproach. Thus although advertisers may, as the Press claims, exert little direct influence on content, it is apparent that their financial role is acknowledged by the careful omission of evaluative critiques. This acknowledgement is what T. Bailey Forman Ltd, in their written evidence to the 1947 Royal Commission, described as the 'negative influence of advertisers':

> . . . In our experience, overt pressure from advertisers is a very rare incident indeed. When it occurs it is faithfully dealt with, even at the risk of losing revenue. The negative influence of advertisers is more subtle and difficult to pin down. It probably does have some effect in producing a disinclination to stir up antagonism when there is no strong consciousness of a public duty to take a positive line which would produce such a

result, but it may fairly be said that advertisers' likes and dislikes rarely obtrude upon editorial consciousness.[41]

Thus, for the proprietors of the Nottingham *Evening Post* at this time, only a 'strong consciousness of a public duty' would cause it to 'stir up antagonism'; what must transpire for 'consciousness' to become 'strong' is a matter for speculation. By and large, it seems that this company—and it can be assessed as continuingly representative —was content to 'play along' with advertisers and to refrain from objective criticism unless this was strikingly necessary in the public interest and, perhaps, inevitable in view of existing rumour and comment in the circulation area. But its dislike of risking antagonistic reaction means, in general, that it will avoid taking up the positive line on commercial practice that characterised the cited article from *The People*. It may also cause the local Press not to probe too deeply into the causes of industrial unrest in the private sector; how often does it present the worker's point of view in a fully documented feature article? Research on this point needs to be carried out.

T. Bailey Forman's claim that advertisers' 'likes' rarely obtrude upon editorial consciousness hardly stands up to examination at the present time. For a second way in which the provincial Press acknowledges the financial contributions of advertisers is by its publication of 'puff' feature articles, which are often, although not always, accompanied by related advertising. Although the bulk of the 'puff' material received by particular newspapers may, as Scarborough and District Newspapers claimed, be consigned to the waste-paper basket, some—for instance about the latest fashions, cosmetics, motor cars, 'pop' records and so on—clearly is utilised by 'puff' feature writers. If the material specially prepared in conjunction with local advertising campaigns is also taken into account, one finds that 'puff' consumer features command about 20 per cent of the evening Press's total feature space.

Many of these consumer features make a 'no holds barred' appeal to the reader's vanity. Thus a *Birmingham Evening Mail* fashion 'puff' on 4 January 1966 was entitled 'The look that turns the head'; it contained the following passages:

... For a woman there is tremendous satisfaction in the right holiday clothes, even though they seem to gobble up a lion's share of the budget. ... Wherever you go this year you will need your slippers, a smart raincoat, an uncrushable dress or suit and a rakish hat.
Outside this basic framework come beach clothes and dance dresses,

lacey wool evening jackets, and brief bistro tunics which slip over your bikini and stop the gendarmes lecturing you if your shorts are too short!
. . .

The text was given a pictorial dimension by four items, including a modelled swimsuit ('this Helanca suit by Nelbarden'—£4 9s. 11d [£4·49½]) and a dress (in 'non-crush Tricel cloque'—£8 18s 6d [£8·92½]). The effect of such clothes on others and the 'tremendous satisfaction' that they are stated to induce in the wearer are judged to outweigh the consideration that they 'gobble up the lion's share of the budget'. The inducement is to spend for effect rather than for necessity, although the incomes of the majority of the *Mail*'s readers hardly permit self-centred extravagance.

Turning to holiday features, one finds the Bristol *Evening Post* (in 'The ABC of choosing a holiday for 1966') taking each letter of the alphabet in turn and recommending a European holiday resort for each one:

> B for Benidorm, between Alicante and Valencia, and one of the most popular resorts in Spain. Fabulous beaches and plenty of evening entertainment. From £35.[42]

In general, holiday features offer alluring descriptions of particular countries, regions or resorts—including scenery, amenities, distinctive food or drink, and prices. Most of them assume a reader seeking a holiday within the typical price range of the advertisers, i.e. from 20 gns (£21) (eight days, Belgium) to 51 gns (£53·55) (fourteen days, Grand Scenic Austria). A few pitch their sights rather higher; one might point to a feature in the *Huddersfield Daily Examiner* recommending a £93 holiday on Corfu ('local dishes include whitebait, fried squid, moussaka, red mullet and spitted meat').[43]

The effect of much 'puff' feature material is to turn options (the very latest swim-suit, central heating, holidays in Spain) in the direction of norms, and therefore to pitch readers' expectations (as consumers) well beyond the sphere of basic necessities. The young wage-earner is soon conditioned if he is a willing recipient of advice like the following—from a *West Lancashire Evening Gazette* feature, 'Teenage choice':

> The carefree days of youth—over too soon—are there to enjoy. The young and fancy-free of today are having a better time than their counterparts of two decades ago.

This is the time when wages tend to burn a hole in your pocket—and so they should. Teenage days are carefree days, days when you can afford to buy the things you like, rather than worry about the next mortgage payment, or the grocery bill.

. . . Obviously a lot of teenage money is spent on clothes, but most teenagers feel that they want to spend their money on other things, too.

What kind of things? Well things which everybody else is buying, of course. Things like tape record players and transistor radios.

This is money soundly spent, for they will continue to give pleasure for many years to come. . . .[44]

This 'puff' was designed to accompany specific advertisements for a discotheque bar, a school of dancing, a local ballroom, a boutique, a hair fashions salon and a shop selling tape recorders, record players and radios; each was accorded its own particular 'plug'. The feature served as an unqualified endorsement of egoistic pleasure-seeking. Youth should be 'carefree'; the days of youth are 'there to enjoy'. Wages should very properly 'burn a hole' in the teenager's pocket; he or she will unquestionably want to spend money in the same way as 'everybody else'—on things that give pleasure ('things' occurs five times in the passage). This is the criterion exclusively formulated; no perspective-yielding hint is given of possible alternative ideals, such as self-sacrifice, charity, thrift or individualism. The basic contention is that spending equals enjoyment; the two sides of this equation are persistently articulated: 'enjoy'; 'wages'; 'buy'; 'money'; 'spent'; 'spend'; 'money'; 'buying'; 'money'; 'spent'; 'pleasure'. The style, crude and repetitive though it is, is no doubt finely calculated to make its mark and stimulate demand.

The inclusion of such a feature in the *Gazette* seems all the more curious when the different scale of values espoused in the paper's leading column is considered. For here some kinds of consumption (and their social effects) are held up to ridicule:

Youths with transistors consistently blaring, whose only visits to the barbers were to get the oil changed, and girls with skirts so short that they instructed the birds and the bees.[45]

For the leader-writing 'gatekeeper', then, transistor radios are an acute irritation and confer no prestige on their possessors; for the 'puff' feature writer they represent 'money well spent, for they will continue to give pleasure for many years to come'. In this area, therefore, the *Gazette* can be said to present mutually conflicting value systems to its readers. Similar self-contradictions as between advertising and leading column content in the provincial Press could be cited; for instance, editorial homilies on the excesses of the permissive society may feature in an issue containing highly emotive advertising on behalf of 'sex and violence' X films or local strip clubs.

It has been shown, therefore, that although the provincial Press does not—if its spokesmen are correct—yield to direct pressure from advertisers (pressure that would be primarily concerned to secure the exclusion of unfavourable news), it nevertheless acknowledges the crucial financial contribution of commercial organisations in two main ways. First, it largely contracts out of the watchdog role that is fulfilled by consumer research, and refrains from adopting an objectively critical stance in relation to consumer goods and services. Second, it actively assists in the promotion of consumer spending by publishing advertising features or 'puffs'.

In practice, advertisers are tacitly assisted by the sheer volume of advertising published. It has been seen that on particular evenings the advertising content accounts for up to 70 per cent of the total space available; it carries the implicit message that money is for spending. Some editors are clearly uneasy about the mass of advertising their newspapers carry. They know that this has been increased as a means of increasing profit margins; they do not wish to increase it to the point at which some readers—even a small minority—become deterred by its spatial dominance. One editor has suggested that the extension of advertising content represents the most noticeable change in the provincial Press in the last twenty years, adding that when advertising commands 70 per cent of a newspaper's space 'resentment . . . becomes very strong'. He continued: 'I am very much concerned that the economics of the newspaper industry have led to the production of unbalanced evening newspapers, carrying masses of advertising in relation to editorial content. As far as I know, no evening newspaper or organisation has carried out research to discover the type of paper their readers would like to have. We have gone on inflating our size (to forty-eight pages) to accommodate more advertising—not to accommodate more news (except as a by-product). There is now talk of introducing machinery to enable us to print up to seventy-two pages and possibly more. But what size of paper does the reader prefer? And what would he or she like to see? At the moment, if editors are honest, we must say that we are only guessing. That our sales remain roughly constant or perhaps increase may be only a result of habit or improved selling techniques. I think there is a tremendous field of inquiry open here.'[46] One implication of these comments is that the newspaper industry has paid far more attention to advertising-oriented research than to research on the editorial side. A further implication is that local newspapers will grow in size primarily to accommodate more and more advertising; additional space for news and features will be merely a 'by-product'.

It is probable that the volume of submitted advertising will increase, gathering considerable momentum as and when reflations of the economy take place. Charles Fenby has expressed the view that both display and classified advertising will expand. The regional organisation of television is the key, in his opinion, to a growing readiness on the part of national advertisers to use local newspapers as the logical medium for 'follow-ups'. Accordingly, he perceives in them 'a positive aggression in the face of the popular nationals' at the present time; the former virtual monopoly of national advertising by the national Press is being broken:

. . . since it seems likely that the TV set-up is a permanent one, it is not fanciful to imagine that more national advertisers having been forced to think regionally by this turn of events will more readily think regionally so far as the Press is concerned. Already, local newspapers are used in conjunction with television to ram the message home, and the question arises whether this movement will reach the point where the most popular newspapers are not the automatic first choice for advertising nationally distributed goods.[36]

This writer is clearly pleased with the prospect that the provincial Press will be increasingly 'used' to 'ram' advertisers' messages home. The phrasing suggests that readers are being thought of primarily as mass consumers, to be bludgeoned until they respond. The exclusiveness of the focus inevitably pushes other purposes of newspapers as communicators into the shadows.

The volume of classified advertising has also increased, and will continue to increase. Fenby notes that this has been brought about 'by the employment of new techniques for a medium which can be shown to work'. Clearly, the provincial Press believes in keeping up to date in areas that will demonstrably augment its revenue. The danger, as Raymond Williams has observed, is that 'all the basic purposes of communication—the sharing of human experience—can become subordinated to this drive to sell'.[47] In rightly ensuring their economic well-being, it is up to local newspaper companies to see that such a subordination does not transpire; it will not if the editorial attitudes of Mr Elliot Dodds (editor of the *Huddersfield Daily Examiner*, 1923–59) predominate. Mr Dodds was writing in the *Examiner's* centenary issue of 28 January 1971:

I am thinking more particularly of local newspapers when I say that a newspaper is (or ought to be) something more than a mere commodity. It is (or ought to be) an artefact with a soul. . . . It must make a profit, or it cannot survive; but profit-making must not be the sole concern of those who are running it . . .

Notes

1 Wiles, *op. cit.*, pp. 152–3.
2 *Ibid.*, p. 142.
3 See *The Daily Telegraph*, 20 December 1966.
4 See statement accompanying the annual accounts of United Newspapers Ltd, year ending 31 December 1966.
5 *The Times*, 25 March 1967.
6 Robert Hornby, *The Press in Modern Society* (London: Frederick Muller, 1965), p. 24.
7 The classification 'non-local' refers principally to specific products not manufactured in the locality; local branches of national or regional retail outlets are classed as 'local'.
8 *Minutes of Evidence* (1947 Royal Commission), 21 January 1948, p. 16.
9 James Grant, *op. cit.*, vol. II, pp. 354–5.
10 *Congleton Chronicle*, 20 November 1964.
11 *Slough Express*, 18 December 1964.
12 *County Express* (Stourbridge), 5 December 1964.
13 *Brighton and Hove Herald*, 11 December 1964.
14 *Surrey Advertiser*, 12 December 1964.
15 *Woodford Express and Independent*, 11 December 1964.
16 *Bucks. Free Press*, 4 December 1964.
17 *Stockport Advertiser*, 10 December 1964.
18 *Mid-Devon Advertiser*, 24 April 1965.
19 *Birmingham Evening Mail*, 2 December 1966.
20 *Wakefield Express*, 5 December 1964.
21 *West Lancashire Evening Gazette*, 2 December 1966.
22 The *West Briton*, 3 December 1964.
23 *Southport Visiter*, 5 December 1964.
24 *Crawley and District Observer*, 11 December 1964.
25 *Burnley Express*, 31 July 1965.
26 *Stockport County Express*, 10 December 1964.

27 *Hayes Gazette*, 11 December 1964.
28 *Staffordshire Advertiser and Chronicle*, 22 July 1965.
29 *Rochdale Observer*, 5 December 1964.
30 *Croydon Advertiser*, 11 December 1964.
31 Grant, *op. cit.*, vol. II, p. 384.
32 *Ibid.*, p. 396.
33 Harold Evans, 'Getting the facts', *The Practice of Journalism*, ed. J. Dodge and G. Viner (London: Heinemann, 1963), pp. 74–5.
34 W. G. Hoskins, *Local History in England* (London: Longmans, 1959), p. 29.
35 Kenneth Wheare, *The Universities in the News* (Cambridge: the University Press, 1967), pp. 17–18.
36 Charles Fenby, 'A deserving share for the regional papers', *Financial Times*, 26 June 1967.
37 *Memoranda of Evidence*, p. 99.
38 *Ibid.*, p. 132.
39 *Ibid.*, p. 169.
40 Bolton *Evening News*, 20 January 1966.
41 *Memoranda of Evidence*, p. 84.
42 Bristol *Evening Post*, 12 January 1966.
43 *Huddersfield Daily Examiner*, 11 January 1966.
44 *West Lancashire Evening Gazette*, 8 November 1966.
45 *Ibid.*, 4 November 1966.
46 Comment submitted in January 1966.
47 Raymond Williams, *Britain in the Sixties: Communications*, p. 24.

III Cultural and political attitudes

The fallacy is to believe that artistic activities, at present supported by us and other local or charitable bodies, could in fact be transferred to commercial managements. The fate of the London theatre has demonstrated that, except in the rarest instances, we have contrived an economic world where it is a simple untruth that worthwhile activities must necessarily succeed . . . No small repertory theatre need reproach itself that its box office receipts cannot maintain the performances even if it is playing to near-capacity, when we realise that newspapers with circulations in the region of two million readers cannot, in the 'Alice in Wonderland' world in which we live, make a sufficient profit to safeguard their survival. . . .

Lord Goodman, in the Introduction to the 1969–70 report
of the Arts Council

The *Gazette* warned the electors of Eatanswill that the eyes not only of England, but of the whole civilised world, were upon them; and the *Independent* imperatively demanded to know, whether the constituency of Eatanswill were the grand fellows they had always taken them for, or base and servile tools, undeserving alike the name of Englishmen and the blessings of freedom. Never had such a commotion agitated the town before.

Charles Dickens, in *The Pickwick Papers*, 1836–67

There is a considerable fund of common imaginative strength in all parts of society. If a thinner consumers' culture is not to spread over all more care will have to be taken in seeking relevant connections, links between things which show this strength (some features of day-to-day life, some work in the arts today, some social organisations, some forms of recreation). It is not possible to define in advance the nature of a good demotic culture. Unless one believes such a culture is not possible, one has to try to keep open all lines which may allow for promising development as well as oppose those likely to lead to a dead smartness . . .

Richard Hoggart, in 'Mass communications in Britain',
Speaking to Each Other, vol. 1

III Cultural and political attitudes

11 Provincial newspaper attitudes to culture, with special reference to television and 'pop' music

1. Attitudes to culture

In practice, there are two main uses of the word 'culture'. It is used in a general, anthropological sense to refer to the commonly shared attributes of a group—its values, attitudes, assumptions, interests, activities, styles, etc. The group may be national, regional, sub-regional, institutional, racial, differentiated by age, sex or physique, and so on; thus 'Nazi culture', 'youth culture' and 'Northern culture'.[1] 'Culture' can also be used to refer to 'a people's achieved works of intellect and imagination'.[2] The influence of Matthew Arnold[3] has greatly helped to equate culture in this sense with the 'serious' arts, thereby pushing other forms of intellectual achievement to the periphery. Hence C. P. Snow's diagnosis of a 'cultural divide' and his plea for more recognition for 'the scientific culture'.[4]

It is the second meaning, equivalent to 'the enlightening arts', that the provincial Press typically attaches to the term culture. One assumption that local newspapers appear to hold in common is that the majority of rate-payers are indifferent, even hostile, to the serious arts. This was apparent in a leader in the weekly *Lincolnshire Chronicle*, written in support of the Lincolnshire Association:

> That new cultural movement the Lincolnshire Association has set itself a target of £50,000 for its first year of operation and half of this it hopes to raise from the rates.
> The county councils of Lindsey, Kesteven and Holland will be asked for a ½d rate, county boroughs will be asked for a farthing rate and the balance will be requested from the remaining local authorities in proportions to be decided.
> Will they get it? You can almost hear every Tom, Dick and Harry chorus the famous phrase of Eliza Doolittle in 'Pygmalion'—'Not (so-and-so) likely.'
> With facile tongues they will argue that everything must be done to cut the rate burden, not increase it . . .[5]

The writer takes it for granted here that 'Tom, Dick and Harry' (or the so-called 'man in the street') will resist any proposed outlay of their money on local culture; in effect, he anticipates a comment in the White Paper *A Policy for the Arts*: 'too many working people have been conditioned by their education and environment to consider the best in music, painting, sculpture and literature outside their reach'.[6]

The presumed majority antipathy to the arts serves as a continuing reference point for those town councillors who object to cultural subsidy, as the following extract from a report in the *Leicester Mercury* shows:

> '*Support the arts' plea is rejected by Bosworth R.D.C.*
>
> A plea for more support for the arts, including a possible contribution to Leicester's Phoenix Theatre, was made by a few members at Market Bosworth Rural Council meeting yesterday, but went unheeded. On a vote it was decided by a big majority not to refer back for further consideration a decision by the Finance Committee not to make a contribution.
>
> The matter was brought to a head by Councillor W. Cushing when he said, 'The council has decided to make no contribution to the National Council for Civic Theatres, the Eastern Authorities Orchestral Association, the Phoenix Theatre, and they have decided they cannot support Enterprise Neptune.
>
> 'If the arts are going to thrive in this country it will be without the assistance of Market Bosworth Rural Council,' he said . . .[7]

The tone of the concluding sentence implies a 'them' and an 'us'. 'They' are the people who would stand to benefit from cultural subsidy; they are perceived by Councillor Cushing as a non-local minority. Local people are collectively assessed in terms of the stereotype of the 'anti-subsidy rate-payer'; another councillor, W. T. H. Cragg, 'urged the members to reflect that they were not spending their own money but money belonging to ratepayers'.[7]

Majority indifference towards the arts is of course sustained—either actively or by the implication of minimal coverage—by the popular national newspapers. Raymond Williams notes that the following proportions of news space were devoted to the arts (including radio and television) in July 1961: *Daily Express*, 2 per cent; *Daily Mirror*, 2 per cent; *Sunday Express*, 2 per cent; *The People*, 2 per cent; *News of the World*, 1 per cent. The average for the 'quality' dailies was 10 per cent, and for the quality Sundays 31 per cent.[8] The *Express* group intermittently publishes features that set the so-called 'highbrow' against the 'average family reader'; thus one finds A. J. P. Taylor portraying an interest in opera as a manifestation of cultural snobbery on the part of a minority:

... One of the most detestable features of our modern world is that minorities think they are virtuous and superior, just because they are minorities.

The man who goes to Covent Garden thinks that he is superior to the family who go to the local cinema. And he even claims that the community should subsidise him, or Covent Garden, for being superior ...[9]

The passing off of assumption as asserted fact in this passage needs no elucidation; the salient point is that this represents an endorsement of the view that the arts should not be subsidised from rates or taxes. The *Daily Telegraph* also deprecates subsidy and would prefer to see the extension of private patronage; it therefore looks with disfavour on the Arts Council's 'tirades . . . directed at the elected representatives of local authorities because they refuse to sanction the disposal of substantial sums for a purpose of which they and (by implication) their electors disapprove'.[10]

The supposed popular view, therefore, is that the arts should stand on their own feet. In order to assess local Press attitudes to culture and its financing, a sample of sixteen evening newspapers was studied over the period 10–22 January 1966. At this time Miss Jennie Lee, as Minister of State with special responsibility for the arts, was touring the regions in an attempt to prime the cultural pump. She was anxious that there should not be a narrow interpretation of culture, and stressed that—to take one example—music in all its forms (classical, jazz, folk, 'pop', etc.) should be encouraged. During this period five of the sampled newspapers offered leading column comment on local culture—four of them in the context of arguments for cultural subsidy. These were the Newcastle *Evening Chronicle*, Darlington *Evening Despatch*, Wolverhampton *Express and Star*, *Oxford Mail* and *Lancashire Evening Post*. In view of the majority attitude discussed above, it is fair to say that these newspapers were making a courageous stand—details of which follow.

The Newcastle leader pleaded with local government and local industry to support the North East Association for the Arts more generously:

... it needs money desperately, and will continue to be impoverished until attitudes towards its financial support change considerably.

The sooner it is accepted generally that culture cannot be had 'on the cheap' the better it will be for the association and the people it has set itself out to serve.

With a few notable exceptions (Newcastle and South Shields, for example) the contributions of local authority members are pitifully small.

Even the best approach nowhere near the sixpenny rate which they could legally apply to such projects as the association is prepared to carry through.

Industry's attitude is even more parsimonious, and can only be interpreted as evidence of a lack of understanding of cultivating the fuller life.[11]

This passage evinces a cogency and incisiveness indicative of real commitment. A 'fuller' community life was also the goal of the *Oxford Mail*'s leader in support of two councils that had voted to assist a local theatre group:

A live theatre

It was enlightened of Bullingdon R.D.C. this week to vote a grant of 100 guineas to the Meadow Players, despite protests from some members. Oxford City Council faced opposition couched in similar terms when it granted the company £500 in addition to the annual £3,000 grant last spring. Other councils in the Oxford area have turned down the request for grants to the Meadow Players.

Most local councillors must be aware that modern thinking—for example, the idea behind Miss Jennie Lee's post as Minister for the arts—advocates more public patronage of the arts and particularly the live theatre.

Against this trend they will argue that there are more urgent matters—dangerous corners, street lights and so on—which councils should spend the ratepayer's money on. But are these bread and butter matters really all that much more urgent?

Communities must keep their physical amenities in good order so that the people in them can lead easier lives. But amenities of this sort do not give the communities their vigour or guts. After all do we remember Elizabethan England because it brought in the Poor Law and water supplies for London or because it gave us Shakespeare and Marlowe, Middleton, Ben Jonson and Beaumont and Fletcher?[12]

This is, clearly, intended as a compelling exhortation, but the writer's rather old-fashioned concept of culture could be said to get him into avoidable difficulties. It causes him to set the arts apart from material amenities; a wider definition of culture would enable him to avoid this 'either . . . or' position. For the physical environment is part of the raw material from which the arts are fashioned; in Emerson's words, 'man's culture can spare nothing, wants all the material'.[13] Or, as the authors of *A Policy for the Arts* put it, 'diffusion of culture is now so much a part of life that there is no precise point at which it stops. Advertisements, buildings, books, motor cars, radio and television, magazines, records, all can carry a cultural aspect and affect our lives for good and ill as a species of "amenity".'[14] Thus local amenities and the arts can be seen as elements making up a whole way of life, or culture in the wider sense discussed at the beginning of this chapter.

One newspaper that had clearly taken to heart Miss Lee's plea for an expansion of the notion of what is cultural was the *Lancashire Evening Post*:

... There are, of course, many versions of what constitutes art and culture. They range much wider than art galleries and museums; it is the narrow interpretation of culture which makes many people shy away from the word.

The joint Ministry circular caught the feeling when it suggested that a promising field of initiative even for small authorities was the provision of an arts centre to cater for all ages and tastes.

And museums surely need to be something more than havens of stuffed birds and dusty collections of Victoriana!

Other countries have shown what can be done by lifting galleries out of the cobweb era and turning them into centres which interest people and sometimes become tourist attractions.

It would be an immense advance if we could get our ideas of art and culture into the twentieth century. We need a hurricane of change.[15]

There is a refreshing attempt here to elicit the causes of indifference to the traditional arts; the writer rightly perceives that the term 'culture' carries many repelling overtones. He implies that most people do in fact see museums as 'havens of stuffed birds and dusty collections of Victoriana' belonging to a 'cobweb era'. 'Shying away' is a phrase that exactly catches a prevalent response; people think of culture as something 'highbrow' and not for them. If the provincial Press as a whole were to adopt the *Lancashire Evening Post*'s approach, considerable impetus would be given to advancing our 'ideas of art and culture'. For as Hall and Whannel point out, the 'cultural map' is undergoing considerable change; 'the older culture has been put under pressure not only from the new media, but also from the art and experiment of the *avant-garde*'.[16]

The five newspapers that commented on local culture showed themselves to be—in principle at least—solidly behind Miss Lee's campaign. No conflicting approaches were in evidence in the sample, and the indications thus far are that when editorial comment is forthcoming it does not toe the assumed majority line on cultural matters. Furthermore the evening Press, taken as a whole, gives quite substantial feature coverage to the traditional arts. A note of the space devoted to book reviewing in a sample of eight evening newspapers must serve to suggest this:

Birmingham Evening Mail ('New books'): 34 column inches.
Bolton *Evening News* ('The world of books'): 70 column inches
Bristol *Evening Post* ('The book page'): 40 column inches.
Cambridge Evening News ('Guide to the new books'): 31½ column inches.
Huddersfield Daily Examiner ('Books of today'): 30½ column inches.
Oxford Mail ('Book page'): 120 column inches.
West Lancashire Evening Gazette: nil
Yorkshire Evening Post: 24½ column inches.
(Average space allotted: 44 column inches)

The critics concerned were clearly aiming to interest the 'intelligent layman' through many of the reviewing choices; however, the range of books considered (including twenty-nine different works of non-fiction) was too wide to facilitate a detailed account. It remains to discuss the critical position adopted towards television and the 'pop' world as a means of assessing more precisely the provincial Press's cultural attitudes.

2. Attitudes to television

Of the sixteen evening newspapers sampled[17] six were found to include television reviews on most nights of the week; two others —the *Oxford Mail* and the *Huddersfield Daily Examiner*—offered one weekly critical feature. Eleven gave previews, nine of these evening by evening. The normal reviewing practice is to select one or two programmes and criticise these in the detail that the allotted space permits. On Monday 10 January 1966 the column inch totals of the reviews were as follows:

Birmingham Evening Mail	5
Bolton *Evening News*	10
Lancashire Evening Post	7½
Leicester Mercury	12
Newcastle *Evening Chronicle*	4
Yorkshire Evening Post	9

The average length of text was therefore 8 column inches—indicating that TV reviewing is not perceived as a function that warrants spatial generosity. Even so, the reviews may well command considerable reader interest. Of course, general trends in television, as well as particular programmes, intermittently prompt leading column comment—some of which is cited below.

Leader writers' and reviewers' attitudes to television are largely predictable from what has already been established about the kind of family and community life that the provincial Press upholds as its ideal, and about its Matthew Arnold-tinged view of culture. Television should aspire to be morally wholesome and intellectually uplifting; it should not just be content to offer the viewing public what the TAM ratings point to as popular. It should not affront the Christian ethic; its programmes should not give grounds for suspicion that sex or violence are being exploited in detachment from a clear moral framework. Nor should language ostracised in the ideal family setting be used unless it can be defended as artistically crucial and as serving a moral end; even then, it should be used very sparingly.[18] There is an evident preference for orthodox structural forms in plot and dialogue,[19] and a dislike of interviewers or raconteurs who 'beat about the bush' and fail to focus incisively on the topic under discussion. All these factors require more detailed substantiation, but summarised in this way they suggest the common front of broad agreement. Much of the illustrative material that follows is drawn from the *West Lancashire Evening Gazette*, which in this respect can be regarded as one of the more conservative evening newspapers—although not so conservative as to be unrepresentative.

At the root of provincial comment on TV are assumptions about the expectations of the family viewing unit. In spite of the obvious disparities in family environment, social status, education and so on, the elements all families are felt to hold in common—and persisting even in this more permissive age—are regarded as justification for the meaningful use of phrases like the 'ordinary family' and 'family values'; amongst the significant values would be the sense of justice, decency, morality and proportion.

During the mid-1960s television drama, and the late-night, 'TW3' type of revue, were frequently criticised for failing to meet the expectations of viewers. Some Press comment alleged an inexcusable discrepancy between the moral tone of particular plays and the tacit morality that sustains family and community life. This was the

charge levelled in a *West Lancashire Evening Gazette* leader, 'Writing
on the wall':

> The BBC advances a strange argument when it says that if it is to
> encourage new writers it must not prevent them from saying what they
> have to say.
> And if what they have to say happens to be a lurid concoction of sex,
> violence and deep depression it apparently does not matter—the little
> dears must be allowed their squeaks.
> Writing, acting and all the creative arts are involved processes, and so
> it is not surprising that the BBC should tend to become somewhat con-
> fused and involved in its attempts to analyse them.
> But the average healthy-minded viewer and listener—and that descrip-
> tion, thank goodness, still applies to most people—sees the matter quite
> simply.
> He and his wife demand entertainment that will give pleasure to them-
> selves, and entertainment that they can watch with their families; not
> spectacles that arouse embarrassment, distaste and repulsion . . .[20]

The 'new writers' are seen as lacking the sense of their audience;
they should reflect that the average viewer is 'healthy-minded' and
is likely to be in the company of his family. The 'lurid concoction'
is felt to denote insufficient maturity and experience on the drama-
tists' part; the writer paternalistically reproves 'Auntie' BBC for
her short-sighted indulgence. The playwrights are accorded the physical stature of five-year-olds in 'the little dears'; 'squeaks' reduces
them even further to the size of mice. This permits the reader to
assume Brobdingnagian dimensions and equate his size with superior
moral wholesomeness.

The trend of the discussion so far makes the *Gazette*'s admiration
for a series like 'Dr Finlay's casebook' fully understandable. Its
moral tone is faultless, its appeal is to the family, and the narrative
line avoids taxing complexities. The *Gazette*'s leader writer drew the
predictable homily:

Real life

Up and up soar the viewing figures of 'Dr Finlay's Casebook'.
> Splendid! For the stories are life as it is lived—life with joy and sorrow,
> comedy and tragedy, happiness and fortitude; the life of ordinary men
> and women in an ordinary place—and yet a microcosm of humanity.
> All purveyors of sleaziness, sordidness and lust—and those who allow
> them to screen it—please note.[21]

There are two assumptions of interest here. One is the view that
television should mirror the normal: 'life as it is lived' or 'the life

of ordinary men and women in an ordinary place'. The patterns of normality ('joy and sorrow, comedy and tragedy, happiness and fortitude') are set over against the abnormal—presumably unrelieved unhappiness, sorrow or tragedy, as well as 'sleaziness, sordidness and lust'. Second, there is the proposition that Tannochbrae is 'an ordinary place'. It is, certainly, ordinary in the sense that the fictional community consists of a complex network of personal relationships within which the individual knows his position exactly, and in that the pattern of events corresponds—after the necessary tailoring—to a pattern of life identifiable with 'life as it is lived' in a real community.

Many viewers may well live in places which, like Tannochbrae, are long established and familiar, with known social gradations and interconnections. They may also be on nodding terms with the local people they rely on in times of crisis—the doctor, the clergyman or the solicitor. But several types of contemporary community do not afford this sort of security, such as new housing estates, tower blocks of flats, demolition zones, or those urban areas that are little more than transit camps for mobile flat-dwellers or young couples saving up for a house in the suburbs. The people who live in such communities are 'ordinary', but 'life as it is lived' by them must seem very different—much more anonymous and impersonal—to life in Tannochbrae. Indeed, Tannochbrae's contrast to it may constitute an additional attraction; the shooting location has in fact become a tourist Mecca, and 'awed sightseers . . . file past Dr Cameron's house and surgery'.[22] The drawback to the *Gazette*'s concept of the ideal 'ordinary place' is that it could easily initiate a prejudice against TV fiction rooted in other, perhaps less attractive —but none the less 'real'—types of community setting.

In pointing to the family unit, and advancing the criteria just sketched out, provincial newspapers are able to command the approval of socio-culturally conservative community leaders. Perhaps a new descriptive phrase needs coining for those local moralists who place great stress on the need for the mass media to inculcate social and ethical values explicitly, and who believe that some aspects of reality (e.g. 'sleaziness' or 'sordidness') should be played down or, better still, screened out; one might refer to them as the 'ultra-conservative moralists'. Another group, probably fewer in numbers, is composed of 'radical realists'; they opt to look at social realities fairly and squarely, and feel that the media should do likewise.

It is the ultra-conservative moralists who seem to write most frequently to the local Press about TV. The TV reviewer who in some respect appears to be failing to conform to their media criteria is likely to be chastised with alacrity. For instance, the *Gazette*'s TV critic was reproved by a local vicar for the following comments on 'Dixon of Dock Green':

New series replaces 'Dock Green'

Lockhart in; Dixon out. That's the latest event in the teletec world.

Different series, different channels, different days. The only point they have in common is that they both look like going on forever.

If I have to choose between the two my hand goes up for George. A little cosy sometimes, often leaden-footed and incorrigibly moral, 'Dixon of Dock Green' has the human touch. . . . Jack Warner's fans need not be dismayed. He will be back in the autumn.[23]

The phrase singled out as objectionable—amidst the personal, chatty commentary characterised by such an 'in group' neologism as 'teletec' and by the colloquial tone of 'my hand goes up for George'—was 'incorrigibly moral', The protesting vicar's letter serves to clarify the standpoint of the ultra-conservative moralists:

The moral Dixon

I was surprised to read your radio and television commentator's complaint that 'Dixon of Dock Green' was 'incorrigibly moral'. How out of character with the general tone of your paper! Incorrigibly moral, forsooth!

In a previous sentence Mr. Boothroyd states that Dixon looks like going on for ever.

Does he not see that it is because he is moral and provides a feast of healthy sense that he so strongly appeals to many? TV has been likened to a mirror reflecting the life and thought of the people, and in 'Dixon of Dock Green' the belief in morality cherished by the vast majority of the nation is faithfully portrayed.

Surely we have more than enough sordid and nauseating stuff without wishing 'Dixon of Dock Green' to descend to an immoral level. To urge that he should do so is to encourage the forces which oppose sound citizenship.

I trust that I am not speaking for myself alone in registering this protest, but if it be so then so be it.[24]

'Incorrigibly moral' has been interpreted as meaning 'moral to a fault' or 'moral to excess'—implying a degree of moral virtue bordering on the unbelievable. The reviewer may well not have intended to point to anything more than Dixon's Aesopian role, whereby events are not allowed to speak for themselves but are briefly sermonised upon in a mildly unctuous, admonitory tone. There is no reasonable ground for reading in—as the vicar did—the suggestion that Dixon should 'descend to an immoral level'.

The significance of this letter lies in its indication of the kind of vigilance and critique that is constantly applied to provincial newspaper content. Total acceptance of the vicar's TV ideal—that it should offer 'a feast of healthy sense'—could lead to every fictional programme containing a predictable homiletic weighting, and aiming at the overt reinforcement of the moral code said to be 'cherished by the vast majority'. The drawback to such an approach is that some aspects of contemporary life must necessarily be falsified in their purged presentation; the viewer is not being allowed to form his own opinion in detachment from judgments explicitly and implicitly incorporated. It is therefore possible to charge the vicar with seeking a simplification of experience which, although it results in wholesome entertainment, may be dishonest as a representation of reality. It is this sort of simplification that worries the 'radical realists'; their position is clarified in the following news report, also from the *West Lancashire Evening Gazette*:

Fleetwood 'gamble' a success

CURATE PRODUCES 'SEAMY' PLAY

Fleetwood Parish Drama Group performed one of the most talked-about plays in Fleetwood at Broadway Rooms, Fleetwood, last night, when they presented *Women of Twilight*—an adults-only production.

The Rev. H. Entwhistle (curate), who produced the play, agreed that the story of a squalid London home for unmarried mothers and unmarried pregnant women and the colourful language had been a gamble.

'I made no alterations to the script and chose the play because of the obvious Christian moral behind it,' said Mr. Entwhistle.

'Christian people, especially, should be aware that this sort of place exists. Without the bawdy language and cockney slang the play would have meant nothing and I took it for granted that an intelligent audience would appreciate its seriousness.'

. . . The general comment from the capacity audience last night was very favourable but a small minority seemed to think some of the language unsuitable . . . [25]

The local Press headline—'Curate produces "seamy" play'—denotes the unusualness of the choice of production and is based on the assumption that curates are not conventionally in favour of plays that contain 'bawdy language'. But the curate stands by the belief that here dramatic realism serves a Christian purpose. He is at pains to stress his view of the audience as an 'intelligent' one, composed of 'serious people'. As such, they need no cushioning; the dramatic material will not undermine their moral fibre. But in spite of the reporter's assessment of audience reactions, it is fair to say that a letter to the local Press would be most likely to come from the dissenting minority.

Thus although both kinds of local opinion former—the ultra-conservative moralist and the radical realist—would agree that a moral end is the crucial criterion, there is an area of major disagreement as to whether this end is best served by an expurgated version of reality or by a more documentary approach which, while fulfilling a moral purpose, attempts to be faithful to the observed facts. Provincial leader writers and TV critics can usually be located in the middle ground between these two wings; 'Dr Finlay's casebook' may approximate to the ideal, but they are at least prepared to be sympathetic towards the radical realists. An interesting test case was afforded by the short play *New Eve and Old Adam*, based on D. H. Lawrence's story. This would certainly have been judged by the critics as unlikely to have struck a sympathetic chord in most viewers, on whose part—as Denis McQuail has shown—there is a strong preference for detection or suspense stories, or romantic comedies, and a strong resistance to plays with 'some element of unfamiliarity of plot or setting' that are found to be 'disturbing or controversial'.[26] However, only one of seven provincial reviews studied indicated total acceptance of known majority attitudes, remaining content merely to play these preferences back:

> It mirrored the disenchantment with human relationships and people of the small screen's drama departments.
> . . . 'What worse bondage can we conceive than the bond of love?' ran the plaintive quotation. Tck! Tck! Isn't life a misery? Where's that handkerchief? I feel the tears are about to flow. . . .[27]

This reviewer plays on the known liking for a measure of comic relief and a happy ending; he feels that a sustained, unmodified depiction of marital misery is not, and ought not to be, dramatically viable. Three other reviewers drew attention to the play's consistent, forbidding seriousness. The *Yorkshire Evening Post* assessed the play as 'poignant, soul-searching stuff unrelieved by humour'.[28] A comparable comment was offered in the *Birmingham Evening Mail*; *New Eve and Old Adam* had been 'deep stuff, with its flashbacks,

Biblical quotations and bedroom philosophising'.[29] (The common term 'stuff' seems to connote 'not my—or, probably, your—sort of stuff'.) The Newcastle *Evening Chronicle*'s critic felt that Lawrence had drawn 'a rather grim picture'.[30]

However, of the six critics who reviewed the play in some detail (the Bolton *Evening News* merely noting that 'ITV's D. H. Lawrence short story adaptations look like turning out winners'), four praised the quality of the production as a whole and five the standard of acting. The story had been 'outstandingly well done'[31] and 'powerfully translated'[29]; 'in spite of a somewhat choppy direction . . . it came across very well, and the repetitive argument was broken up sufficiently to keep it fresh'.[30] The *Leicester Mercury*'s reviewer was far from seeing the play as just another 'long moan about life': 'Lawrence's treatment of the age-old theme was remarkable for the dignity and depth. It contrasted with the shallow way so many modern authors handle similar situations.'[32]

Furthermore, the play had been 'excellently acted';[30] Pauline Devaney and Bernard Brown had given 'effective performances of sustained yet restrained power'[28] and 'beautifully sensitive, well-rounded pieces of acting'.[31] The *Birmingham Evening Mail* felt that the lead actors had 'sensitively conveyed the gulf between the Eve who wanted to be more than a mate and the Adam who could only try to comprehend'. Thus although four reviewers stated or implied that they felt the play's theme and mood had been too insistently lodged ('deep stuff', 'rather grim picture'), five of the six found much to commend in this production of a 'sad study of a newly married couple faced with the agonising dilemma that they were unhappy together but miserable apart'.[28] A theme of this kind is hardly acceptable to that kind of ultra-conservative moralist who fully endorses the critical canons of Mrs Whitehouse and the NVALA; amongst the many forms of 'high-spot drama' she would banish from TV is the play that suggests 'that relationships are more likely to disintegrate than to mature'.[33] She would be extremely reluctant, one suspects, to see anything meritorious in a play about the 'agonising dilemma' posed by an unhappy marriage.

The analysis of the reviews of *New Eve and Old Adam* has shown that the majority were not content merely to echo the widely assumed viewing preferences of the 'average viewer'. The critics' cultural horizons are wider, and they afford the radical realist grounds for moderate optimism; he can feel that 'good' realism (one thinks of a play like *Cathy, come home*) is more likely to be well received—albeit with some reservations—than condemned.[34]

To sum up, the provincial Press clearly attaches crucial importance to 'patterned, family viewing'.[35] Essential elements in this pattern are the 'popular series and comedy shows'. It was noted that the *West Lancashire Evening Gazette* regards 'Dr Finlay's casebook' as an ideal series for family viewing; it is seen as portraying 'life as it is lived' and as 'a microcosm of humanity'. Television is not deemed a suitable medium for all forms of documentary or dramatic realism; 'sleaziness, sordidness and lust', 'the expletives of the gutter' and 'deep depression' are amongst the kinds of content cited as objectionable. Although exceptions are made, it is thought that in general realism should be modified in ways that will give the viewer a feeling of reassurance; good ought to triumph over evil, optimism should prevail over pessimism, and a positive morality be endorsed. But family values are not seen as quite the rigid cultural determinants that they represent for Mrs Whitehouse; the distinction was made in a *Gazette* leader, 'Offensive': '. . . This column is no Mrs. Whitehouse, but it does feel entitled to object to a most offensive word that was used several times last night in a gratuitous BBC television puff for a new theatrical venture . . .'[36]

The analysis of the reviews of *New Eve and Old Adam* showed that most critics keep the door open for modes of realism that strike them as sincere and qualitatively convincing; but the radical realist's case is far from being accepted *carte blanche*. The *Gazette*'s opinion that 'moderation in all things is the best policy'[37] would command widespread assent in the provincial Press.

Audience research sponsored by ITV has shown that watching television is 'easily the most popular leisure activity in the country';[38] in view of this, it is surprising that only half the newspapers sampled published TV reviews on a regular nightly or weekly basis. It can also be seen as regrettable for, as Denis McQuail points out, 'something of a common culture is represented already by the widely shared interest in certain kinds of mass media content . . . what is at issue is the level at which it will be set'.[39] The evening Press could do much to influence the nature and the level of its mass readership's viewing expectations.

3. Attitudes to the 'pop' world

The general level of 'pop' music (after due allowance for the exceptions that Wilfrid Mellers would rightly make[40]) and its social milieu—the discotheque, the coffee bar and the 'pop' festival—would seem to be alien both to the provincial Press's concept of culture and to its formulation of family values. This proposition is discussed below; first, it must be re-asserted that the leading exponents of the 'pops' are certainly regarded by the majority of evening newspapers as newsworthy—even when the news is as orderly as a Beatle's wedding. Disorder news about 'pop' performers commands even more prominence; for instance, the Rolling Stones' drug trial was adjudged to be worth the main headlines of six out of eleven evening newspapers sampled on 28 June 1967. The headlines of all the reports and the number of column inches each report received are summarised in table 15.

Table 15

Name of newspaper	Headline (MH: main headline)	Total column inches
Manchester Evening News	'Stones: "A strong, sweet smell of of incense"' (MH)	59
Newcastle Evening Chronicle	'Nude girl at Stones' party, say police' MH)	58
Oxford Mail	'Court story of Stones' party' (MH)	47
Nottingham Evening Post	'Stones: QC tells of girl in rug' (MH)	40
Lancashire Evening Post	'Stones drug jury told of girl in a fur rug' (MH)	23
Leicester Mercury	'Nude woman at Rolling Stones' party, says QC' (MH)	22
Bolton Evening News	'"Naked woman at drug party"'	14½
Bristol Evening Post	'"Stones" court told of girl in fur skin rug'	14
Yorkshire Evening Post	'Nude at Stones party says QC'	10½
Huddersfield Daily Examiner	'Woman in fur rug at Stones' party'	9*
Cambridge Evening News		nil

Average front page column inch allocation : 27

* Back page.

Four newspapers referred to the 'nude' or 'naked' woman: the Bolton *Evening News, Leicester Mercury,* Newcastle *Evening Chronicle* and *Yorkshire Evening Post*. These could be said to have maximised the sensational potential of the case, either for the sake of sensation or for the purpose of bolstering an eventual watchdog leader about the 'pop' world—or for both reasons. The girl in question was in fact presented contrastingly as clothed (if only in a fur rug) in the newspapers of Bristol, Huddersfield, Nottingham and Preston. The two newspapers that gave George Harrison's wedding least space—the *Huddersfield Daily Examiner* and the *Cambridge Evening News*— were also the two to give this court case least attention. The *Examiner* accorded it 9 column inches on its back page, whilst the Cambridge 'night final' edition failed to mention it at all. All the city newspapers, apart from those of Leeds, Bristol and Cambridge, gave the Rolling Stones' trial their main headline. The *Yorkshire Evening Post* (main headline 'Yorkshire troops in dash back to Aden') and Bristol *Evening Post* ('Widow found strangled in Bristol') both gave priority to local stories.

Only two of the evening newspapers sampled in January 1966 published leading column comment about 'pop' culture: the *Yorkshire Evening Post* and *Leicester Mercury*. These evinced a tonal animosity that could—it seems fair to say—be regarded as representative of only the most socially and culturally conservative sector of the provincial Press. The *Post*'s leader ('Pop age') opened by approving a Hull headmaster's expressed determination not to appease the 'pop age' but 'to fight against long hair, drainpipe trousers, uncouth speech, coffee bar manners and so forth'. It did not approve, however, of his warning to parents that they should nevertheless be prepared to 'recognise new modes of living, new styles of thinking, and make allowances for "the teenage revolution" ': 'What are these reservations but veiled obeisance to youth? Surely if new modes of living violate well-tried precepts they should be smartly denounced, not recognised . . .'[41]

The *Post* associates 'pop' culture with a stereotype recognisable by long hair and drainpipe trousers; the 'teenage revolution' is set against 'well-tried precepts' and found wholly wanting. The tone is assertive and uncompromising. Yet in its previous week's Friday feature 'Young outlook' the *Post* devoted 37 column inches to a description of the TV programme 'Top of the pops'—including a small photograph of Jimmy Saville; on the day of this leader the

Post's 'Records' feature focused solely on the 'pops' and ended with the sentence 'It will be interesting to see who gets higher in the charts—Dusty or Sandie'. This newspaper's ego seemed interested in the 'pop' world while its super-ego was busy denouncing it.

The *Leicester Mercury* similarly disapproved of the supposed social influence of the 'pop' cult, and felt that the necessary corrective should be supplied by parents:

Pop go the pundits!

The only obvious connection between the pop stars and the rising crime rate is that they are both making new records. But a Conservative study group looking at crime figures and tracing their root cause consider they are closely related.

The long-haired kings of the discs with their aura of audience hysteria have been blamed for many things but this is the first time they have been singled out in what purports to be a serious survey into the underworld of crime.

But let that point go. The long-haired, guitar-playing creatures might be an influence for the worse for the facts are that half of today's offences against society are being committed by the under-21s.

We need to look further back than the kind of youth-culture indicated by girlish locks, back to the sad decline in the influence of the family. Today, the interests of the young people are no longer shaped by their parents and their fun and games are not channelled into constructive outlets. Where they are there are no juvenile delinquents . . .[42]

The *Mercury* did not commit itself to an unqualified acceptance of the Conservative study group's theory, but does suggest that pop groups might be 'an influence for the worse'. The groups are held up to ridicule as 'the long-haired, guitar-playing creatures'. Long hair seems to exasperate the writer particularly, and it came first in the *Yorkshire Evening Post*'s list of specific criticisms. It was a Puritan characteristic to stress sober uniformity of appearance, although one should recall that hair length has typically become shorter since the seventeenth century. The *Mercury* also objects to the alleged negative quality of pop culture; it is not perceived as a 'constructive outlet'. In referring to the 'sad decline in the influence of the family' the *Mercury* is evidently trying to prompt parents to 'stop the rot'— its own concept of ideal family values serving as the measuring rod.

The *Yorkshire Evening Post* and *Leicester Mercury* were two of the four newspapers to include the emotive word 'nude' in their headlines for the Rolling Stones' trial, and also two of the three to refer to the QC—thereby, perhaps, endeavouring to underscore the magnitude of the alleged disorder:

'Nude at Stones party says QC' (*Yorkshire Evening Post*).

'Nude woman at Rolling Stones' party, says QC' (*Leicester Mercury*).

These headlines can be seen as serving a double purpose. First, they maximise the sales possibilities in the story; second, they are available as reference data for leading column admonitions of the kind cited.

It was suggested above that the *Yorkshire Evening Post* and *Leicester Mercury* are—or, at least, were at this time[43]—amongst the more conservative evening newspapers; others, perhaps, would give more assent to the proposition in *A Policy for the Arts* that 'pop' culture is in part a justified 'revolt . . . against the drabness, uniformity and joylessness of much of the social furniture we have inherited from the industrial revolution'.[44] But to defend it in these terms may seem to many editors to carry the undesired risk of affronting socioculturally conservative local opinion, and few, if any—to the writer's knowledge—appear to have adopted this approach.

Even so, the evening Press concedes that there is sufficient reader interest in the pop and jazz scene to warrant quite extensive feature coverage—the average space allocation being 45 column inches weekly. This being the case, it seems rather hard on the pop groups that their contribution to 'disorder' should be so amply publicised and that editorial comment (when offered) should be so unswervingly censorious. The weakness in this position is exposed by the adulatory treatment that *local* groups receive when they achieve some measure of national acclaim; thus a successful record by the Spencer Davis group was given front page attention in the *Birmingham Evening Mail*; headlined 'City group top of pop parade', the report opened by immediately identifying the group with Birmingham: 'The first change in the 1966 hit parade puts Birmingham at the top. . . . They become the second "Brum Beat" group to claim the supreme spot in the national hit parade.'[45] It seems that whatever reservations particular newspapers may have about the pop world in general, these are readily jettisoned when the 'local lads make good'.

A more open-minded attitude to the 'pop' world and its music, and less dependence than most feature articles show on clichéd evaluation ('great beat', 'great arrangement', 'great blues singer') would help to enlarge the cultural map in one of the ways that the authors of *A Policy for the Arts* recommend. The problem is very much one of 'bridging the gap between what have come to be called the "higher" forms of entertainment and the traditional sources— the brass band, the amateur concert party, the entertainer, the music hall and pop group—and to challenge that a gap exists'.[46] A wider definition of culture does not mean assenting to a debasement of standards; it does mean removing the artificial wall between the 'serious' and the rest, and then, in an unprejudiced way, advancing informed and qualitative judgments.

The evidence in this chapter suggests that the local Press is enthu- siastic about the traditional arts and more liberal in its taste than the group described as ultra-conservative moralists; but its very proper concern for family values seems to cause it to be exaggeratedly antagonistic and condescending towards 'pop' culture.

Notes

1 See T. S. Eliot, *Notes towards the Definition of Culture* (London: Faber & Faber, 1962), p. 22.
2 See Lionel Trilling, *The Opposing Self* (London: Secker & Warburg, 1955), p. x.
3 Matthew Arnold, *Culture And Anarchy*, ed. J. Dover Wilson (Cam- bridge: the University Press, 1963), p. 6.
4 C. P. Snow, *The Two Cultures: and a second look* (New York: Cam- bridge University Press, 1963), p. 22.
5 *Lincolnshire Chronicle*, 11 December 1964.
6 *A Policy For The Arts*, Cmnd. 2601 (London: HMSO, 1965), p. 5.
7 *Leicester Mercury*, 20 January 1966.
8 Raymond Williams, *Communications*, pp. 33–6.
9 *Sunday Express*, 8 January 1967.
10 *Daily Telegraph*, 17 July 1970. For the other side to this argument the reader is referred to two stimulating essays in *Libraries and the Arts* (London: Clive Bingley, 1970): 'Society's responsibility', by Aneurin Thomas and 'Maisons de la culture', by A. C. Charpentier.
11 Newcastle *Evening Chronicle*, 18 January 1966. See also Darlington *Evening Despatch*, 11 January 1966; Wolverhampton *Express and Star*, 14 January 1966.
12 *Oxford Mail*, 15 January 1966.
13 R. W. Emerson, *The Conduct of Life, Nature and Other Essays* (London: J. M. Dent, 1908), p. 216.
14 *A Policy for the Arts*, pp. 15–16.

15 *Lancashire Evening Post*, 22 October 1965.
16 Stuart Hall and Paddy Whannel, *The Popular Arts* (Boston: Beacon Press, 1967), p. 22.
17 See list on p. 67.
18 See 19 January 1966 issues of the *Cambridge Evening News* and Bolton *Evening News*—the latter observing that 'the English language is rich enough in invective without needless recourse to the expletives of the gutter'.
19 See, for instance, the *West Lancashire Evening Gazette*'s TV feature, 19 December 1964: 'Viewers are weary of plays without plots, plots without plays . . . plots without endings'; similarly, 18 January 1969: 'We have wasted too much time on plays which pose a problem and never hint at an answer . . .'
20 *West Lancashire Evening Gazette*, 18 November 1964.
21 *Ibid.*, 16 March 1964.
22 See *Daily Telegraph*, 'TV and radio topics', 10 February 1969.
23 *West Lancashire Evening Gazette*, 7 May 1966.
24 *Ibid.*, 11 May 1966.
25 *Ibid.*, 9 June 1966.
26 Denis McQuail, 'The audience for television plays' in *Media Sociology*, ed. J. Tunstall (London: Constable, 1970), p. 342. He notes that 'the continuum along which plays were judged seems to reflect a movement from the conventional and familiar to the unexpected, violent and morally repugnant'.
27 *Lancashire Evening Post*, 18 January 1966.
28 *Yorkshire Evening Post*, 18 January 1966.
29 *Birmingham Evening Mail*, 18 January 1966.
30 Newcastle *Evening Chronicle*, 18 January 1966.
31 *Huddersfield Daily Examiner*, 22 January 1966.
32 *Leicester Mercury*, 18 January 1966.
33 Mary Whitehouse, *Cleaning up TV* (London: Blandford Press, 1967), p. 174.
34 See, for instance, the *West Lancashire Evening Gazette*'s leader 'Home truths to shock', 17 November 1966: 'The BBC did a notable public service by presenting the play "Cathy, come home" last night. The plight of this homeless family must have struck a chill of horror in many happy, settled households . . .'
35 *Birmingham Evening Mail*, 1 June 1966.
36 *West Lancashire Evening Gazette*, 3 April 1967.
37 *Ibid.*, 3 November 1969.
38 See *Daily Telegraph* report, 30 December 1966, on *ITV 1967—A Guide to Independent Television*.
39 McQuail, *op. cit.*, pp. 349–50.
40 See, for instance, Wilfrid Mellers, 'The scope of school music: notes on a university course', *Music in Education*, vol. 32, No. 331, May–June 1968, pp. 130–3, and *Music in a New-found Land* (London: Barrie & Rockliff, 1964).
41 *Yorkshire Evening Post*, 22 January 1966.

42 *Leicester Mercury,* 22 January 1966.
43 Both newspapers have become members of chain groups since—the *Leicester Mercury* is owned by Northcliffe Newspapers, and the *Yorkshire Evening Post* by United Newspapers. There has also been a change of editor in each case.
44 *A Policy for the Arts,* p. 20.
45 *Birmingham Evening Mail,* 10 January 1966.
46 *A Policy for the Arts,* p. 16.

12 The extent and nature of political partisanship

In this chapter an analysis is made of the degree of support for each of the three main political parties at the time of the general election of 1970—with particular reference to the evening Press. It was assumed that partisan newspapers would, with very few exceptions if any, show their political colours at such a time. A sample of twenty-five evening newspapers was taken, representing a third of the English total. They were chosen so as to reflect the available range in terms of types of community served and circulation sizes. Following the analysis of the evening Press, a brief survey of the weeklies and a discussion of local Press influence on political attitudes are carried out.

The evening Press

The following evening newspapers were taken on 16 and 17 June 1970:

North: *West Lancashire Evening Gazette, Lancashire Evening Post, Lancashire Evening Telegraph, Manchester Evening News, Oldham Evening Chronicle, Huddersfield Daily Examiner*, Bradford *Telegraph and Argus, Yorkshire Evening Post, Yorkshire Evening Press, The Star* (Sheffield), Hull *Daily Mail*, Darlington *Evening Despatch*, Newcastle *Evening Chronicle*.

Midlands and South: Stoke *Evening Sentinel*, Wolverhampton *Express and Star, Birmingham Evening Mail, Leicester Mercury, Oxford Mail*, Reading *Evening Post, Cambridge Evening News, Eastern Evening News* (Norwich), Brighton *Evening Argus, Southern Evening Echo* (Southampton), Bristol *Evening Post*, Exeter *Express and Echo*.

In order to determine whether or not a partisan position was held by a newspaper at this time, particular (but not exclusive) attention was paid to leading column comment. The findings that resulted are grouped under four headings: (1) support for the Conservative Party, (2) support for the Liberal Party (3) support for a general radical, or Lib.–Lab., position and (4) neutral. The size of each grouping is then assessed in percentage terms.

1. Support for the Conservative Party Of the twenty-five evening newspapers, nine explicitly supported the Conservative Party—those of Leeds, Bradford, York, Blackpool, Birmingham, Wolverhampton, Leicester, Cambridge and Brighton. A further one, the Exeter *Express and Echo*, could be seen as hinting at a Conservative preference.

Six of the ten newspapers listed did not refer to the local scene in their leaders, preferring to concentrate on the election in national terms. Thus the *Yorkshire Evening Post* made the italicised claim on 17 June that 'the biggest development of the last seven days has been the emergence of the real strength and character of the Tory case'. Mr Edward Heath's campaign had been 'consistently serious and honest', Mr Harold Wilson's 'superficial—putting forward no new policies to deal with the coming problems'. The *Post* concluded: 'Look at the last six years of mismanagement, broken promises, and government by publicity machine. There is little doubt who deserves to lose this election.'

The same points were made, but in more detail, in the Wolverhampton *Express and Star*. Mr Heath was presented as 'essentially honest' and as a man of 'courage and ability'; Mr Wilson, in contrast, had been a twister of facts ('Was there ever a man slicker at twisting the facts to suit his case?') and had 'propounded no constructive programme'. The leader went on to relate the balance of payments surplus to devaluation and warned that 'from now onwards the benefits from devaluation will diminish and galloping inflation if not stemmed will seriously affect our ability to export'. It concluded:

The Conservative Party have spelt out in some detail how they propose to deal with the problems of the future. We have confidence that under the leadership of Mr. Heath, a man of great ability, courage and integrity, no effort would be spared to carry out the programme.

The *Express and Star* did not refer to the local candidates and so no mention was made of Mr Enoch Powell.[1]

The *Leicester Mercury*'s eve-of-poll leader focused on an incident at one of Mr Wilson's meetings. A lady had stood up, with her hand raised and 'clearly wanting to ask a question': 'Mr Wilson addressed her. It was all right, he said. He had a schoolmaster on the platform and he knew what she wanted when she raised her hand. (Laughter.)' The *Mercury* continued: 'This is not an isolated example of his election style, or, in charity, we would have forgotten it. But it is a pity and a calamity that a Prime Minister should aim so below the belt.' Mr Wilson might be able to outshine Mr Heath on 'the box' but, the *Mercury* warned, 'those with votes to cast will also remember the things that have made Britain great and will keep Britain great— among them the virtues of dignity and integrity'.

The merits of Mr Heath and the demerits of Mr Wilson played little part in the leading column material shared by the two West-minster Press newspapers (of four sampled), the *Yorkshire Evening Press* and Brighton *Evening Argus*. Labour's economic record was critically examined at length; a brief extract follows:

> Labour has tried to fight the election without answering for the economic blunders of the past four years or offering any convincing economic policy for the next four years. To claim a balance of payments surplus is not to offer a policy, and is selective almost to the point of dishonesty. The £ was devalued to get it, yet the poor trade figures for April and May are evidence enough that the over-all surplus is far from safe.

After referring to the feeling of 'some' that Labour's 'social aspira-tions' deserved support, the two newspapers warned that 'unless we avoid another blistering economic crisis—and the signs of one are extremely disturbing—all our social aspirations will fade . . . The Conservatives have a notably better record on economic growth and it would be logical to turn to them now.' The word 'logical' epito-mises the leader's 'armchair statesman' tone;[2] it offers a quiet, delib-erative conclusion.

The evening newspapers of Birmingham and Bradford set much of their editorial comment in a regional context. The *Birmingham Evening Mail*, noting that Marplan surveys had indicated that the Conservatives could win three out of four West Midlands marginals (Oldbury, Dudley and Perry Barr), conjectured that 'it may be that West Midlanders have been thinking a bit harder about the election issues that have been so studiously glossed over in Labour's cam-paign'. Perhaps it was that 'living close to the car industry, which is customarily kicked around in times of economic stress, encourages longer memories'. Readers were urged to 'look behind the complacent Labour line-up for the people who have been significantly silent during these last few weeks—the Left-wing trade union leaders who have sometimes seemed to be running the country'. Mr Enoch Powell was referred to, and presented as an unknown quantity in the sense that his influence 'cannot be ignored, but it is open to argument. Those Midlanders who respect Mr. Powell for his out-of-line frankness do not necessarily swallow Powellism whole.' But presumably the same Midlanders would not regard 'out-of-line frankness' as a euphemistic description, and so be tempted to vote for Mr Wedgwood Benn's party.

The Bradford *Telegraph and Argus* opened its eve-of-poll leader on an uncompromising note: 'West Yorkshire has one very good reason for not voting Labour tomorrow, and that is to preserve the essentially local character of our local government.' Local voters now had their 'only opportunity to show what we think of Labour's proposal to take power from the localities and give it to a remote metropolitan authority'. Moving on to some kind words about Mr Heath ('the depth of feeling which . . . clearly motivates him', etc.), the *Argus* then turned its attention to Mr Wilson—jocularly making a tentative, yet accurate, prognostication:

> Mr. Wilson has chosen to fight the election on a low key, visiting party workers rather than making major speeches, relying on sunshine, the World Cup and the balance of payments to return him to No. 10. He may well be in for a shock. England are out of the World Cup and, yesterday, it rained.
> . . . Mr. Wilson has deliberately over-simplified the economic situation to his own advantage. He has glossed over problems of wage inflation and —Labour's biggest failure—trade union reform . . . What about the money we borrowed to balance the books? What about the fast declining balance? Is the electorate really fooled so easily?

A different approach was adopted by the *Cambridge Evening News* and *West Lancashire Evening Gazette*; these offered both a general political case for voting Conservative and a specific recommendation of the previous (Conservative) local Members. The former paper felt that in Cambridge there had been 'little to upset the atmosphere of calm, serious debate'; the two candidates were 'old adversaries who do not conceal a degree of mutual respect' and 'treat electors in the same manner'. Addressing the floating voter, the *News* declared its support for the Conservatives: 'We believe there is one overriding reason for returning the Conservatives and that is the threat to industry imposed by Labour's policies. Britain cannot ignore the danger signs shown by those firms which have had to beg finance from the Government, who have drained them of their working capital.' Furthermore, the Conservative candidate (David Lane) had 'proved himself a first-rate constituency MP'—a man 'so knowledgeable' about Cambridge's 'major problems and the personal difficulties of its organisations and individuals'.

The *West Lancashire Evening Gazette* felt that although the election campaign had been 'just about the quietest in recorded history' the issue was nevertheless 'stark indeed': 'Conservatism means the survival of what remains of private enterprise and personal freedom of thought and action within the law. Socialism means simply increasing personal regimentation within a framework of "Whitehall knows best".' Turning to the local scene, the *Gazette* suggested that there was 'every reason why the present Members of Parliament should be returned to carry on their good work': 'they have acquitted themselves with credit both in Parliament and in their constituencies. They have looked after all their constituents regardless of politics or creed.'

Finally, it was noted above that the Exeter *Express and Echo* appeared to show Conservative leanings. In a leader about wildcat strikes on 16 June it concluded that 'what is wanted is a Government prepared to govern in the interests of all, and not to run away when the going becomes rough'. In view of the Conservatives' stand on trade union reform, the hint seems clear enough.

To sum up, the pro-Conservative newspapers adopted a variety of approaches making systematic comparison pointless. Four of them introduced local angles, but local candidates were always treated with restraint and courtesy; no Eatanswill-style rhetoric was apparent.

2. Support for the Liberal Party Three evening newspapers explicitly supported the Liberal Party: the *Huddersfield Daily Examiner*, *Oldham Evening Chronicle* and *Eastern Evening News* (Norwich). The first two of these are amongst the very few survivors from the nineteenth-century Liberal Press, and act in concert with pro-Liberal weeklies (the *Rochdale Observer* and the *Colne Valley Guardian*) in the same region.

The *Huddersfield Daily Examiner*, with the opinion polls in mind, suggested that 'so far from there being no change, there could even be a massive strengthening of the Labour Party in the House'; this would be 'quite disastrous for the country' as 'the Government would acquire several fresh coats of glossy complacency which a demoralised Opposition would not have the spirit to remove'. In such a context 'the clear independent thinking and strength of purpose of a well-founded Liberal Party' would be vital, and the electors of Huddersfield and district had 'a prime opportunity to contribute towards this end'. The 'two impressive young campaigners' in the Huddersfield constituencies would be 'sure to bring in a solid Liberal vote' and in the Colne Valley division voters 'will not need to be reminded of the services . . . that Mr. Richard Wainwright has rendered during the four years that he has been their MP'. Parliament needed a strong body of Liberals, forming a group that was 'neither hamstrung and demoralised by a hat trick of defeats and leadership crises nor soused in complacency'. In fact, the Liberal candidates came a poor third in both Huddersfield constituencies, polling no more than 13 per cent of the total votes cast.

The *Oldham Evening Chronicle* opened its leader ('End of deadlock') with a question: 'Has there ever been an election in living memory in which the voter finds it so difficult to do the right thing?' The *Chronicle*'s diagnosis of this difficulty was 'the Wilson credibility gap'; this had 'spilled over to all other parties and politicians . . .' The only way to 'break the unholy deadlock of the bitter and cynical battle for power between the two main parties' was to return a strong third party in the Commons: 'If ever there was a time to vote Liberal, this is it. Everyone has been saying that Jeremy Thorpe, the Liberal leader, has made the best impression on TV of all the three leaders. Certainly, he was the only one who concentrated on policies without too much talking about the failures of the other parties. . . .'

The *Eastern Evening News* (Norwich) saw the election campaign as 'in many ways . . . unsatisfactory'; 'the trivial and the dog-eared have played too big a part, and there has been too much looking back at the expense of looking forward'. The Liberals—'in their best election voice for some years'—were probably right to feel that 'a good many people may be fed up with aspects of the cases and the bickering of the main parties'. The *News* concluded:

> The Liberals put themselves forward as the party of common sense, able to keep the other parties on their toes, and maintain that they could have sufficient strength in the House to do this if all their sympathisers voted for them.

Such a proposition would be true most of all if the main parties were finely balanced, and this—despite the polls—is by no means an impossible outcome.

The three Liberal-supporting newspapers, therefore, stressed the alleged drawbacks of the two main parties and their tactics ('the bickering' and 'the bitter and cynical battle for power') and the benefits attendant on a strong, independent body of Liberals.

3. Support for a general radical, or Lib.–Lab., position Two of the newspapers sampled can fairly be ascribed to this category: the *Evening Despatch* (Darlington) and the *Manchester Evening News*. The *Despatch* eve-of-poll leader was headed 'A vote for Enoch is a vote against democracy'. After attacking Mr Powell for trying to 'exploit race in the most outrageous manner', and on other grounds, it suggested that more 'Powellites' might well be returned to Parliament; if so, 'Mr Heath will have to watch out for the knives'. This proposition of a split Conservative Party would certainly not be intended to assist the Tory cause, but the leader did not specify a particular radical platform. This represented a change from 1966, when the *Despatch* had a kind word both for Mr Heath and the Liberal Party.

The *Manchester Evening News*, under its new editor, Brian Redhead, has adopted a more radical outlook, and a shift in position as between 1966 and 1970 was apparent. In 1966 the *News* claimed to be independent, but hints of Tory leanings were evident in statements like the following:

> ... This election needs to throw up a real leader who will compel people to believe in Britain a little more, and persuade all sections of the nation to show character by giving an honest day's work for a good day's pay.
> We need the sting of individual competition and rewards for enterprise . . .[3]

The first sentence implies that Mr Wilson did not, in his first period of office, measure up to the *News*'s idea of 'a real leader'; the second is a straightforward statement of an unmistakably Conservative attitude. In 1970 the burden of the *News*'s leader was to point to 'the absence of conspicuous differences between the two principal parties' and to suggest that 'the weak and all who need help' seemed to be being unduly neglected by both. It ended in this way:

> It looks still as if Mr. Wilson will win. If so, we shall have a competent government, for after its early blunders in the last Parliament, Labour put

up a reasonable show. The Tories seem to have failed to make good use of their time in Opposition, so that they have never looked quite ready to take office. Mr. Grimond shrewdly sounded the most telling note for the Liberals when he said every vote for them was a vote for good sense and humanity . . .

This passage came closer to explicit support for Labour than any of the leaders sampled; the Liberals are also recommended, and a general 'Lib.–Lab.' position is appropriately ascribed.

4. Political neutrality There was no indication of any political partisanship in the leading column comment of ten of the evening newspapers sampled—those of Preston, Blackburn, Sheffield, Hull, Newcastle, Stoke, Oxford, Reading, Bristol and Southampton. All, however, considered the election from some standpoint. The Sheffield *Star* and the *Lancashire Evening Post* took pains to stress that their neutral position should be seen as a virtue:

> On the eve of polling in the general election this newspaper, unlike a number of others today, is not about to tell the voters which party they should choose as the next government tomorrow. We are content to have presented what facts were available as adequately and fairly as possible during the campaign . . . [*The Star*]

> We do not intend to give advice on how to vote. We do not regard that as a newspaper's job. For the past fortnight we have been printing the parties' views; we have ranged from Ministerial to local candidate level. Any reader who does not know what the election is about has not read or is not interested.
> Our only appeal is: GO OUT AND VOTE . . . [*Lancashire Evening Post*]

The *Post* also listed some questions for its readers to ask themselves, amongst which was: 'Which has a policy which strikes you as workable, not a negative policy or a soft policy, but one which shows some realism?' Conservatives might well have felt that this hinted at a Conservative preference on the *Post*'s part, but the fact that Labour supporters might not agree has to be decisive, and the claim of neutrality allowed to stand.

Six of the neutral newspapers urged their readers to go out and vote; this was their 'duty' (Bristol *Evening Post*) and a 'precious opportunity' (*Southern Evening Echo*). The Newcastle *Evening Chronicle* stressed that 'no vote is wasted. So make sure you use yours tomorrow.' The three Thomson newspapers (of Reading, Blackburn and Newcastle) all paid some attention to what they saw as an unhealthy election atmosphere; the *Evening Telegraph* (Black-burn) asserted that 'people simply do not trust political leadership any more', the Newcastle *Evening Chronicle* alluded to an 'undoubted cynicism' on the voters' part, and the Reading *Evening Post* defended opinion polls on the ground that they at least maintained interest 'when it has been sapped by the reiterations of weary propaganda by the parties'.

The *Lancashire Evening Post*, Hull *Daily Mail* and Stoke *Evening Sentinel* leaders concentrated on the economy and noted two versions of it: Mr Wilson's and Mr Heath's. The electorate's task was 'to decide which of the two men is right' (Hull *Daily Mail*). But the *Southern Evening Echo* felt that there had been too much emphasis on domestic issues; little had been heard about Britain's international role, and more should have been heard about the Common Market, 'a subject which divides the electorate while uniting the parties'. Finally, the *Oxford Mail*'s long leader, evincing the moderate, judicial style of the armchair statesman, saw points for and against both main parties on several issues:

> . . . The Conservatives have made a bid to be considered as the party that would help the really poor, but have not eradicated the feeling that Labour is best for the social services. The Labour record—for all its failings, notably housing—suggests it can provide reasonable, civilised government in the social sphere. What is has yet to show is that it can provide the economic growth it promised and failed to achieve since 1964. Yet this provides the resources for social welfare.
> Whether Labour or Conservatives win, it seems important that, pro-vided there is a working majority, the swing should not go too far. It would be tragedy if the Liberal voice were eliminated. And the fewer Conservative supporters of Mr. Enoch Powell that are returned, the better.

In making this last point, the *Oxford Mail* was echoing its West-minster Press stable-mate, the Darlington *Evening Despatch*; but the two other newspapers sampled from this group (those of York and Brighton) ignored Mr Powell in their 17 June leaders.

Conclusions on the evening Press The analysis of evidence for partisan-ship or neutrality has been carried out solely in terms of leading column comment. Careful study of the extensive reporting of local candidates' meetings suggested that the local scene was impartially covered, although the prominence given by the Brighton *Evening Argus* to left-wing demonstrators could be construed as a pro-Conservative tactic. Partisanship did, however, frequently express

Another· clash over devaluation

(a)

Under fire — but unrepentant

DIAMOND BLAMES 'SCARE'

Daily Telegraph Reporter

THE "last-minute scare" over devaluation helped the Conservatives to win votes, said Mr Jack Diamond, Chief Secretary to the Treasury in the Labour Government, yesterday.

His 13 years as M.P. for Gloucester had ended a few hours earlier.

"As a Treasury Minister, it strikes me as laughable," he said to me during a pause in his tour around the constituency to thank his supporters.

Mr Diamond was defeated by the Conservative candidate, Mrs Sally Oppenheim, by 1,061 votes. His 20,777 votes was 174 fewer than at the 1966 General Election, while Mrs Oppenheim increased the Conservative poll by 6,160. Liberal votes were down 2,605.

On the devaluation issue, Mr Diamond said: "It seems incredible that this should have made any headway, but it seems to have done. The polls indicate that there was a last-minute shift." (f)

DEVALUATION: HEATH STICKS TO FORECAST

(b)

Devaluation –Heath says it again

(c)

Tory chief repeats charge over devaluation

(d)

Heath attacked on devaluation charge...

(e)

Fig. 12 The 'second devaluation' controversy: a sample of main headlines from the evening Press, 17 June 1970. (a) *West Lancashire Evening Gazette*, (b) *Leicester Mercury*, (c) Bristol *Evening Post*, (d) Stoke *Evening Sentinel*, (e) *Huddersfield Daily Examiner*, (f) *Daily Telegraph*, 20 June 1970. Reproduced half actual size. *By courtesy of the Daily Telegraph, Evening Post (Bristol), Evening Sentinel (Stoke on Trent), Huddersfield Daily Examiner and West Lancashire Evening Gazette*

itself in the selection and wording of main headlines. For instance, eight of the ten newspapers classed as Conservative focused on the 'row' or 'storm' provoked by Mr Heath's charge that a second devaluation might follow in the wake of another Labour government, whereas only four of the ten neutral papers selected this story; four of the five remaining papers (Liberal or Lib.–Lab.) also chose it. A list of these headlines follows—all published on 17 June 1970:

Conservative newspapers

'Row flares on Heath devaluation speech' (Leeds).
'Devalue hint "despicable"—Callaghan' (York).
'Devaluation: Heath sticks to forecast' (Leicester).
'Storm over pound flares again' (Cambridge).
'Ted makes his claim again' (Wolverhampton).
'Heath rapped in pre-poll row' (Brighton).
'Poll seesaw as bitterness boils over' (Bradford).
'Leaders slug it out in last rounds' (Blackpool).

Liberal and Lib.–Lab. newspapers

'Heath attacked on devaluation charge' (Huddersfield).
'Heath slammed by Wilson on sterling' (Darlington).
'Combined attack on Heath' (Oldham).
'The final fling' (Manchester).

Neutral newspapers

'Heath hits back at party leaders' condemnation' (Stoke).
'Sterling attack wrangle' (Southampton).
'Two party heads round on Heath' (Oxford).
'Heath claim "on a par with Powell" ' (Reading).

Clearly, Conservative-supporting newspapers considered that there was much 'political mileage' in this story; interestingly, only two Conservative newspapers—those of York and Brighton—presented Mr Heath as the recipient of censure, whereas five of the remaining eight put him in this position. The contrast is apparent in 'Ted makes his claim again' (Wolverhampton) as against 'Combined attack on Heath' (Oldham). In the sixteen reports listed above, the word 'devaluation' appeared in the first sentence in nine and the second sentence in five. As the opening paragraphs of the *Leicester Mercury* and *Oldham Evening Chronicle* were identical, it would seem correct to suppose that both were using a Press Association wired report *verbatim*—the same report supplying the basic material for the rest; the paragraphs ran as follows:

> Harold Wilson, James Callaghan and Jeremy Thorpe rounded on Edward Heath today for his warning that Labour policies could lead to another devaluation. But the Conservative leader was unrepentant—and repeated the charge at his London press conference.
>
> In Manchester, the Prime Minister accused Mr. Heath of basing irresponsible comments on sterling on the flimsy evidence of one month's trade figures . . .

It is, of course, impossible to assess the impact of this eve-of-poll report on readers; in any case, the evening Press is only part of the total coverage afforded by Press and television. There were those, like Mr Edward Short in the early hours of 19 June, who ascribed the Conservative win to the 'devaluation scare'. But it is doubtful whether the precise causes can ever be established beyond dispute; what can be said here is that Conservative-supporting evening newspapers clearly saw the devaluation charge as deserving of maximum prominence.

It remains to present the findings about partisanship and neutrality in tabulated form. Before doing so, it is worth noting that existing knowledge about the political attitudes of the provincial Press is very sketchy indeed—even within the Press itself; hence the partial inaccuracy of the following passage from a *Bury Times* leader. It was discussing the effects on the 1970 election from a prolonged close down—if this took place—of the national Press: 'Coverage of the campaign will of course continue to be given by the provincial and local Press and the radio and TV, but traditionally, these media do not, like the national Press, take sides in the conflict; they merely inform . . .'[4] How far this comment is true for the weekly Press will be considered below; it is applicable to, at most, no more than half the evening newspapers with circulations over 25,000. In order to express the evidence from the sample in statistical terms, scores of 4 or 2 were allocated to each paper in relation to the following criteria:

> Explicit, or strongly implied, support for one party: a score of 4 to that party.
> Explicit or implied support for two parties: a score of 2 to each party.
> Non-partisanship: a score of 4 under the heading 'neutral'.

The following scores resulted:

Conservative   40 (per cent)
Liberal   16 (per cent)
Labour   4 (per cent)
Neutral   40 (per cent)

Thus 60 per cent of the sample showed some sort of political preference; 40 per cent favoured the Conservatives and 20 per cent a
radical position, predominantly Liberal. Only 40 per cent conformed
to the neutral role thought to be predominant by the *Bury Times*.

A final point concerns the performance of the 'chain' newspapers
sampled, since it certainly seemed to be assumed at the time of the
first Royal Commission (1947) that a uniformity of political outlook
was a 'danger' attendant upon chain control. The facts do not point
to any such uniformity. The three Thomson newspapers (of Blackburn, Newcastle and Reading) were classed as neutral; four of
United Newspapers (Blackpool, Preston, Sheffield and Leeds) included two Conservative and two neutral; four of the Westminster
Press group (York, Brighton, Darlington and Oxford) showed two
Conservative, one radical and one neutral. Of four Northcliffe newspapers at Stoke on Trent, Hull, Norwich and Leicester, two were
neutral, one Conservative and one Liberal. Overall, the 'chain'
newspapers only differ from the sample as a whole in that there is an
increase in the neutral position (up 13 per cent).

The weekly Press

The sample of evening newspapers taken was large enough to provide
reasonably conclusive figures for the distribution of partisanship or
neutrality in the evening Press. The number of weeklies is too large
to permit more than a tentative assessment to be made from a small
sample—chosen so as to reflect the diversity of constituencies in
terms of politics and location. Twenty-five weeklies were taken from
the following county, city or town circulation areas: Buckinghamshire, Sussex, Essex, mid-Devon, Durham, Hereford, the Colne
Valley, Salford, Bury, Rochdale, Altrincham, Stockport, Buxton,
Nelson, Barnsley, Whitby, Nuneaton, Warley, Evesham, Reading,
Leyton and Brighton.

Of the twenty-five papers, twenty took up a neutral position; these would presumably agree with the explanation offered by the *Salford City Reporter*: 'Like all local weekly newspapers the *City Reporter* exists to serve the whole of its community, compounded of people of many beliefs and convictions, and it is none of our business to come out in favour of one party or candidate.'[5]

The remaining five newspapers included three Conservative supporters (the *Stockport Advertiser, Reading Mercury* and *Brighton and Hove Herald*) and two Liberal (the *Rochdale Observer* and *Colne Valley Guardian*). The *Reading Mercury* cast Mr Wilson as an evader of issues: 'at least the Conservatives have hammered away at Labour in an endeavour to probe the difficulties which they suspect face the nation economically in the immediate future'.[6] The *Brighton and Hove Herald* itemised three ways in which it felt that Labour had failed to remedy the local housing problem—after each one posing the question 'Is this the record Labour is so proud of?'[7] The *Stockport Advertiser* criticised a local Labour candidate for objecting to the Conservatives' use of the union jack on their party propaganda: '. . . the comment by the Stockport Labour candidate revealed the distinction between the parties. He said, "The Conservatives do not control Britain or Stockport." How right he is! If there is any control it has come from the Labour Government. They have clamped down on this nation and strangled it with controls of one sort or another. Socialism . . . means control from the cradle to the grave.'[8]

This sort of spirited partisanship is now something of a rarity in the local Press, harking back as it does to the emotive interchanges of Dickens' Mr Pott and Mr Slurk. But the Liberal *Rochdale Observer* remains briskly vigorous. Casting Mr Wilson as Tweedledum and Mr Heath as Tweedledee, it reviewed their 'antics . . . on the Westminster seesaw'. Its Liberal stand was pressed in this way:

WE NEED A CHANGE—A CHANGE IN VOTING HABITS AS WELL AS A CHANGE OF GOVERNMENT.
This is a Liberal newspaper, but it is no mere act of duty which makes us say: VOTE LIBERAL. There are parts of Liberal policy—the Common Market, for instance—with which we find it hard to agree.
But we do believe that if the one-time respect for Parliamentary government is to be restored and deep unrest over the dwindling value of money is to be avoided, the eternal seesaw of Tweedledum and Tweedledee has got to be broken.
The only party in the country with any hope of doing it is the Liberal Party . . .[9]

Across the Pennines the *Colne Valley Guardian* joined forces with
the nearby *Huddersfield Daily Examiner* on the Liberals' behalf.
'This has been a rum election,' said the *Guardian*; 'there has not
been the traditional feeling of involvement.' The fine weather was
partly responsible, and perhaps the World Cup; 'and then there is
the growing feeling that Britain has now moved decisively into the
American presidential type of election with a brace of gladiators
fighting it out between themselves with little that happens at local
level being of any great matter'. The leader concluded, as in 1966,
with a cogent endorsement of the Liberal candidate Mr Richard
Wainwright: 'He has served this constituency well for four years
and would do so again. He put the constituency on the map with his
victory and would keep it there with another . . . at the end of the
second day we hope and expect that Richard Wainwright will again
be on his way to Westminster.'[10]

In 1966 the *Guardian*'s hopes were fulfilled; in 1970 Mr Wainwright was narrowly defeated.

The general picture of political partisanship or neutrality for the
weekly Press is easily summarised. There is a scatter of Conservative
weeklies (perhaps as many as 10 per cent of all weeklies), located in
seaside resorts and established 'county' areas. There is a strong
pocket of Liberal support in the area running from Rochdale to
Huddersfield. The rest plough an independent furrow, and constitute as many as 90 per cent of the weekly newspapers published. In
respect of the weekly Press, therefore, the *Bury Times*' view that
they do not take sides is certainly true of the vast majority.

Postscript: the political influence of the provincial Press

Whether or not Samuel Smiles was correct in his claim that 'the *fiat*
of the *Leeds Mercury*' was 'decisive' in its circulation area in 1842[11]
his view contrasts strikingly with that held by the typical provincial
editor of modern times. In reply to one of the 1947 Royal Commission's written questions, in which newspaper companies were invited
to gauge their influence, not a single provincial or national company
claimed to exert any significant influence so far as national politics
are concerned. The eleven of the fifty-nine provincial companies (i.e.

18 per cent) that offered comment on political influence were unanimously sceptical about their opinion-forming power in this respect. Walter Reid & Sons Ltd felt that Press influence had declined: 'its influence in moulding people's opinions by direct argument and persuasion is now less than it was'.[12] The Bristol Evening Post Ltd assessed its political influence as 'little';[13] Mackie & Co. Ltd stated that 'if by the influence of the newspaper and periodical Press is meant the ability to sway public opinion in a *desired direction* the answer is that for the daily Press it is almost non-existent . . . and that for the periodical and local weekly Press such influence is hardly won and can only be exerted in special circumstances'.[14] For instance, the local Press may be able to assist in mobilising a protest vote—as in the Colne Valley constituency in 1966.[15]

Academic research in recent years has corroborated the view that the media do not have the power to 'sway public opinion in a desired direction'. R. S. Milne and H. C. Mackenzie studied the voting behaviour of a random sample of 528 electors in the Bristol Northeast constituency at the 1955 general election; after analysing the 'reasons for voting' of 480 of these electors, they reached the following general conclusion about the influence of propaganda sources: 'Only 4 per cent . . . cited a propaganda source as an explanation of their voting decision. The most frequently mentioned source was television, followed by newspapers and election literature.'[16] It is unlikely that the percentage would have been higher had the two evening newspapers, the Bristol *Evening Post* and *Bristol Evening World*, been partisan and not neutral. For one of the findings of J. Trenaman and D. McQuail in their study of the impact of television on the 1959 general election, with special reference to a sample of 661 voters in the Leeds West and Pudsey constituencies, was that partisan newspapers not only failed to persuade readers to their viewpoints but even created a weakening of loyalties: 'the inference is that the average reader was slightly repelled rather than persuaded by what often appeared to be a partisan presentation of political news in the Press'.[17]

Yet in spite of editorial and academic pooh-poohing of the likelihood of influence, partisan newspapers continue to publish editorial persuasions and, in some cases, to present the news in the way that seems mostly likely to promote the favoured party's interests. Provincial newspapers have little to lose, as their respective advocacies do not appear to affect circulation.[18] Furthermore, Conservative newspapers will enjoy the bonus of approbation on the part of the business community. They may also attach some credibility to the theory of a cumulative effect, as proposed by the Leeds Labour Publishing Society and Tribune Publications Ltd in their evidence to the 1947 Commission:

> ... The *Yorkshire Post*, the *Yorkshire Evening Post* and the *Yorkshire Evening News* all supported Conservative policy at the General Elections. Five of the six Leeds seats are now Labour. The circulations of these papers per week must be 100 times that of the *Leeds Weekly Citizen*. I therefore think that the effect of newspapers is comparatively small at election times; but, on the other hand, the continual criticism of the government and of the local council in the local Press is likely to have a cumulative effect and to help the inevitable swing.[19]

> ... It is probably true to say that the popular Press does not in the final analysis decide a man's vote, but it does shape opinions every day on a hundred and one issues that may seem sometimes trivial and sometimes not even apparent. This comes about ... mainly through the presentation of news and not through expression of opinion ...[20]

The result of the 1970 general election threw into disarray many existing assumptions about the formation and predictability of the electorate's voting decisions. Events in the period immediately before polling day clearly played an unanticipated and crucial role. It is fair to suppose that much of the 'cumulative effect' of news and opinion unfavourable to the Government during 1968–69 was arrested and partially dissipated in the spring and early summer of 1970; however, in the final stages of the election the news appears to have reactivated enough disaffection to produce a good Conservative turn-out and a weakened Labour one. The main headlines of the *West Lancashire Evening Gazette* may well tell the tale of the 1970 election as well as it will ever be told:

15 June: 'Britain's trade deficit worse'.
16 June: 'Hard facts have sunk Labour—Mr Heath'.
17 June: 'Leaders slug it out in last rounds'.
18 June: 'Young voters lead the way'.
19 June: 'Ted's triumph'.

Provincial Press spokesmen are probably right to be sceptical about the efficacy of partisan argument, but both they and opinion researchers need to consider the possibility that there can be a sudden, short-term revival of an earlier 'cumulative effect'—erroneously assumed to have been dissipated by intervening events, but in fact merely dormant. In 1970 the right short-term events came to hand for the Conservative sector of the regional Press and maximum use was made of them.

Notes

1 The *Express and Star*'s attitude to 'Powellism' is referred to on pp. 139–44.
2 See Graham Martin, 'Public voices' in *Your Sunday Paper* ed. Richard Hoggart (London: University of London Press, 1967), pp. 45–7.
3 *Manchester Evening News*, 30 March 1966.
4 *Bury Times*, 13 June 1970.
5 *Salford City Reporter*, 12 June 1970.
6 *Reading Mercury*, 13 June 1970.
7 *Brighton and Hove Herald*, 12 June 1970.
8 *Stockport Advertiser*, 11 June 1970.
9 *Rochdale Observer*, 13 June 1970.
10 *Colne Valley Guardian*, 12 June 1970.
11 See p. 8.
12 *Memoranda of Evidence*, p. 163.
13 *Ibid.*, p. 57.
14 *Ibid.*, p. 128.
15 In March 1966 the Liberal *Colne Valley Guardian* was able to assist the local Liberal organisation in mobilising a protest vote; there follows an extract from its leading column of 25 March 1966: 'Our second reason for preferring Mr. Wainwright is that his election, after so many years of Labour representation of the division, would instantly focus attention on the Colne Valley and its problems. So long as the representation remains unchanged the tendency at county and national level will be to assume that Colne Valley folk are satisfied with their lot and that they are prepared to go on being taken for granted. . . .' The Liberal was elected, but failed (as did Eric Lubbock and Michael Winstanley) to hold the seat in 1970.
16 R. S. Milne and H. C. Mackenzie, *Marginal Seat, 1955* (London: Hansard Society for Parliamentary Government, 1958), p. 161.
17 J. Trenaman and D. McQuail, *Television and the Political Image* (London: Methuen, 1961), pp. 189–90.
18 See p. 21.
19 *Memoranda of Evidence*, p. 121.
20 *Ibid.*, p. 184.
   See also Colin Seymour-Ure, *The Press, Politics and the Public* (London: Methuen, 1968), pp. 283–4.

13 Conclusions

This study of the contemporary provincial Press has now fulfilled three broad aims; it has considered the functions the local newspaper performs in its community setting, illustrated the kinds of content—both typical and untypical—that ensue, and attempted to determine the nature of the system, or controlling factors, that influence the interpretations of function. It remains to summarise the findings and briefly consider their implications, with special reference to the evening Press.

1. Summary of controlling factors and functions

(a) The factor of localness The provincial evening newspaper is predominantly local in its content; its front page news may suggest a degree of non-localness that is not corroborated elsewhere in the newspaper. Thus analysis of the forty-five reports of 10 column inches or more length in three evening newspapers revealed that only three (i.e. 6·6 per cent) were non-local.[1] It must be added, however, that two-thirds of the sixteen evening newspapers sampled for chapter 7 dealt with more non-local than local topics in their leading columns; the range was from 94 per cent non-local (*Manchester Evening News*) to 92 per cent local (Newcastle *Evening Chronicle*). Non-local leaders, and much of the non-local news, undoubtedly carry a prestige element—as well as informational value—by denoting that the newspaper's sights extend well beyond the parish pump.[2] But readers of the weekly Press neither expect, nor are given, non-local news; further, 87 per cent of its leading column comment was found to be local in reference.

It was apparent that the nature of the news reported varies according to the type of newspaper (evening or weekly) and its circulation size. In general, the proportion of disorder news[3] increases, and that of secondary order news decreases, as one moves from the small circulation weekly to the large circulation evening newspaper. Thus in a sample of three weekly papers the overall ratio of order to disorder news (with reference to total column inches) was 3 : 1; in a sample of three evening newspapers the ratio was 1 :1·6. The weekly, by including a relatively greater proportion of institutional order reports, will therefore seem a more intimate form of communication to the reader who is an active participant in community life. The larger evening newspapers can be seen as offering some compensation for their greater social distance from readers by regular inclusion of the light-hearted story, cartoons and diversions (e.g. crosswords, 'spot the ball') and locally rooted feature articles. They can also be relied upon to give high prominence to the more sensational kinds of non-local event.

The version of local life that is variously reflected can be seen as a confrontation of the agencies of community order and disorder. On the side of order are the community leaders, local heroes and achievers, and those who attain a transient celebrity status in the context of home or work: centenarians, non-retirers, lucky winners, etc. News of such order figures, as Morris Janowitz has noted, may have an important effect on the reader's emotional attitude to his newspaper:

Local news incorporates a strong feeling of local pride and personal respect which print enhances. . . . If the individual has any personal knowledge of these persons and institutions close at hand or any sense of identification with them, he in turn feels a sense of solidarity and cohesion well beyond being merely informed.[4]

Community disorder manifests itself in reports about the agents and victims of disasters, accidents, crimes and institutional discord or neglect. The presence of such reports in the local Press should not be allowed to mask the fact that it presents institutional leaders in their normal, positive roles with much greater frequency than the popular national dailies.

The functions of local watchdog, pump-primer, booster and reflector are fulfilled by means of news reports, features, leaders or correspondence. The four roles enable the provincial newspaper to project itself as a community conscience, idealist, standard bearer of local pride and recorder. The degree to which the watchdog role is fulfilled will in part be determined by the editor's (and proprietor's) view of his paper's *raison d'être*; some editors will wish to campaign vigorously, others will prefer to damp down controversy in the interest of a peaceful consensus, and yet others to adopt an intermediary position between these two extremes.

(b) Local mass circulation A second controlling factor that applies especially to the predominant monopoly situation is the occurrence of high household coverage. It was noted that in the case of thirty-two out of the forty-eight members of the Evening Newspaper Advertising Bureau, household coverage is over 75 per cent. It was also shown that for every middle-class (i.e. ABC1) reader there are 2·6 working class (C2DE) readers of the evening newspaper. The assumed interests and preferences of this majority must, therefore, be one of the key influences on content; hence the prominence that most of the evening newspapers accorded to distinctively sensational non-local crimes and trials. The 'second body' story was given main headline coverage in 71 per cent of papers outside the West Midlands conurbation where the crime occurred; 55 per cent gave their main headlines to the Rolling Stones' drug trial. Of course, full response to the assumed interests of the majority may, in the case of particular newspapers, be modified by the adoption of the 'educator' role—a point that is taken up again below.

The collective local knowledge of community readerships makes the maintenance of accuracy and reliability crucially important; a spate of slips or misinterpretations would create an undesirable lack of confidence on the readers' part. Finally, it is the latter's expectations as rate-payers that are perceived as the mandate for the Press's watchdog surveillance of the town council. One of the most important functions of the correspondence column is that it enables protesting rate-payers to communicate publicly with community leaders, and the evidence indicates that this form of protest is far from being the sole preserve of the more educated members of the middle classes.

(c) Minority interests Within the local readership there are the so-called intelligent minority and minority groups with particular social, political, cultural or religious commitments. As readers, their interests have to be taken into account; hence the inclusion of much non-dramatic, purely informational order news from the local institutions.

There is some evidence to suggest that the immigrant minority has suffered from the high proportion of disorder news—involving prominent ethnic specification—about a small fraction of its members; but there are clear signs that the provincial Press is trying to remedy this. There is also strong editorial support for liberal attitudes and an evident dislike of extremist positions.[5]

So far as local cultural activity is concerned, the provincial evening Press was, on the whole, found to be well disposed to fostering its progress; during one period of survey 40 per cent of the newspapers sampled published leaders supporting increased subsidy for the arts via the rate levy. The majority give feature space to both old and new cultural forms; for example, of the eight newspapers discussed in chapter 11, all eight offered weekly features on 'pop' music and seven contained book reviews—the odd one out being the *West Lancashire Evening Gazette.*

In theory, minority opinions can be voiced through the correspondence column—provided they are not treasonable, blasphemous, libellous or unacceptably offensive. In practice, some editors do screen out particular categories of correspondence (e.g. religious controversy) on the ground that they lack wide public interest. The editorial prerogative of closing a debate is intermittently exercised for the same reason.

The provincial Press claims that it fairly reflects news and views from minority political groups, and, although further validation of this claim is desirable, it is fair to say that complaints from such groups are infrequent. To take one example, in September 1970 an official at the Communist Party's headquarters stated that 'in general local newspapers are prepared to publish correspondence from local Party spokesmen'—adding that 'whenever the local Party is deeply involved in local campaigns, local elections and Parliamentary elections, then the provincial Press is usually quite reasonable'. But there were exceptions, and more needs to be known about them.

(d) The local institutions and their leaders It was shown in chapter 3 that the local Press attaches great importance to the opinion that community leaders hold of it; these leaders are important as the controllers of much community news, and as key influencers of local attitudes to the newspaper. Typically, the Press co-operates with the institutions and feels a 'sense of responsibility' towards them.[6]

Detailed research into the effects of a political antipathy as between the local Press and the town council would result in a desirable enlargement of existing knowledge.[7] In general, the tone of

watchdog comment addressed to local councils is equable and circumspect; sternly censorious leaders appear to be reserved for situations where culpability is both proved and already in the open. As
a rule, editors evidently prefer correspondents to shoulder much of
the burden of direct, uncompromising criticism of the institutions;
they claim that this may well be the most effective form of criticism
in any case.

The ways in which the local Press co-operates with commercial
concerns were outlined in chapter 10. Amongst them are its 'disin-
clination to stir up antagonism' (where there is 'no strong consciousness of a public duty to take a positive line which would produce
such a result'), and its inclusion of 'puff' features about consumer
goods or services. For the most part, it leaves evaluative appraisals
of these to local and national consumer research organisations, and
campaigning national newspapers like *The People* and that highly
individual Scottish newspaper *The Sunday Post*. In practice, therefore, watchdog surveillance tends to be confined to the standard of
public amenities (e.g. transport, housing, leisure facilities)—whether
nationally or municipally controlled.

(e) **Family values** The local newspaper aspires to be a family newspaper—one which 'parents can have about in the home without fear
of children picking it up and reading something distasteful, indecent
or horrifying'.[8] No material describable in these terms (unless one
includes items like the Moors murders trial) came to hand during
the period of survey in the provincial newspapers examined; it
should be added, however, that a few failures to meet the criteria
appropriate to a family newspaper have been censured by the Press
Council. H. Phillip Levy, in his study of the Press Council's judgments, cites the Hull *Daily Mail* report (in 1955) of a case of criminal
assault upon a girl of eleven; the newspaper was judged to have
'failed to observe the bounds of decency in publishing extensive
details of the evidence'. Deviations of this kind are of infrequent
occurrence, but need to be recorded as part of the total picture of
provincial newspaper practice.

The more paternalistic newspapers, such as the *West Lancashire
Evening Gazette* and *Yorkshire Evening Post* during the late 1960s,
were found to use their leading columns to enjoin and reinforce
family values. In the case of the *Gazette* these values include the
Christian ethic, a hierarchy of prides and loyalties (in and to Queen

and country, the North, Lancashire and Blackpool), community service, work, courage and heroism. The same values would be endorsed generally within the provincial Press, but urged upon readers less frequently and, in many cases, less insistently. Family values serve as crucially important criteria for the selection, prominence and presentation of much news and feature content.

By formulating a network of ideal values for their readers, provincial newspapers assume the role of a socialising medium. The more paternalistic the newspaper, the more antagonistic it will tend to be towards social groups and influences that it sees as a threat to family cohesion. Thus television is widely judged as desirable or undesirable in relation to its presentation of, and impact on, family life. In general, it can be said that provincial reviewers and leader-writers are more open-minded about some forms of documentary or fictional realism than the National Viewers' and Listeners' Association, but they tread warily.

(f) The roles of educator and political persuader In chapter 5 it was suggested that in their coverage of non-local events and issues the majority of evening newspapers can be located in the middle ground between the popular and quality national dailies. Seven of the sixteen newspapers sampled were assessed as giving 'high prominence' to the news story of Mrs Gandhi's election: the Darlington *Evening Despatch*, *West Lancashire Evening Gazette*, *Manchester Evening News*, Bolton *Evening News*, Newcastle *Evening Chronicle*, Nottingham *Evening Post* and *Huddersfield Daily Examiner*. A further five —the *Yorkshire Evening Post*, *Lancashire Evening Post*, *Birmingham Evening Mail*, Wolverhampton *Express and Star* and Bristol *Evening Post*—signalled the importance of this election by publishing leaders and/or features about it. This sort of evidence is, of course, too limited to permit firm conclusions, but taken in conjunction with the generally impressive coverage of the arts (see chapter 11) it suggests that the possible role of public enlightener is still actively pursued—even if, in most cases, without the altruistic panache of the *Leeds Mercury* under Edward Baines Jr.

It has been shown that there is a continuing debate within the provincial Press as to whether or not it should be politically committed or neutral. In practice, sampling indicated that about 40 per cent of evening newspapers and up to 90 per cent of weeklies take up a non-partisan position. This should not, one feels, be categorically condemned by those who yearn for the 'challenge and counter-challenge' of the nineteenth-century competitive situation; it is not so much the position taken up, as the use that is made of it, that should form the basis for assessment. For instance, if a neutral stance is accompanied by a genuine intention to evaluate political developments without fence-sitting or 'tactful' side-stepping, then it may well be much more helpful to the average reader than mere tub-thumping partisanship. This last description, fortunately, does not apply to more than a handful of the committed newspapers.

Even so, it seems reasonable to suppose that the more politically aware and active provincial readers would prefer to take a politically congenial newspaper if one were available. For this reason, and in spite of the community-unifying value of the monopoly newspaper, a return to the competitive situation remains as an ideal to be worked for.[9] Contemporary working-class equivalents to, say, the readers of O'Connor's *Northern Star*—the Chartist newspaper—must now depend solely on a general altruism, a Dickensian social conscience, on the part of the local Press; no evidence came to light that any provincial newspaper of today is specifically committed to championing their interest—and only a very small minority support a radical ideology at all.

Indeed, this study of the provincial Press has revealed that it is essentially a conservative communications medium. It strongly upholds family and institutional life; it typically demands discipline in relation to penology and education; it values conventions and traditions. Broadly speaking, it endorses capitalistic assumptions and the Protestant ethic. The value of a competing, radical Press would lie in its stimulus to debate; one has in mind the antithesis between the radical Bentham and the Conservative Coleridge that John Stuart Mill regarded as so beneficial to society at large: 'the one pressing the new doctrines to their utmost consequences; the other reasserting the best meaning and purposes of the old'.[10] For this reason it is a matter for regret that the monopoly situation seems likely to continue in the foreseeable future.

(g) Summary of functions The primary aim of this study has been to clarify the role of the local Press and therefore to put on record its particular contribution to local life. Four functions stand out:

(i) The promotion of a sense of community identity and cohesion, and the fostering of the individual's integration within
local society.

(ii) The provision of political, institutional and cultural information, together with varying kinds of background analysis and
interpretation. This in turn serves as a permanent record
of community affairs; a number of contemporary studies that
draw heavily on this record (such as Paul Foot's *The Rise of
Enoch Powell*) testify to its importance.

(iii) The provision of a platform for debate and complaint, acces-
sible to institutional spokesmen, minority groups and individuals.

(iv) The publicising of goods and services available, situations
vacant, announcements and notices.

The value of these services to the community needs no underlining.

2. The provincial Press in the 1970s

(a) The watchdog role There is clearly considerable scope for
expanding the watchdog function to cover—with greater range and
penetration—the field of consumer goods and services. Such a surveillance could have many desirable effects, as Raymond Williams
has noted:

The communication of real information, and the continual challenge to
make judgments of quality, could make a radical difference to our whole
economic life, in a proper combination of freedom and responsibility. . . .
The gimmicks and false appeals which have given affluence a bad name
must be challenged in the interests of real use, good design, and a sense
of proportion about commodities.[11]

In fairness to the Press, Williams also points out that the seeming
reluctance to offer critical comment on consumer goods and services
is partly accounted for by editorial nervousness *vis-à-vis* the defama-
tion laws. In this respect, Cecil King has observed that a newspaper
cannot use the defence of qualified privilege because 'the law does
not recognise that newspapers have a duty to publish matters which
are of public interest'.[12] He notes approvingly that in 1965 a joint
working party of Justice and representatives of the British committee

of the International Press Institute, chaired by Lord Shawcross, declared that 'the law should recognise such a duty and such an interest'. Yet little progress has as yet been effected, as the Gros *v.* Crook libel case of 1969 showed.[13] Indeed, the defeated 'right of privacy' Bill (January 1970) was seen as potentially tying the Press's hands even further, since it would inhibit the practice of investigatory journalism.[14]

The same point—that the law needs to be clarified—arises in the context of the Press's relationship with other local institutions. One outstanding provincial editor, David Hopkinson of the *Birmingham Post*, displayed the tenacity of the great eighteenth-century printers in his decision to publish documentary material that came to light in the Warwick University saga.[15] An interim injunction was served on 12 February 1970, aimed at suspending activities which might interfere with the rights the University was claiming. The national Press evidently regarded the publication of extracts from the documents[16] as too much of a risk and, as the authors of *Warwick University Ltd* point out, 'only the local press, and especially the *Birmingham Post*, upheld the journalist's tradition of publication without fear when the public interest so requires'.[17] After analysing the legal niceties, the same authors conclude that the nationals 'might well have found the law to be less inimical to publication in the public interest than their lawyers supposed'.[18] The stand taken by Mr Hopkinson was not unfamiliar to him; as editor of the *Sheffield Morning Telegraph* he had been the publiciser of the 'rhino whip' charges against the police in 1963. Of course, in the Warwick episode he had the substantial assets and influence of the Birmingham Post and Mail group behind him; the editors of smaller provincial journals might, in similar circumstances, feel obliged to proceed more cautiously. This does not detract from Mr Hopkinson's achievement, but serves rather as a measure of the shackling power of legal phraseology.[19] Once the Press's watchdog rights have been legally clarified and codified, it will be easier to assess which newspapers are the real laggards in exercising one of their socially most important rights.

In respect of local news, the challenge in the 1970s will be to enlarge yet further the scope and penetration of the coverage of local life. More particularly, the whole area of local government reporting will need careful reappraisal, and more effort should be made to enable readers to understand the structure and functions of local authorities in detail. Such a reappraisal will be even more necessary as and when the proposals outlined in the White Paper on local government reorganisation (Cmnd. 4583, February 1971) are put into effect —not least in those city, county borough and municipal borough circulation areas (e.g. Plymouth, Stoke on Trent, Nottingham, Blackburn, Darlington) due for demotion to district council status within a larger, two-tier county structure. The size of county authorities and the range of their responsibilities (including roads, social services, education and planning—but not housing development) will make the watchdog vigilance of the local Press crucially important. For one danger attendant on reorganisation is that many people will feel confused (even disorientated), and disarmed by the seeming remoteness of their regional overlords; they will look to the local newspaper to safeguard their interests and voice their worries and problems.

Of course, as the report of the Skeffington Committee stressed— with particular reference to the publicising and debate of plans for urban change—the authorities will need to provide full information and the opportunity for public participation (e.g. community forums and community development officers).[20] But leading column comment published in the North-west seemed unanimous in fearing that the Skeffington proposals might well be 'slipped into a pigeonhole'[21] never to come out again; 'remote control' by 'officials . . . in their ivory towers' is seen as an alarming but very real prospect[22] (see Fig. 6).

Inevitably, evaluative feature articles of greater informational thoroughness about local life and institutions necessitate the employment of senior journalists educated well beyond the minimum professional entry requirement of five O levels. But to attract and retain such men in the required numbers presents the problem of increased salary costs, and for this reason they are rather thinly spread within the provincial Press. This point has been explored by Oliver Boyd-Barrett in a stimulating survey of journalism recruitment and training:

Several lecturers in journalism stress the fact that provincial newspapers are very dependent on juniors for general reporting work. In 1967 figures for all weekly newspapers show that amongst editorial staff there were 1·37 seniors to every junior only, compared with a ratio of 2·36 to 1 for all staff of all newspapers. Almost 30% of the total labour force of journalists (NUJ members) are aged between 16 and 23. Of these, almost half are aged 20 years or under. In raising educational qualifications further, they feel, the NCTJ would be imposing increased salary costs on the provincial press. Additionally, more highly educated trainees might be less willing to accept the type of work expected of them on such newspapers. It could therefore become more difficult to find staff, which would also affect salary costs.[23]

Even if the present entry standard is adequate for routine reporting work,[24] it is essential that the evening Press in particular should be able to hold a sufficient proportion of senior journalists for more complex assignments—and find the money to do so.

At the time of writing the whole question of relevant training standards is being reviewed by the recently established Printing and Publishing Training Board; the National Council for the Training of Journalists (formerly responsible for training) continues to supervise the 'selection, examination, registration and certification of trainees'.[25] Some leading editors are unhappy about recent trends in training, and feel that it is becoming too theoretical and too far removed from their control. Peter Harland, editor in chief of the Bradford *Telegraph and Argus*, would like to see a comprehensive induction course of about three months for all recruits, run by the newspaper in conjunction with college lecturers and emphasising (in English studies) 'recognition of the cliché, good and bad intros, good and bad headlines, economy of words, consistency of style and grammar, the art of précis, and so on'.[26] Literary appreciation would be ruled out. Mr Harland feels that the ties between the NCTJ and the colleges have been weakened in the period of uncertainty following the establishment of the Industrial Training Board. Journalism training is in a rather uneasy transitional stage, and it is to be hoped that the eventual solution will prove acceptable to provincial editors and beneficial to journalism. The vocational exclusiveness recommended by Mr Harland should, one feels, be a matter for continuing debate; the outsider is entitled to wonder whether the spirit of Mr Gradgrind looms too dominantly in the understandable emphasis on essential professional skills.

Given a clear legal framework and a steady supply of recruits aware of the tradition represented by Andrew Brice, C. P. Scott and, in our own times, J. Clement Jones and David Hopkinson, there is no good reason why the editorial content of local newspapers in the 1970s should not be far removed from the nightmare vision of 'one big shopper' sketched out in a recent, pessimistic appraisal of the provincial Press.[27] There is, however, a proviso; the finances of the local Press must be in a healthy state.

(b) Commercial viability in the 1970s There are no indications at present that the 1970s will witness a spate of closures of the dimensions of the early 1960s, when the weaker competing evening newspapers went to the wall. Nevertheless, many of the smaller provincial groups must be apprehensive about the period immediately ahead. At this point it is worth referring to the late John F. Goulden's analysis of an unspecified evening newspaper's revenue in a sample week in March 1965; the newspaper's average daily circulation was 99,896. Its net revenue from sales was £6,530, and its advertising revenue was £11,130. Its expenditure totalled £14,114, leaving a profit of £3,546, or 20 per cent of revenue. The main items of expenditure were wages (editorial, production, distribution, advertising, etc.) at £6,007 and newsprint at £4,000. These two items accounted for about 70 per cent of total expenses.[28]

A rise of 20 per cent or more in costs would, therefore, eliminate profit. Assuming annual rises in costs as low as 5 per cent, a newspaper seeking to maintain its profit margins has to find the extra 5 per cent from increased advertising revenue and/or sales price. The fall-off in sales that occurs after a price rise proves difficult to recoup, and increased advertising rates (especially at a time of economic stagnation) may lead to a decline in volume and frequency. In 1969–70 it is the smaller groups that seem to have been most vulnerable to rising costs—two examples being Home Counties Newspapers (owners of weeklies in Bedfordshire, Hertfordshire, Essex and Buckinghamshire) and F. J. Parsons (owners of weeklies in south Kent). The former group's pre-tax profits for the half year to 30 June 1970 were £86,000, compared with £99,000 for the same period in 1969; the latter's pre-tax profits for the half year to 31 March 1970 were £138,081, as against £152,123 in 1969. Many of the larger independent groups reported higher pre-tax profit margins during 1969–70, examples being The Bristol Evening Post Ltd (up 4 per cent) and The Liverpool Daily Post and Echo Ltd (up 16 per cent). However, The Birmingham Post and Mail Ltd sustained a drop of 20 per cent. The provincial newspaper contribution to chain group profitability showed steadiness or improvement, as in the case of United Newspapers, whose pre-tax interim profits to June 1970 showed an increase of 30 per cent. But this company's chairman sounded a warning note in May 1970; profit margins were proving difficult to maintain. Associated Newspapers, experiencing acute difficulties with its national newspaper sector, reported a 22 per cent drop in profits for the half year to 30 September 1970. With few exceptions, proprietors representing the entire range of provincial companies saw 1970–71 as a period when the rising cost of wages, newsprint and ink, distribution and news agency services would constitute a significant threat to existing margins, and make increased profitability difficult or unlikely in many cases.[29]

It is in this context that the impact of the 'give-away' newspaper can be quite serious in certain types of circulation area. It has been estimated that there are now over a hundred of these free, advertising-financed tabloids. They require a closely packed, densely populated circulation area which minimises distribution costs and maximises their attractiveness to small advertisers, and they need vigorous commercial management. The reaction of the larger provincial Press groups has been varied, as the following extract from an *Observer* article suggests:

> . . . Murdoch was just beaten to the biggest give-away in Britain, the *ABC Weekly Advertiser*, by the Birmingham Post and Mail group. 'We would rather have it in our hands than someone else's,' says Post chairman Sir Eric Clayson.
> Westminster Press, which has 80 local papers . . . is using them to build the circulation of its paid-for papers, and to 'soak up the overspill of advertising from lack of press capacity'.
> United Newspapers, which has many very profitable provincial papers, says 'we might be driven into giveaways as a defensive gesture, but it is doubtful if we would go for them on a large scale'.[30]

Groups as large as these have the resources to buy up existing give-aways or establish new ones; smaller owners—especially in the London area—are finding the give-away's encroachment on advertising revenue a serious matter, as the editor of the *South London Press* (H. H. Wall) pointed out in the BBC2 'Money' programme on 2 July 1970. It would indeed be tragic if the comprehensive news service afforded by such weeklies were to be impaired or even extinguished by pseudo-newspapers whose editorial content is highly selective and often brash in tone and style—a style epitomised by the free *Blackpool and Fylde Journal* main headline ' "Oil town" pundits must be bonkers!'[31] The *South London Press* employs twenty-one journalists; its give-away competitor, the *South Londoner*, seven. In all probability the give-away may well ultimately survive only in the more densely populated areas of London and the Midlands; the reasons given for the News of the World Organisation's closure of its Merseyside give-away suggest why: 'Merseyside was not a good area for give-aways . . . we were losing money, so we decided to pull out. We would rather concentrate our efforts on the major population centres like London than put more money into a loss-making situation.'[32]

Wage demands, price increases in materials and, in some places, the advent of the give-away are the current causes of inroads on profit margins. A further 'threat' (as some see it) is the imminence of commercial radio; the former Postmaster-General (Mr Stonehouse) has suggested that this 'could do critical damage to many local journals'.[33] But the White Paper *An Alternative Service of Broadcasting* (Cmnd. 4636) of March 1971, forecasting a network of up to sixty commercial radio stations throughout the United Kingdom, says of local newspapers: 'Such evidence as there is does not suggest . . . that the impact of independent radio will necessarily be damaging to local newspapers.' Arthur Sandles, writing in the *Financial Times*, has speculated that in the long term the local Press will not be harmed: 'Commercial radio will give advertisers a new outlet, and initially at least will probably rob the local newspapers of some of their revenue. However, there is good reason to believe that with this extra arm in local coverage, national advertising campaigns will be increasingly backed up by local efforts using both Press and radio as media.'[34]

All that can be said at this stage is that for newspaper companies with a stake in local commercial radio, advertising profit should not contract if the stations prove successful; the position of newspapers without this stake is impossible to predict. 'Successful' here denotes commercial and not cultural 'success'; commercial radio may well be 'viable only when it . . . relies on the cheapest pop music/news formulae, spiked with such items of local interest or origin as can be obtained free'.[35] Mr Christopher Chataway (Minister of Posts and Telecommunications) has gone on record as concerned to protect local newspapers, and it is to be hoped that his Labour predecessor's fears are unfounded. Certainly MPs of all parties have much to lose in terms of publicity if the local Press in their constituencies 'dies'— and, ironically perhaps, the Conservatives are the main beneficiaries of partisan support. Thus self-interest (if no higher motive) should result in the necessary degree of protection; the White Paper states that 'the Government accepts the case for giving special consideration to the local and provincial Press'.

In conclusion, then, the provincial Press will do well to maintain its 1969–70 profit margins in the immediate future, and the crucially important contribution that the *Manchester Evening News* and *Birmingham Evening Mail* make to the survival of their morning sister papers—*The Guardian* and the *Birmingham Post*—must, it would seem, remain static at best until the economic climate improves and the Press as a whole starts to reap the benefit.[36]

The preceding considerations relate to the decade ahead; on the more distant horizon lie technological and social changes of such magnitude that their nature and effect can hardly be imagined. Christopher Johnson, managing editor of *The Financial Times*, has sketched out the technological possibilities:

> If communications technology ever achieves its dream, the distinction between Press and television will not last for ever. Every home will have a video screen which can take television programmes, cassette video recordings, or newspapers, with print-out machinery to deliver them in something like the traditional form.[37]

This may be the long-term prospect; at present, however, it is still appropriate to discuss the provincial Press in terms of an editorial and publishing tradition of over 250 years' continuity. The expressed ideals of contemporary editors are the same in essence as those of early printers like Andrew Brice; the passage that follows was written by the editor of the Darlington *Evening Despatch* in 1968, when outlining the functions and duties of a local newspaper:

> . . . its purpose is not only to present and project the news objectively and imaginatively, but to help its readers to express themselves more effectively, canalizing their aspirations, making more articulate their demands. A newspaper should reflect the community it serves—warts and all. When a mirror it holds to society reveals neglect, injustice, inhumanity, ignorance, or complacency, the mirror should not be clouded but polished, so that these things can be eradicated rather than ignored. And the newspaper should help to eradicate them. It would be pretentious to think that a local paper (or even a national) can change the course of world affairs—but at the local level it can exert influence, it can probe, it can help to get things done. Though, of necessity, it must concentrate on local affairs it should also try to broaden its readers' horizons, discarding the parish-pump mentality. In its columns its readers should be encouraged to express their opinions, their fears, their hopes—and, just as important, air their grievances. . . . A citizen with a grievance can always write to his local paper.

If the newspaper is doing its job properly, that grievance will be investigated—and the paper will help to put it right. It can persuade, shame, cajole and criticise as well as inform and entertain.[38]

These editorial guidelines must command the assent of all who have the interests of the local Press at heart; they embody the true principles of community journalism, and consensus-seeking market journalism—the world of candy floss and puff—is tacitly rebuffed. Assuming the continued absence of competitive situations, monopoly newspapers that act upon these principles will be offering an alternative so invaluable as to make their preservation a matter for national, as well as local, concern.

Notes

1 See p. 85.
2 See pp. 123-4.
3 See pp. 84-8.
4 Janowitz, *op. cit.*, pp. 156-7.
5 See chapter 7.
6 See p. 43.
7 See pp. 112-13.
8 *Memoranda of Evidence*, p. 93 (submitted by the Holmesdale Press Ltd).
9 See Raymond Williams, 'Radical and/or respectable', *The Press we Deserve*, ed. Richard Boston (London: Routledge & Kegan Paul, 1970), pp. 25-6.
10 F. R. Leavis (ed.), *Mill on Bentham and Coleridge* (London: Chatto & Windus, 1962), p. 140.
11 Raymond Williams, *Communications*, pp. 128-9.
12 King, *op. cit.*, p. 104.
13 See 'Libel—must publishers always be responsible?' *The Financial Times*, 5 May 1969.
14 See *The Times*, 16 January 1970.
15 *Birmingham Post* editorial, 'The right to publish', 24 February 1970.
16 *Warwick University Ltd*, ed. E. P. Thompson (Harmondsworth: Penguin Books, 1970), chapter 6.
17 *Ibid.*, p. 97.
18 *Ibid.*, p. 101.
19 See Quintin Hogg, 'Language and law', *Times Literary Supplement*, 22 January 1970, *passim*.
20 See *People and Planning*: report of the committee on Public Participation in Planning (London: HMSO, 1969), pp. 19-20, 47-8.
21 See *Manchester Evening News* editorial, 18 September 1969.
22 See leaders in the *Lancashire Evening Post*, 26 June 1970, and *West Lancashire Evening Gazette*, 9 July 1970.

23 Oliver Boyd-Barrett, 'Journalism recruitment and training: problems in professionalization', *Media Sociology*, ed. J. Tunstall, p. 192.
24 *Ibid.*, p. 188.
25 See Printing and Publishing Training Board *Newsletter 4*, November 1969.
26 Peter Harland, 'Training: off the rails', *UK Press Gazette* No. 243, 17 August 1970.
27 A. C. H. Smith, 'Provincial Press: towards one big shopper', *The Press we Deserve*, pp. 132–43.
28 John F. Goulden, *Newspaper Management* (London: Heinemann, 1967), pp. 132–43.
29 The financial data are taken from, or based on, Moodies news cards.
30 *The Observer*, 14 September 1969.
31 *Blackpool and Fylde Journal*, 9 January 1970.
32 See the *Daily Telegraph*, 19 September 1970.
33 *Financial Times*, 17 March 1970.
34 *Ibid.*, 21 July 1970.
35 See letter from the Secretary of the Radio Writers' Association, *Daily Telegraph*, 14 September 1970.
36 See Clive Irving, 'The last days of Fleet Street', *The Listener*, 16 July 1970. Noting that *The Guardian* lost £600,000 in 1966, he writes: 'It has got by until now largely on infusions from the profits of the *Manchester Evening News*, its sister paper, but they are not what they were and meanwhile *The Guardian*, like *The Times*, knows that the basic sums are wrong and that unless costs can be checked and selling prices substantially increased only death can follow.'
37 'World Press', *Financial Times* survey, 17 March 1969.
38 Arnold Hadwin, 'The teacher and the journalist', *Times Educational Supplement*, 22 March 1968.

Appendix

Survey of the reading choices of a sample of *West Lancashire Evening Gazette* readers, April 1971

The emphasis of chapters 5–10 was on the nature of the content available for reading in local newspapers; it remains to give some indication of the reading choices of a sample of local Press readers. During the first week of April 1971, 450 questionnaires were despatched to 225 homes in all parts of the *West Lancashire Evening Gazette*'s circulation area. 260 were sent to the homes of members of the *Gazette*'s 26,000-strong Women's Circle; 100 were distributed through two local schools, thirty through newsagents, twenty to members of a local church and forty to runner-up winners of the *Gazette*'s 'Mark the ball' competition. By the closing date for reply (21 April), completed questionnaires had been returned by 100 women readers and seventy men. As the basic pattern of reading choices had become virtually settled after twenty-five replies had been analysed, it seems reasonable to suppose that the results of this survey carry a high degree of reliability. They certainly provide valid pointers.

Respondents were asked to indicate their ages within one of three groups: 18–30, 30–50 and over 50. The resulting distribution was as follows:

Men		Women	
18–30:	11	18–30:	14
30–50:	24	30–50:	40
Over 50:	35	Over 50:	46
Total:	70	*Total*:	100

In percentage terms, the 18–30 age group constituted 15 per cent, the 30–50 group 38 per cent, and the over-50 group 47 per cent. Ideally, percentages of 20, 40 and 40 respectively would have been preferable; it should be noted, therefore, that the over-50 group is over-represented by 7 per cent, and the 18–30 group under-represented by 5 per cent.

The methods adopted for distributing the questionnaire succeeded in drawing in a satisfactorily wide range of occupations and income groups. Their diversity can be suggested by noting the occupations of the twenty-one (out of twenty-four) men aged 30–50 who specified them: company director, hoteliers (two), school bursar, senior engineer (aircraft), chief estimator (building firm), civil servant, teacher, driving instructor, sales representative, clerk, butchery manager, master butcher, security supervisor, mechanical fitter, electrician, process worker, postman, council cleansing officer, welder and flagger.

The questionnaire listed forty-one items of content, and readers were asked to show how often they read each item by selecting one of the following scores: 4 for ALWAYS; 3 for USUALLY (say, four out of six occasions); 2 for OCCASIONALLY (say, two out of six occasions); 1 for

INFREQUENTLY and 0 for NEVER. This method was devised to provide more helpful information than would have resulted from a simple 'read' or 'don't read' alternative; it does not, of course, indicate the thoroughness of reading nor the degree of enthusiasm with which an item is read.

Table 16 presents the detailed scores for men and women respondents and the total scores. The total score is reached by multiplying the ALWAYS score by six, the USUALLY score by four, the OCCASIONALLY score by two and the INFREQUENTLY score by one, and adding the resulting figures together. The actual total score is then expressed as a percentage of the maximum possible score—600 for women, 420 for men. The final column shows the average percentage for men and women readers combined, and assumes equal numbers of each. The table contains three sections: (i) news, editorial column, letters to the editor and selected features, (ii) information, diversion, entertainment, and (iii) notices, announcements and advertising (selected categories). Fig. 13 shows the ten items most read by men, women and all readers respectively.

Observations Table 16 shows that front-page news (predominantly non-local) and the main local news page were rated as read by 93 per cent and 90 per cent respectively of the 170 adult readers who returned completed questionnaires. The desire for printed news about international, national and local affairs clearly remains very powerful. Editorial comment (centre page, left) was noted as read by 59 per cent of respondents, and other items regularly placed on the same page—Letters to the Editor (65 per cent), Seasider's Diary (54 per cent) and most local features (53·5 per cent)—are also read by a majority. It is possible that the percentages in these cases are assisted by the very high readership for the facing main local news page. It is relevant to note that the readership for the editorial column, correspondence column, town diary and most local features was lowest in the 18–30 age group, and highest in the over-50 group; thus the editorial column had a readership of 30 per cent in the 18–30 group, 54 per cent in the 30–50 group and 74 per cent in the over-50 group.

The distinctive interests of women readers are indicated by the high readership for the Women's Circle Magazine (91 per cent), Births, Marriages and Deaths (85 per cent), Your Stars (72 per cent), fashion display advertisements (67 per cent) and food display advertising (62 per cent). The particular interests of men readers are sports news (76 per cent) and Jimmy Armfield's weekly sports feature (54 per cent). The provision of TV and radio programme details (77 per cent of all) and of local entertainment advertisements (55 per cent) is evidently valued by a majority of both men and women readers.

The low figure for the non-local feature 'Westminster Notebook' (18 per cent) suggests that the *Gazette*'s readership is largely resistant to political discussion that can be seen in many ways as a duplication of material available in the national daily Press. A low readership for such minority sports as golf (15 per cent of men) and angling (19 per cent of men) was anticipated.

Features about the natural environment (In the Country—47 per cent)

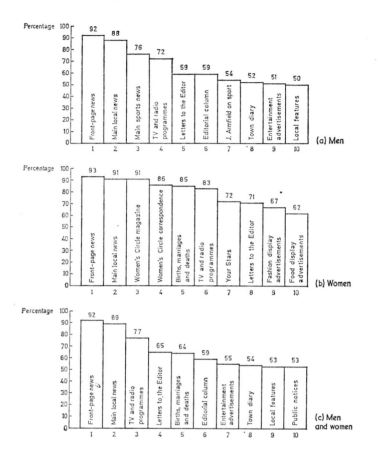

Fig. 13 The ten most frequently read items of content (see Table 16): (*a*) men readers, (*b*) women readers, (*c*) men and women readers, assuming equal numbers of each. For comparative purposes a controlled sample of 100 of the 170 respondents was also taken, so that the following weighting of age groups was achieved:

    (i) 18–30: ten men, ten women (20 per cent).
   (ii) 30–50: twenty men, twenty women (40 per cent).
  (iii) Over 50: twenty men, twenty women (40 per cent).

The percentage differences as compared with the full sample were—where more than 2 per cent—as follows (referring to the items in Fig. 13 only):

    (i) Men: Sports news, +3 per cent.
           Letters to the editor, editorial column and local features, all −3 per cent.
   (ii) Women: fashion display advertising, +4 per cent.
  (iii) Men and women: all variations under 2 per cent.

Note: 'Today's sunbeam'—a daily joke or witticism appended to Seasider's Diary (overall readership: 56 per cent)—is not included.

Table 16 Readership for selected items

	Numbers of men scoring 0, 1, 2, 3 or 4 (max. 70)							Numbers of women scoring 0, 1, 2, 3 or 4 (max. 100)							Average (%)
	0	1	2	3	4	Total (of 420)	% of max.	0	1	2	3	4	Total (of 600)	% of max.	
(i)															
Front-page news	0	1	3	9	57	385	92	0	2	1	14	83	558	93	92·5
Main local news page	0	1	6	11	52	369	88	0	3	3	14	80	545	91	89·5
Editorial column	3	8	20	17	22	248	59	6	10	28	25	31	352	59	59
Letters to editor	4	10	16	17	23	248	59	2	8	19	24	47	424	71	65
Seasider's Diary	10	9	18	13	20	217	52	14	12	16	27	31	338	56	54
Local features[1]	11	10	16	15	18	210	50	9	10	25	27	29	342	57	53·5
*In the Country[2]	20	11	16	7	16	167	40	18	12	19	19	32	318	53	46·5
*25 Years Ago[3]	10	12	20	18	10	184	44	26	16	28	18	12	216	36	40
*Northern Sketchbook[4]	23	13	19	10	5	121	29	23	16	31	13	17	232	39	34
*You and the Law[5]	12	14	18	13	13	180	43	32	16	27	16	9	188	31	37
*TV topics	10	12	18	17	13	194	46	16	12	27	20	25	296	49	47·5
*POPscene	40	8	14	4	4	76	18	50	20	13	13	4	122	20	19
*Taking Stock[6]	27	11	8	13	11	145	35	57	17	15	6	5	101	17	26
*Westminster Notebook[7]	29	16	13	8	4	98	23	66	13	12	6	3	79	13	18
*Women's Circle magazine[8]	41	9	9	2	4	65	16	2	0	9	15	80	546	91	53·5
Women's Circle Correspondence[9]	38	14	14	4	0	58	14	2	2	9	13	74	516	86	50
Sports news (esp. football)	5	3	8	11	43	321	76	52	18	18	7	5	112	19	47·5
*Jimmy Armfield on the sporting scene	15	6	10	16	23	228	54	73	13	9	2	3	57	10	32
*Golf feature	44	11	7	5	3	63	15	73	11	12	2	2	55	9	12
*Angling feature	44	11	4	3	8	79	19	84	4	8	2	2	40	7	13

(ii)

Category														
TV and radio programmes	4	3	14	12	37	301	72	3	3	7	20	67	499	83	77·5
*Film notes	14	18	14	12	12	166	40	14	9	26	23	28	321	53	46·5
Published Wills	24	14	11	10	11	142	34	14	7	27	27	25	319	53	43·5
Weather notes	15	20	13	8	14	162	39	26	15	22	12	25	257	43	41
City Prices	33	13	8	7	9	111	26	73	12	8	4	3	62	10	18
Today's Sunbeam	10	16	10	8	26	224	53	15	12	20	20	40	358	60	56·5
*Prize Crossword	53	6	5	1	5	50	12	61	7	13	10	9	127	21	16·5
*Family Quiz	24	18	14	6	8	118	28	31	13	21	20	15	225	37	33
*Your Stars	33	9	12	7	9	115	27	7	8	10	22	53	434	72	49·5

(iii)

Category														
Births, Marriages and Deaths	15	20	10	5	20	180	43	2	5	6	13	74	513	85	64
Entertainment ads.	8	6	23	17	16	216	51	3	13	27	31	26	347	58	55
Public Notices	8	13	15	24	10	199	47	8	6	26	29	31	360	60	53·5
Houses for Sale	22	9	26	9	4	121	29	12	24	26	15	10	222	37	33
Situations Vacant	25	18	10	9	8	122	29	25	14	34	14	13	216	36	32·5
Miscellaneous for Sale	12	14	26	8	10	158	38	6	16	37	21	20	294	49	43·5
Car display ads.	23	11	17	8	14	155	37	52	25	15	5	3	93	15	26
Carpets, Furnishings (Display)	24	19	17	7	3	99	24	9	10	35	25	21	306	51	37·5
Food display ads.	25	16	17	6	6	110	26	8	7	21	30	34	373	62	44
Ladies' Fashion display ads.	51	11	3	4	1	39	9	5	3	19	38	35	403	67	38
Auctions	25	25	8	9	3	95	23	31	26	24	14	5	160	27	25
Lost and Found	26	16	14	7	7	114	27	19	7	29	22	23	291	48	38

Notes

* Published once each week.
[1] Refers to series of watchdog, pump-priming, reflector or booster features about local life. Two series published in March 1971 were given as examples in the questionnaire.
[2] See pp. 193-6.
[3] Diary paragraphs referring to local, national and international events of 1946.
[4] Describes and illustrates local or regional scenes of interest to the artist.
[5] Written locally.
[6] Money matters: investment, saving, mortgages, etc.
[7] Parliamentary affairs (non-local origin).
[8] A four-page tabloid-size pull-out that publicises Women's Circle activities; it may include features on make-up, fashion, cooking, cleaning etc. and contains a correspondence column and a personal or practical problems column.
[9] Included two or three times each week.

and TV programmes (48 per cent) enjoy solid support; features about recent history (25 Years Ago—40 per cent), the law (37 per cent) and money matters (35 per cent of men) also command followings that would seem to justify their inclusion. Although the 'POPscene' feature had a low overall rating (19 per cent), its readership within the 18–30 age group was 50 per cent.

Local commercial advertisers can derive satisfaction from the readership for displayed advertising. The percentage of women readers for carpets and furnishings advertising was 51, for food 62 and for ladies' fashions 67. The men's readership for car display advertising was lower at 37 per cent, but it should be noted that in response to the question 'If you were thinking of buying a car, would you look at the *Gazette*'s motor car advertisements?' 83 per cent of men answered 'yes'. Similarly, although the regular readership for 'Houses for Sale' was established as 33 per cent, 163 (or 98 per cent) of the 166 readers who answered the question 'If you were looking for a house, would you consult the *Gazette*'s "Houses for Sale" section?' replied 'yes'.

The average percentage readership for five categories of classified advertising (Public Notices, Lost and Found, Situations Vacant, Houses for Sale and Miscellaneous for Sale) was 40, with 'occasional' readers being the most numerous in the cases of Houses for Sale and Miscellaneous for Sale. The readership for Public Notices (54 per cent) was higher than anticipated; in this respect, as in much editorial content, the local Press is serving as a vital link between the local institutions and the community at large.

Reading time Respondents were also asked to estimate the length of time that they would usually spend on reading the *West Lancashire Evening Gazette*; the results were as follows:

(a) Less than 10 minutes: 3 (two men, 1 woman).
(b) 10–20 minutes: 44 (eighteen men, twenty-six women).
(c) 20–30 minutes: 67 (twenty-seven men, forty women).
(d) Over 30 minutes: 56 (twenty-three men, thirty-three women).

If the four categories are allotted five, fifteen, twenty-five and thirty-five minutes respectively, the average reading time works out at twenty-five minutes. This is a slightly higher figure than was expected, and suggests that readers try to obtain full value for their current outlay of 3*p*. It also hints at the likelihood of editorial content being quite thoroughly perused where readership is claimed.

Selective bibliography

Press studies (historical, sociological, autobiographical etc.)

ABRAMS, Dr Mark, *Education, social class and reading of newspapers and magazines*. IPA booklet No. 5, January 1966.
—— *The newspaper-reading public of tomorrow*. London: Odhams Press, 1964.
ANDREWS, Alexander, *The history of British journalism*, vols. I–II. London: Richard Bentley, 1859.
ANDREWS, Sir Linton, *Autobiography of a journalist*. London: Ernest Benn, 1964.
—— *Problems of an editor*. London: Oxford University Press, 1962.
BENNETT-ENGLAND, Rodney (ed.), *Inside journalism*. London: Peter Owen, 1967.
BERELSON, Bernard, 'What "Missing the newspaper" means', *The process and effects of mass communication*, ed. W. Schramm. New York: Harper, 1965, pp. 36–47.
BOYD-BARRETT, Oliver, 'Journalism recruitment and training: problems in professionalization', *Media Sociology*, ed. J. Tunstall. London: Constable, 1970, pp. 181–201.
BRENNAN, James, 'Journalists condemn discrimination', Institute of Race Relations *News Letter*, March 1966.
CHRISTIANSEN, Arthur, *Headlines all my life*. London: Heinemann, 1961.
CRANFIELD, G. A., *The development of the provincial newspaper, 1700–1760*. Oxford: Clarendon Press, 1962.
CUDLIPP, Hugh, *At your peril*. London: Weidenfeld & Nicolson, 1962.
EVANS, Harold, 'Getting the facts', *The practice of journalism*, ed. J. Dodge and G. Viner. London: Heinemann, 1963, pp. 64–83.
EVENING NEWSPAPER ADVERTISING BUREAU, *Where? An analysis of regional evening newspaper sales*. London: 1970.
GALTUNG, J. and RUGE, Mari H., 'The structure of foreign news', *Media sociology*, ed. J. Tunstall. London: Constable, 1970, pp. 259–98.
GOULDEN, John F., *Newspaper management*. London: Heinemann, 1967.
GRANT, James, *The newspaper Press: its origin, progress, and present position*, vols. I–III. London: Tinsley Brothers, 1871.
HADWIN, Arnold, 'The teacher and the journalist', *Times Educational Supplement*, 22 March 1968.
HORNBY, Robert, *The Press in modern society*. London: Frederick Muller, 1965.

JANOWITZ, Morris, *The community Press in an urban setting*. Glencoe, Ill.: Free Press, 1952.

KING, Cecil, *The future of the Press*. London: MacGibbon & Kee, 1967.

LEVY, H. Phillip, *The Press Council*. London: Macmillan, 1967.

MADDEN, Lionel, *How to find out about the Victorian period*. Oxford: Pergamon Press, 1970, pp. 22–38.

MARTIN, Graham, 'Public voices', *Your Sunday paper*, ed. Richard Hoggart. London: University of London Press, 1967, pp. 43–56.

MORRIS, Claud, *I bought a newspaper*. London: Arthur Barker, 1963.

NATIONAL COMMITTEE FOR COMMONWEALTH IMMIGRANTS, *Survey of four local London newspapers*, 1967.

READ, Donald, *Press and people, 1790–1850*. London: Edward Arnold, 1961.

ROYAL COMMISSION ON THE PRESS, 1947, *Memoranda of evidence submitted to the Royal Commission on the Press*. London: HMSO, 1947.

—— *Minutes of evidence taken before the Royal Commission on the Press*. London: HMSO, 1948.

—— *Report*. London: HMSO, 1949.

SCOTT, C. P., *C. P. Scott, 1846–1932: the making of the 'Manchester Guardian'*. London: Frederick Muller, 1946.

SCOTT, George, *Reporter anonymous—the story of the Press Association*. London: Hutchinson, 1968.

SMITH, A. C. H., 'Provincial Press: towards one big shopper', *The Press we deserve*, ed. Richard Boston. London: Routledge & Kegan Paul, 1970, pp. 132–43.

WHEARE, Kenneth, *The universities in the news*. Cambridge: University Press, 1967.

WHITE, David M., 'The "Gatekeeper": a case study in the selection of news', *People, society and mass communications*, ed. L. A. Dexter and D. M. White. Glencoe, Ill.: Free Press, 1964, pp. 160–71.

WILES, R. M., *Freshest advices: early provincial newspapers in England*. Columbus, Ohio: Ohio State University Press, 1965.

WILLIAMS, Francis, *Dangerous estate*. London: Arrow Books, 1959.

WILLIAMS, Raymond, *Britain in the 'sixties: communications*. Harmondsworth: Penguin Books, 1962.

—— 'Radical and/or respectable', *The Press we deserve*, ed. Richard Boston. London: Routledge & Kegan Paul, 1970, pp. 14–26.

WORPOLE, K., and HUDSON, R., 'Community Press', *New Society*, 24 September 1970.

Background studies

A policy for the arts. Cmnd. 2601. London: HMSO, 1965.

ARNOLD, Matthew, *Culture and anarchy*, ed. J. Dover Wilson. Cambridge: University Press, 1963.

BOORSTIN, Daniel, *The image*. Harmondsworth: Penguin Books, 1963.

ELIOT, T. S. *Notes towards the definition of culture*. London: Faber & Faber, 1962.

GERARD, David E. (ed.), *Libraries and the arts*. London: Clive Bingley, 1970.

HALL, S., and WHANNEL, P., *The popular arts*. Boston: Beacon Press, 1967.

HOGGART, Richard. *The uses of literacy*. London: Chatto & Windus, 1957.

HOSKINS, W. G., *Local history in England*. London: Longmans, 1959.

LEAVIS, F. R. (ed.), *Mill on Bentham and Coleridge*. London: Chatto & Windus, 1962.

McQUAIL, Denis, 'The audience for television plays', *Media sociology*, ed. J. Tunstall. London: Constable, 1970, pp. 335–50.

MILNE, R. S., and MACKENZIE, H. C., *Marginal seat, 1955*. London: Hansard Society for Parliamentary Government, 1958.

People and Planning, report of the Committee on Public Participation in Planning. London: H M S O, 1969.

SNOW, C. P., *The two cultures: and a second look*. New York: Cambridge University Press, 1963.

THOMPSON, E. P. (ed.), *Warwick University Ltd*. Harmondsworth: Penguin Books, 1970.

TRENAMAN, J., and McQUAIL, D., *Television and the political image*. London: Methuen, 1967.

TRILLING, Lionel, *The opposing self*. London: Secker & Warburg, 1955.

WHITEHOUSE, Mary, *Cleaning up TV*. London: Blandford Press, 1967.

WILLIAMS, Raymond, *The long revolution*. London: Chatto & Windus, 1961.

Newspaper index

This index lists references to recently published and contemporary morning evening and weekly provincial newspapers, and to national newspapers; newspapers referred to on pages 24–5, 30–2 only are not included.

General index